First World War
and Army of Occupation
War Diary
France, Belgium and Germany

30 DIVISION
Divisional Troops
202 Field Company Royal Engineers
9 November 1915 - 20 March 1919

WO95/2323/1

The Naval & Military Press Ltd
www.nmarchive.com
Published in association with The National Archives

Published by

The Naval & Military Press Ltd

Unit 10 Ridgewood Industrial Park,

Uckfield, East Sussex,

TN22 5QE England

Tel: +44 (0) 1825 749494

www.naval-military-press.com

www.nmarchive.com

This diary has been reprinted in facsimile from the original. Any imperfections are inevitably reproduced and the quality may fall short of modern type and cartographic standards.

Contents

Document type	Place/Title	Date From	Date To
Heading	WO95/2323/1 202 Field Coy Nov 15-Jly 19		
Heading	30th Division Divl. Engineers 202nd Fld Coy R.E. Nov 1915-Jly 1919		
Heading	30th Division 202nd F.C.R.E. Vol I 121/7795 Nov 15-Jly 19		
Heading	War Diary of 202nd Field Company (CP) R.E. from Nov 9th 1915 to Nov 30th 1915 (Volume-One)		
War Diary	Larkhill	09/11/1915	09/11/1915
War Diary	Le Havre	10/11/1915	10/11/1915
War Diary	Bettencourt	11/11/1915	11/11/1915
War Diary	Villers Le Bocage	17/11/1915	17/11/1915
War Diary	Candas	28/11/1915	29/11/1915
Miscellaneous	O.C., 202nd Field Co. (C.P.) R.E. Appendix 1	05/11/1915	05/11/1915
Miscellaneous			
Miscellaneous	Move Of Division A.L. 1632	05/11/1915	05/11/1915
Miscellaneous	O.C. 202nd Fd. Co. R.E. Appendix II	04/11/1915	04/11/1915
Miscellaneous	202nd Field Coy. R.E. Appendix III	09/11/1915	09/11/1915
Operation(al) Order(s)	91st Infantry Brigade Order No. 1 Appendix IV	16/11/1915	16/11/1915
Miscellaneous	1st. Day March Table for 17th November 1915. (Issued with 91st Inf. Bde. Order No 1)	17/11/1915	17/11/1915
Miscellaneous	202nd Field Coy. R.E.	16/11/1915	16/11/1915
Miscellaneous	Reference 30th Division Operation Order No. (1) Para. 4 Transport And Supply Arrangements During The Move Of The Division.	16/11/1915	16/11/1915
Operation(al) Order(s)	90th Brigade Operation Order No. 2 App V	27/11/1915	27/11/1915
Operation(al) Order(s)	90th Brigade Operation Order No. 2	27/11/1915	27/11/1915
Miscellaneous	March Table For 28th Novr Issued With 90th Infantry Brigade Order No. 2	28/11/1915	28/11/1915
Miscellaneous	202nd Field Coy. R.E.	28/11/1915	28/11/1915
Heading	30th Div. 202nd F.C.R.E. Vol 2. Dec		
Heading	Volume 2 War Diary of 202nd Field Coy (C.P) R.E. for December 1915		
Miscellaneous	C Form (Original). Messages And Signals		
Miscellaneous	A Form. Messages And Signals.		
Operation(al) Order(s)	Operation Order No 2 (Cont) App 1	03/12/1915	03/12/1915
Operation(al) Order(s)	202nd Field Co. R.E. Operation Order No. For March On 5-12-1915	05/12/1915	05/12/1915
Operation(al) Order(s)	Extract from Supply And Transport Arrangements Issued In Accordance With 30th Division Operation Order No. 4 Dated 2nd December 1915. App Vol 2	02/12/1915	02/12/1915
Miscellaneous	Attachment of 202nd Field Coy. R.E., 30th Division to 48th Division App I	02/12/1915	02/12/1915
Miscellaneous	March Table Issued With C.R.E. Operation Order No. 2		
Operation(al) Order(s)	C.R.E's Operation Order No. 2 App I	03/12/1915	03/12/1915
War Diary	Candas	05/12/1915	05/12/1915
War Diary	Louvencourt	06/12/1915	06/12/1915
War Diary	Hebuterne	07/12/1915	18/12/1915
War Diary	Louvencourt	20/12/1915	20/12/1915
War Diary	Candas	21/12/1915	30/12/1915
Miscellaneous	202nd Field Company, R.E. App 2	05/12/1915	05/12/1915

Miscellaneous	1st O.C., 2nd Field Co. 202nd App 3	15/12/1915	15/12/1915
Miscellaneous	C Form (Duplicate). Messages And Signals App 4		
Miscellaneous	C Form (Quadruplicate). Messages And Signals App 4		
Miscellaneous	A Form. Messages And Signals App 5		
Miscellaneous	C.R.E. 30th Div		
Miscellaneous	A Form. Messages And Signals. App 5		
Miscellaneous	C.R.E. 30th Divn		
Heading	202nd F.C.R.E. Vol 3 Jan		
Heading	War Diary of 202nd Field Compy R.E. month of January 1916 Volume 3		
War Diary	Candas	03/01/1916	03/01/1916
War Diary	Wargnies	04/01/1916	04/01/1916
War Diary	Pont-Noyelles	05/01/1916	05/01/1916
War Diary	Bray Sur Somme	06/01/1916	31/01/1916
Miscellaneous	March Order for Jany 3rd, 4th & 5th 1916 App 1	03/01/1916	03/01/1916
Operation(al) Order(s)	Operation Order No. 1. by Lieut Col. E H. Trotter, D.S.O. Commanding No. 2 Column		
Miscellaneous	March Table 1st Day Jany 3rd 1916	03/01/1916	03/01/1916
Miscellaneous	G 794 30th Dec. 1915. Communication during Move.	30/12/1915	30/12/1915
Operation(al) Order(s)	Transport and Supply arrangement issued with Operation Order No. 6 dated 29th December 1915	29/12/1915	29/12/1915
Operation(al) Order(s)	21st Infantry Brigade Operation Orders No. 106	03/01/1916	03/01/1916
Miscellaneous	March Table		
Operation(al) Order(s)	C.R.E's Instructions to Field Companies R.E. Supplementary to Div. Operation Order No. 6 Operation Order No 2	30/12/1915	30/12/1915
Miscellaneous	Table B.1 No. 1 Column. Commander Brig. General C.J. Steavenson.		
Miscellaneous	Table B. 2 No. 2 Column Commander Lt. Col E.H. Trotter. D.S.O., 18th. L'pool R		
Miscellaneous	Table B. 3 No. 3 Column. Commander Lt. Col. H.K. Welsh, 2nd. R. Scots. Fus.		
Operation(al) Order(s)	Transport And Supply Arrangement Issued With Operation Order No. 6, dated 29th December 1915	29/12/1915	29/12/1915
Miscellaneous	Supplementary table of moves-(Issued in Connection with 5th Div O.O. 79)		
Miscellaneous	Q.4608 No 77 App 2	15/01/1916	15/01/1916
Miscellaneous	A Form. Messages And Signals. App 3		
Heading	202nd Field 1/2/16-29/2/16 Vol 4		
Heading	War Diary Of 202nd Field Coy. R.E. From 1/2/16 To 29/2/16 (Volume No 4)		
War Diary	Bray Sur Somme	01/02/1916	29/02/1916
Miscellaneous	C Form (Duplicate). Messages And Signals Appendix 2		
Heading	202 Lab Coy R.E.		
Miscellaneous	C Form (Duplicate). Messages And Signals Appendix 1		
Heading	202nd Fd Co R.E.		
Heading	202 Field Coy 1/3/16-31/3/16 Vol 5		
Heading	War Diary Of 202nd Field Coy. Royal Engineers From March 1st 1916 To March 31st 1916 Vol 5		
War Diary	Bray	03/03/1916	31/03/1916
Heading	202 Field Coy 1/4/16-30/4/16 Vol 6		
Heading	War Diary of 202nd field Company Royal Engineers from April 1st 1916 To April 30th 1916 Volume 6		
War Diary	Bray	01/04/1916	07/04/1916
War Diary	Frechencourt	08/04/1916	11/04/1916
War Diary	Bertangles	12/04/1916	26/04/1916

War Diary	Corbie	28/04/1916	30/04/1916
Heading	War Diary Of 202nd Field Coy Royal Engrs. From May 1st 1916 To May 31st 1916 Volume 7		
War Diary	Bray Sur Somme	01/05/1916	28/05/1916
Miscellaneous	Officer Commanding 202nd Field C.R.E. App 1		
Heading	War Diary of 202nd Field Coy Royal Engineers Volume 8 from June 1st 1916 to June 30th 1916		
War Diary	Bray Sur Somme	01/06/1916	30/06/1916
Heading	War Diary of 202nd Field Company Royal Engineers From:- July 1st 1916 To:- July 31st 1916 Volume 9		
War Diary	Bray Trenches	01/07/1916	10/07/1916
War Diary	Bray to Vaux	11/07/1916	18/07/1916
War Diary	Vaux	19/07/1916	19/07/1916
War Diary	Bray	20/07/1916	20/07/1916
War Diary	F. 16	21/07/1916	21/07/1916
War Diary	Silesia Trench	22/07/1916	23/07/1916
War Diary	Bray	24/07/1916	29/07/1916
War Diary	Caftet Wd Bray	30/07/1916	31/07/1916
Heading	30th Divisional Engineers 202nd Field Company R.E. August 1916		
War Diary	Bray-Sur-Somme	01/08/1916	01/08/1916
War Diary	Mericourt l'Abbe	02/08/1916	02/08/1916
War Diary	Hocquincourt	03/08/1916	05/08/1916
War Diary	Robecq	06/08/1916	09/08/1916
War Diary	Gorre	10/08/1916	31/08/1916
Heading	202 Field Coy 1/10/16-31/10/16 Vol 12		
Heading	War Diary of 202nd Field Company R.E. for the month of September 1916 Volume 11		
War Diary	Gorre	02/09/1916	21/09/1916
War Diary	Wargnies	22/09/1916	29/09/1916
War Diary	Montauban	30/09/1916	30/09/1916
Heading	War Diary of 202nd Field Company R.E. for the month of October 1916 Volume 12		
War Diary	Montauban	01/10/1916	21/10/1916
War Diary	Pommiers Rot	22/10/1916	26/10/1916
War Diary	Lucheux	27/10/1916	30/10/1916
War Diary	Bailleulmont	31/10/1916	31/10/1916
Heading	War Diary of 202nd Field Coy R.E. for month of November 1916 Vol. 13		
War Diary	H.Q. Bailleulmont Sections at Berles-Au-Bas	01/11/1916	17/11/1916
War Diary	Bailleulmont Sections at Bellacourt and Berles	18/11/1916	30/11/1916
Heading	War Diary of 202nd Field Coy, Royal Engineers for the month of December 1916 Volume 14		
War Diary	H.Q. Bailleulmont Sections at Bellacourt & Berles-Au-Bois	01/12/1916	31/12/1916
Miscellaneous	Report on Raids night of 16/17 Nov. 1916	18/11/1916	18/11/1916
Heading	War Diary of 202nd Field Company. Royal Engineers for the month of January 1917 Volume 15		
War Diary	Bailleulmont	01/01/1917	08/01/1917
War Diary	Brevillers	09/01/1917	31/01/1917
Heading	War Diary Of 202nd Field Coy. Royal Engineers. From 1st February 1917 To 28th February 1917. Volume No. 16		
War Diary	Brevillers	01/02/1917	09/02/1917
War Diary	Achicourt	10/02/1917	26/02/1917
War Diary	Agny	27/02/1917	28/02/1917

Heading	War Diary of 202nd Field Coy R.E. from March 1st to March 31st 1917 Volume 17		
War Diary	Achicourt	01/03/1917	14/03/1917
War Diary	Agny	15/03/1917	22/03/1917
War Diary	Blaireville	23/03/1917	31/03/1917
Heading	War Diary of 202nd Field Company R.E. from:- April 1st 1917 to:- April 30th 1917 Volume 18		
War Diary	Blaireville	01/04/1917	11/04/1917
War Diary	Bailleulmont	12/04/1917	12/04/1917
War Diary	Monchy-Au-Bois	13/04/1917	14/04/1917
War Diary	Pommier	15/04/1917	18/04/1917
War Diary	Beaurains	19/04/1917	27/04/1917
War Diary	Ococbe	28/04/1917	30/04/1917
Heading	202 Field Coy 1/May/16-31/May/16 Vol 19		
Heading	War Diary of 202nd Field Coy, Royal Engineers from May 1st 1917 to May 31st 1917 Volume No. 19		
War Diary	Ococbe	01/05/1917	02/05/1917
War Diary	Neulette	03/05/1917	20/05/1917
War Diary	Gauchin	21/05/1917	21/05/1917
War Diary	Equirre	22/05/1917	22/05/1917
War Diary	Flechinelle	23/05/1917	24/05/1917
War Diary	Les Ciseaux	25/05/1917	25/05/1917
War Diary	Le Brearde	26/05/1917	26/05/1917
War Diary	Winnezeele	29/05/1917	29/05/1917
War Diary	Brandhoek	30/05/1917	30/05/1917
War Diary	Ypres	31/05/1917	31/05/1917
Heading	202 Field Coy 1/june/17-30/june/17 Vol 20		
Heading	War Diary of 202nd Field Company R.E. from:- June 1st 1917 to:- June 30th 1917 Volume 20		
War Diary	Ypres	01/06/1917	30/06/1917
Heading	202 Field Coy 1/July/17-31/July/17 Vol 21		
Heading	War Diary of 202nd Field C.R.E. from July 1st 1917 to:- July 31st 1917 Volume 21		
War Diary	Ypres Area H 26b 3.7	01/07/1917	05/07/1917
War Diary	H13d 6.2. and H 21d 5.2	06/07/1917	06/07/1917
War Diary	Ypres Area H 13d 6.2 and H 21b 5.2	07/07/1917	11/07/1917
War Diary	H 31b 3.5	12/07/1917	20/07/1917
War Diary	Ypres Area H 31 b 3.5	21/07/1917	23/07/1917
War Diary	H 26 b 3.7 & Chateau Segard	24/07/1917	31/07/1917
Heading	202 Field Coy 1/8/17-31/8/17 Vol 22		
Heading	War Diary of 202nd Field Company Royal Engineers from 1st August 1917 to 31st August 1917 Volume No. 22		
War Diary	H 26 b 3.7 & Chateau Segard	01/08/1917	04/08/1917
War Diary	Steenvoorde Area	05/08/1917	06/08/1917
War Diary	Merris Area	07/08/1917	10/08/1917
War Diary	Mont Vidaigne	11/08/1917	14/08/1917
War Diary	M21 b 3.2	15/08/1917	15/08/1917
War Diary	N 17C 1.1	16/08/1917	21/08/1917
War Diary	N 28 a 8.4	22/08/1917	31/08/1917
Heading	202 Field Coy 1/Sep/17-30/Sep/17 Vol 23		
Heading	War Diary of 202nd Field Coy R.E. from:- Sept 1st 1917 to:- Sept 30th 1917 Volume 23		
War Diary	N 28a 8.4 (Ypres Area)	01/09/1917	18/09/1917
War Diary	N 28a 8.4	19/09/1917	30/09/1917
Heading	202 Field Coy 1/Oct/17-31/Oct/17 Vol 24		

Heading	War Diary of 202nd Field Company Royal Engineers From 1st October 1917 To 31st October 1917 Volume No. 24		
War Diary	N 28a 8.4	01/10/1917	31/10/1917
Heading	202 Field Coy 1/Nov/17-30/Nov/17 Vol 25		
Heading	War Diary of 202nd Field Coy Royal Engineers from 1st Nov. 1917 To 30th Nov 1917 Volume No 25		
War Diary	N 28a 8.4	01/11/1917	30/11/1917
Heading	202 Field Coy 1/Dec/17-31/Dec/17 Vol 26		
Heading	War Diary of 202nd Field Coy Royal Engineers from 1st December 1917 to 31st December 1917 Volume No. 26		
War Diary		01/12/1917	31/12/1917
Heading	202 Field Coy 1/Jan/17-31/Jan/17 Vol 27		
Heading	War Diary of 202nd Field Co Royal Engineers from 1st Jan 1918 to 31st Jan 1918 Volume No. 27		
War Diary		01/01/1918	31/01/1918
Heading	202 Field Coy 1/2/18-28/2/18 Vol 28		
Heading	War Diary of 202nd Field Coy Royal Engineers from 1st February 1918 To 28th February 1918 Volume No. 28		
War Diary		01/02/1918	01/02/1918
War Diary	Nesle	02/02/1918	14/02/1918
War Diary	Roupy	15/02/1918	28/02/1918
Miscellaneous	Method of Detonating Ammonal Safe App 1	17/12/1916	17/12/1916
Heading	30th Div. War Diary 202nd Field Company, R.E. March 1918		
Heading	War Diary of 202nd Field Co R.E. from 1st March 1918 to 31st March 1918 Volume No. 29		
War Diary	Roupy	01/03/1918	31/03/1918
Heading	War Diary of 202nd Field Coy R.E. From 1st April 1918 to 30th April 1918 Volume No. 30		
War Diary		01/04/1918	30/04/1918
Heading	202 Field Coy 1/May/18-31/May/18 Vol 31		
Heading	War Diary of 202nd Field Coy R.E. May 1st 1918 to May 31st 1918 Volume 31		
War Diary		01/05/1918	06/05/1918
War Diary	Steenvoorde Area	07/05/1918	09/05/1918
War Diary	Lederzeele Area	10/05/1918	11/05/1918
War Diary	Eu	12/05/1918	12/05/1918
War Diary	Eu Area	13/05/1918	31/05/1918
Heading	202 Field Coy 1/Jun/18-30/June/18 Vol 32		
Heading	War Diary of 202nd Field Coy R.E. from June 1st 1918 to June 30th 1918 Volume 32		
War Diary	Eu Area	01/05/1918	19/05/1918
War Diary	Nolettes	20/05/1918	20/05/1918
War Diary	Fontaine-Sur-Maye	21/05/1918	26/06/1918
War Diary	Forest-Montiers	27/06/1918	27/06/1918
War Diary	Ganspette	28/06/1918	30/06/1918
Heading	202 Field Coy 1/July/18-31/July/18 Vol. 33		
Heading	War Diary of 202nd Field Coy Royal Engineers from 1-7-18 to 31-7-18 Volume No 33		
War Diary	Ganspette	01/07/1918	08/07/1918
War Diary	Steenvoorde Area	09/07/1918	11/07/1918
War Diary	Godewaersvelde Area	12/07/1918	31/07/1918
Heading	202 Field Coy 1/8/18-31/8/18 Vol 34		

Heading	War Diary of 202nd Field Coy R.E. From 1st August 1918 To 31st August 1918		
War Diary	Godewaersvelde And Boeschepe Area	01/08/1918	08/08/1918
War Diary	Westoutre And Locre Area	09/08/1918	31/08/1918
Heading	202 Field Coy 1/sep/18-30/sep/18 Vol 35		
War Diary	Westoutre Area	01/09/1918	07/09/1918
War Diary	Kemmel Area	08/09/1918	25/09/1918
War Diary	Westoutre Area	26/09/1918	27/09/1918
War Diary	Kemmel Area	28/09/1918	30/09/1918
Heading	War Diary 202nd Field Company Royal Engineers. From 1st October to 31st October 1918 Volume 36		
War Diary		01/10/1918	31/10/1918
Heading	War Diary of 202nd Field Co R.E. from 1st November to 30th November 1918 Volume 37		
War Diary		01/10/1918	30/10/1918
Heading	War Diary of 202nd Field Coy R.E. From Decr 1st 1918 To Decr 31st 1918 Volume 39		
War Diary	Croix Du Bois	01/12/1918	01/12/1918
War Diary	Bac St. Maur	02/12/1918	02/12/1918
War Diary	St. Floris	03/12/1918	03/12/1918
War Diary	Aire	04/12/1918	30/12/1918
War Diary	Dunkirk	31/12/1918	31/12/1918
War Diary	War Diary of 202nd Field Coy R.E. from 1st Jany 1919 to 31st Jany 1919 Vol 39		
War Diary	Dunkirk	01/01/1919	01/01/1919
War Diary	Malo-Les-Bains	02/01/1919	31/01/1919
Heading	War Diary of 202nd Field Coy Royal Engineers February 1919		
War Diary	Malo Les Bains	01/02/1919	28/02/1919
Heading	War Diary of 202nd Field Coy R.E. for Feb 1919		
War Diary	Malo Les-Bains	01/03/1919	31/03/1919
Heading	War Diary of 202nd Field Coy RE for March 1919		
War Diary	Dunkirk	01/03/1919	17/03/1919
War Diary	Beaumarais	18/03/1919	18/03/1919
War Diary	Dunkirk	20/03/1919	20/03/1919

WO 95/2323/1

202 FIELD COY

NOV 15 – JLY 19

30TH DIVISION
DIVL ENGINEERS

202ND FLD COY R.E.

NOV 1915-JLY 1919

30th Division

202nd F.C.R.E.
Vol: I

121
7795

Nov. 15
|
Jly 19

Confidential

War Diary

of

202nd Field Company (CP) R.E

From Nov. 9th 1915 To Nov. 30th 1915

(Volume One)

Volume 1

Instructions regarding War Diaries and Intelligence Summaries are contained in F. S. Regs., Part II. and the Staff Manual respectively. Title pages will be prepared in manuscript.

WAR DIARY
or
INTELLIGENCE SUMMARY.
(Erase heading not required.)

Army Form C. 2118.

Place	Date	Hour	Summary of Events and Information	Remarks and references to Appendices
Larkhill	9/11/15	9.45 am	Entrained Amesbury. Arr: Southampton 12.0 m'day. Departed by Steamer 4.30 pm	App I & II
Le Havre	10/11/15		Disembarked 12.0 m'day. Entrained Gare du Merchandises Havre 9.0 pm. Departed 11.50 pm.	App III
Bettencourt	11.11.15		Detrained Pont Remy 12.0 m'day. Marched to Bettencourt (Dpt de la Somme) arr 7.30 pm to billets (close). Snow fell night 15/16th & 16/17th.	
Villers le Bocage	17/11/15.		Departed from Bettencourt by road at 8.0 am. Hard frost. Roads bad. 4" snow on ground. Arrived Villers-le-Bocage at 1.0 pm, to close Billets. Came into 90th Bde area.	App IV
Candas	28/11/15		Departed Villers Bocage by road 9.15 am. Hard Frost, clear, roads excellent. Arr Candas 1.0 pm. Billeted.	App V
Candas	29/11/15	—	Opened R.E. Divisional Stores at CANDAS for collection of Constructional material and preparation of and issue of finished articles. Timber plentiful in neighbourhood, stone scarce. Commenced manufacture of Samples & bought material (timber etc) in locality.	

H O Wraith Major R.E.
O.C. 202ND FIELD CO., (COUNTY PALATINE) R.E.
29/12/15.

Appendix 1.

SUBJECT: TIME TABLES - MOVE OF DIVISION.

Secret

OCX

O.C.,

202nd Field Co. (C.P.) R.E.

The attached extract from time-table is forwarded for your information and guidance.

R.J.[illegible]

Lieut.R.E.

Adjutant - 30th Divisional (County Palatine) Engineers.

Larkhill Camp,
SALISBURY PLAIN.
5th November, 1915.

SECRET.

Train No.	UNIT.	O.	O.R.	H.	Vehicles 4-Wh.	Vehicles 2-Wh.	From	To	Starting Times. Day NOV.	Starting Times. Time.	Arrival Times. Day NOV.	Arrival Times. Time
X.176.	H.Q.Div.R.E. & Cyclist Co.	8	193	3	1	1 (204 bikes)	Amesbury	Southampton Docks.	7th	1 pm.	7th	2-45 p.m.
X.195	½ 200th Fd.Co.R.E.	3	113.	39	5	4	"	--- do ----	"	11.30 pm	8th	1-15 a.m.
X.196	½ -- do ----	3	113	40	5	5	"	"	8th	12.45 am	"	2-30 a.m.
X.198	½ 201st "	3	113	39	5	4	"	"	"	2-45 am	"	4-30 a.m.
X.200	½ " "	3	113	40	5	5 Bikes	" ~~Bikes~~	"	"	3.45 am	"	5-30 a.m.
X.216.	½ 202nd "	3	113	39	5	4 16	" ~~16~~	"	9th	9-45 am	9th	11-30 a.m.
X.217	½ 202nd " ~~66~~	3	113	40	5	5 14	" ~~14~~	"	"	10.40 am.	9th	12.25 p.m.

SUBJECT: MOVE OF DIVISION.

A.L.1632.

Attached are Time Tables for the move of Division.

Full instructions as to entrainment, embarkation, the voyage, disembarkation, entrainment at the Base, and detrainment in the area of concentration have already been issued in book form. It is of the utmost importance that these instructions are fully and carefully complied with in every respect.

DRESS. All men will parade wearing their greatcoats. All water bottles will be filled.

ENTRAINING. In entraining at Amesbury the following points will be observed:

Horses and Vehicles and Baggage will be at the Station 1½ hours and Men 30 minutes before the departure time of the train. A Mounted Officer will be sent ahead to ascertain from the R.T.O. the platform from which the troops will entrain.

A loading party of 50 men, under an Officer, will be detailed for each train and this party must arrive at the Station in advance of the Horses and Vehicles. The R.T.O. will issue all instructions to this party, part of which will be utilised for loading the vehicles and the remainder for the Baggage.

Care must be taken to see that all Vehicle Poles can be readily removed.

No Rifles are to be left on Transport Vehicles - each man will take his rifle into the carriage with him.

HORSES. Horse wagons will usually be found at head of the trucks for transport wagons. All riders and spare horses must be sent ahead to the leading horse wagons and entrained without delay. The men so released will give a hand with the Team Horses which will be led forward as soon as unhooked well clear of all Transport Wagons.

Bits will be removed and girths slightly loosened, nose bags will be secured to truck rails in rear of the horses.

BAGGAGE. Requisitions for transport for baggage will be forwarded to the O.C., A.S.C., No.2 A Camp, Canada Lines, Larkhill, immediately on receipt of these instructions. In no case will the Baggage sent by Units exceed in amount and weight the scale authorised to be carried in the Baggage Section of Train as laid down in the Field Service Manuals, plus such articles carried in the Supply Section as are articles of Regimental Equipment.

RATIONS. Attention is drawn to para.5 of the "Instructions for Entrainment and Embarkation", and to para.5 of "Instructions for the Voyage" &c. already issued.

H S Clarke
Captain.
D.A.A. & Q.M.G., 30th Division.

LARKHILL.
5/11/1915.

Appendix II

Secret

O.C.

O.C. 202nd Fd. Co. R.E.

The following extract from Orders for Embarkation of the Divn. is forwarded for your information.

Fourth Day. Nov. 9th Southampton to Havre

11 202nd Fd. Co. R.E.

40th mobile Vet. Sect.

34th Casualty Clearing Stn.

70th Sanitary Sect.

H.Q. M.G. section + 1 squadron Lancs. Hussars.

4/11/15

R.J. Stone Lieut.

~~SADWAIN.~~ R.E.

Adjutant, 30th Divisional (County Palatine) Engineers.

Appendix III

30 34

Officer Commanding 202nd Field Coy. R.E.

1. Please note that the Field Coy.

under your command will entrain as detailed in Para. 4 below.

2. Units must be very careful that every man in their unit is told the station and "point of Entrainment" before marching off from camp. Most of the numerous cases of men left behind have occurred through neglect of this precaution.

3. The entrance to Points Nos. 1, 2, and 4 is at No. 70 Cours de la République and to Point 3 at the Boulevard d'Harfleur.

4. Place of entrainment **Gare des Merchandises.**

~~Gare Maritime.~~ Point No. 1

Time 21-00 p.m. Date 10/XI/15

Rayner

Ration Party (strength 1 officer 10 men) to report to Officer i/c Detail Issue Store at **Gare des Merchandises.**

~~Gare Maritime.~~ ~~Point 6.~~

Time 20-30 p.m. Date 10/XI/15

N.B.—The time given is the hour at which units are to arrive **AT THE POINT** specified (*i.e.*, place of entrainment).

5. As soon as orders for entrainment are received the units will at once notify the strength of the unit to the Officer i/c Detail Issue Store at place of entrainment.

6. Your attention is directed to the **"Special Orders for Units Passing through Havre Base,"** especially para. 6 and to **"Standing Orders for Entrainment."**

Any further information about Entrainment can be obtained from the D.A.D.R.T., GARE DES VOYAGEURS.

The Orderly Room Serjeants, if any, should report to this office, at ...... ready in all respects for immediate entrainment on being posted to the D.A.G., 3rd Echelon, for duty.

[signature]

Issued at 14-30 ......CAPTAIN,

Date 9/XI/15 D.A.Q.M.G., Havre Base.

Stationery Services Press, P 420, 1000. 9/15.

Appendix IV

SECRET. Copy No 8

91st Infantry Brigade Order No 1.

16th November, 1915.

(Reference 1/80,000 AMIENS Sheet 12).

-:-:-:-:-:-:-:-:-:-:-

1. The 91st Inf.Bde.and attached troops will march on the 17th and 18th instants to a new billeting area, in accordance with attached March Tables - March Table for 18th instant will be issued later.

2. Officers Commanding Units will on this and all future occasions report:-
(i) When they have established their Headquarters in new billets, and
(ii) When the whole of the unit has arrived in the New Area.

3. A separate order will be issued regarding Supplies.

4. 1st Line Transport and Train Wagons will march with Units.

5. Bde.Headquarters will open at VAUX EN AMIENOIS at 3-0 p.m. at which hour it will close at GORENFLOS.

A.K.GRANT Major
Bde.Maj.91st Inf.Bde.
12-15 p.m.

Copy No 1 Filed
2 Filed
3 30th Division.
4 20th Mchr R
5 21st Mchr R
6 22nd Mchr R
7 24th Mchr R
8 202nd Fd.Coy.R.E.
9 No 4 Coy.Div.Train
10 O.C.Supplies
11 97th Fd.Amb.

SECRET.

Copy No 8

1st Day.
March Table for 17th November,1915.
(Issued with 91st Inf.Bde.Order No1)

UNIT.	FROM.	STARTING POINT	HOUR.	ROUTE.	DESTINATION OR BILLETING AREA.	REMARKS.
20th Mchr R	HOUFLERS & BOUCHON,	Level Crossing FLIXECOURT.	9-30 am	FLIXECOURT & BELLOY.	ARGOEUVES	
21st Mchr R	VAUCHELLES & SURCAMPS	-do-	9-45 am	-do-	ST.SAUVEUR	
22nd Mchr R	BRUCAMPS	Cross Roads at 2nd S of SURCAMPS	9-10 am	ST.OUEN VIGNACOURT	ST.VAST	22nd Mchr R march thro' SURCAMPS
24th Mchr R	ERGNIES	-do-	9-20 am	-do-	FLESSELLES	
No 4 Coy. Div.Train	LA HUIE FERME.	-do-	9-30 am	-do-	VAUX EN AMIENOIS	
202nd Fd.Coy R.E. & 97th Fd.Amb.	BETHENCOURT			VIGNACOURT &FLESSELLES	VILLERS BOCAGE	To clear FLESSELLES by 12nn & Cross Roads at S of ST.OUEN by 9-45 am. These Units march under O.C? 202nd Fd.Coy.R.E.
91st Bde.H.Q.	GORENFLOS	-do-	9-35 am		VAUX EN AMIENOIS	

90th Brigade.
202nd Field Coy.R.E.
201st Field Coy.R.E.
C.R.E.

With reference to the "Transport and Supply arrangements during the move of the Division" issued with 30th Divisional Operation Order (1), the following alterations will be made:-

No.201 Field Coy. R.E. will be in the Divisional Troops Area, and No.202 Field Coy. R.E. will be in the 90th Brigade Area.

[signature]

Captain.

16-11-15. D.A.A. & Q.M.G. 30th Division.

REFERENCE 30TH DIVISION OPERATION ORDER NO. (1) PARA. 4.

TRANSPORT AND SUPPLY ARRANGEMENTS DURING THE MOVE OF THE DIVISION.

---

1 BAGGAGE WAGONS will remain with Units until the move is completed.

BLANKET WAGONS will be issued today at the following scale:-

2 per Infantry Battalion.
1 per Infantry Brigade Headquarters.

These wagons will be returned to the Headquarter Company, Divisional Train at FLESSELLES immediately after the move is completed.

SUPPLY WAGONS will join their units this evening loaded with rations for consumption on the 18th instant; these wagons will march on the 17th with their units until the Units arrive at their billets allotted to them that night, they will issue the rations as soon as possible after the units have reached their billets; stay the night with the unit and will be led by an Officer on the 18th instant to the re-filling point for the Brigade Area. Refilling points as under:-

2 DIVISIONAL TROOPS at the Junction of the FLESSELLES - VIGNACOURT-CANAPES ROADS. (¼ mile N.E. of OLINCOURT CH^au)
89TH BRIGADE point 70 on the VAUX-FLESSELLES cross roads. (¾ mile N of VAUX)
90TH BRIGADE at the cross road from COISY to BERTANGLES and in VAUX PONTAMEVILLE to VILLERS BOCAGE.
91ST BRIGADE at the entrance to PIERREGOT on the RAINNEVILLE road.

3 No. 202 Company R.E. will be in the Divisional Troops area.

No. 98th Field Ambulance and 200 Field Company will be in the 89th Area.

No. 96th Field Ambulance and the 201st Field Company will be in the 90th Area.

No. 97th Field Ambulance in the 91st Area.

4 O.C. Units will be responsible that men falling out do not ride on the Supply wagons, and that the Supply wagons reach the re-filling point for the Brigade Area concerned not later than 3.0 p.m. on the 18th. inst.

5 The following units will be issued with 2 days rations today for consumption on the 17th and 18th instants. The Supply wagons of these Units will return to the Headquarter Company of the Train after issuing rations tonight:-

Divisional Headquarters;	Headquarters, R.E.
Sanitary Section;	Signal Company.
A.K. Cable Section;	Mobile Veterinary Section.

6 All Units will arrange to draw soft-soap for their horses feet from D.A.D.O.S. at 5.0 p.m. today.

This soft-soap is used to prevent balling.

16th November, 1915.

J.H. Humphrey [signature]
Lieut. Colonel,
A.A. & Q.M.G. 30th Division.

App V

Copy no 6.

90TH BRIGADE OPERATION ORDER NO.2.

(Refs. to 1/80,000 AMIENS, Sheet 12).

27.11.15.

1. The 90th Inf.Bde. and attached Troops will move into the FIENVILLERS Area on 28th inst. in accordance with the attached March Table.

2. SUPPLY. The arrangements for supply are attached

3. TRANSPORT.WAGONS will march with their own Units.

4. On arrival at CANAPLES the personnel and baggage of the Grenadier Coy. will re-join their own Units.

5. MEDICAL ARRANGEMENTS. The O.C. 96th Field Ambulance will arrange to pick up casualties as far as road junction 1 mile N.W. of FLESSELLES. From thence and onwards this duty will be carried out by the 97th Field Ambulance.

6. BRIGADE HEADQUARTERS. will open at the road junction about 600x S.W. of the C of CANAPLES at 11.30 am on th 28th inst. at which hour it will close at MONTONVILLERS.

H Montgomery
MAJOR
BRIGADE MAJOR
90TH INFANTRY BDE.

Issudd to Signalsat 10.25 am.

No.	
No.1 copy to	30th Division.
2	16th B.Mnhr.R.
3	17th "
4	18th "
5	19th "
6	202nd Field Coy. R.E.
7	96th Field Ambulance.
8	97th " "
9	No.3 Coy Div.Train.
10	No.4 " " "
11	Signal Section.
12	File.
13 & 14	War Diary.

90TH BRIGADE OPERATION ORDER NO.2.

SUPPLY AND TRANSPORT ARRANGEMENTS.

1. In addition to the Train Transport wagons allotted to Units by War Establishment, the following Units will receive G.S.Wagons on the evening of the 27th. inst. for the carriage of blankets, etc, as follows:-

Field Coys. R.E.	2 wagons per Coy.for baggage blankets etc.
Infantry Battns.	2 wagons per Bn.for blankets.
Bde. H.Q.	1 wagon for blankets.

2. Units will march on the 28th instant with remaining portions of the day's rations in the Cookers, Supply wagonsw will march with their Units empty, and may be used for the conveyance of bl-nkets, Light Stores, etc, and will be sent under an Officer to the Refilling Points for the Brigade Area concerned so as to reach the Refilling Points not later than 3 pm. to draw rations for consumption on the 29th inst.

3. The Refilling Points will be as under:-

89th Brigade. BERNAVILLE.
90th Brigade. CANAPLES.
~~Divisional Troops BERNEUIL.~~

4. The Brigade Supply Officers will post an orderly at the Main Door of the Church in each village in which the Refilling Points are situated to direct Supply Wagons to the Refilling Points.

5. All Train baggage and blanket transport will remain with Units to which they are attached until 9 am on 29th inst. when they will be returned to their Train Coys. which will be billetted in the same village as the Refilling Point in the Area to which they belong.

Supply Wagons will go to the Refilling Points at 10 am 29th inst. to refill for consumption on the 30th inst.

6. 202 Field Coy.R.E. and the 97th Field Ambulance will draw supplies from the 89th Bde.Area until the 91st Bde. returns to 30th Div.Area.

96th Field Ambulance will draw supplies from the 90th Bde.Area.

7. Refilling from the 29th inst. inclusive will be at 10 am.

Montgomery BRIGADE MAJOR,

27-11-15.

90th (late ...) INFANTRY BRIGADE

SECRET.

~~FIRST DAY.~~

COPY NO. 6

MARCH TABLE FOR 28th Novr ISSUED WITH 90TH INFANTRY BRIGADE ORDER NO. 2.

UNIT.	FROM.	STARTING POINT.	Time Head of Unit passes starting point.	ROUTE.	DESTINATION.	REMARKS.
Brigade Hqtrs & Grenadier Co.,	MONTONVILLERS.	North exit from village.	9.20.am.	FLESSELLES-HAVERNAS.	CANAPLES.	Cross roads at F of FLESSELLES not to be reached before 10.am.
16th Bn Mchr R.	VILLERS BOCAGE.	Cross roads at Pt 130 N.W.of VILLERS BOCAGE.	9.15.am.	FLESSELLES-HAVERNAS-CANAPLES.	BONNEVILLE.	To march in rear of Bde Hqtrs.
17th " "	BERTANGLE.	Cross roa ds 400x west of the B of BERTANGLE.	9.25.am.	FLESSELLES-HAVERNAS.	MONTRELET.	To march in rear of 16th Bn Mchr R after passing cross roads at F of FLESSELLES.
19th " "	COISY.	" "	9.30.am.	BERTANGLE-FLESSELLES-HAVERNAS.	CANAPLES.	
18th " "	CARDONNETTE.	" "	9.35.am.	COISY-BERTANGLE-FLESSELLES-HAVERNAS.	"	
No 3 Co Div Train	COISY.	" "	9.40.am.	FLESSELLES-HAVERNAS-CANAPLES.	HALLOY-LES)PERNOIS.	
96th Field Ambulance.	POULAINVILLE.	" "	9.43.am.	Cross roads 1 mile S of B of BERTANGLE-FLESSELLES-VIGNACOURT.	BERTEAUCOURT.	
Details No 4 Co., Div Train.	PIERREGOT.	Western exit from village.	9.0.am.	TALMAS-CANDAS-FEINVILLERS.	BOISBERGUES.	
202nd Field Co.R.E.	VILLERS BOCAGE.	Cross roads at Pt 130 N.W.of VILLERS BOCAGE.	9.30am.	TALMAS-LA VICOGNE.	CANDAS.	
97th Field Ambulance.	" "	" "	10.15.am.	FLESSELLES-HAVERNAS-CANAPLES	CANAPLES	To march independently on the 29th to LE MEILLARD

Map Reference 1/80,000 AMIENS. Sheet 12.

202nd Field Coy. R.E.

Secret.

March Orders. 28.11.15.

1. Transport & Supply. The copy of Transport and Supply arrangements is attached.

The extra G.S. Wagons will be billeted by 202nd Field Coy. R.E.

2. Rations Each man will carry a havers[ack] ration, and cooks will prepare a h[ot] meal as soon as possible after arriv[al] at destination.

3. Advance Party. Lieut Rayner, with 2 N.C.O's & 4 Sapper Cyclists, and Interpreter Mar[illegible] will leave the Parade Ground at 8-45 on 28th Nov. to arrange billets at CANDAS.

[4]. Destination The Company will march to CANDAS. and will be billeted as near as possible to the existing R.E. workshop the[re].

[5]. Route. TALMAS, LA VICOGNE.

[6]. Time. The Company will parade at:-

Drivers: 8.30. a.m.

Sappers: 8.45. a.m. for the Compa[ny] to move off at 9-15. a.m.

The Company will pass the Startin[g] Point at the Cross Roads; VILLERS BOCAGE, FLESSELLE, & TALMAS to POULINVILLE at 9-30 a.m. following the 16th Battalion Manchester Regiment.

27.11.15.

H.O. Spratt [signature]

Major. R.E.

O.C. 202nd Fld. Coy. R.E.

30th Div

202nd F.C. R.E.
Vol: 2
Dec.

Confidential

VOLUME 2

WAR DIARY OF

202nd FIELD Coy (C.P.) R.E.

For

DECEMBER 1915

"C" Form (Original).

Army Form C. 2123.

MESSAGES AND SIGNALS.

No. of Message 77

Prefix Code Words 49

Charges to collect

Service Instructions.

Received From By

Sent, or sent out At m. To By

Office Stamp. Vol 2

Handed in at Office m. Received m.

TO 202 Fd. Co. R.E.

*Sender's Number	Day of Month	In reply to Number	AAA
K. 158	4th		

202nd Field Co will be accomodated at LOUVENCOURT instead of COUIN on night 5/6th Dec aaa An R.E officer will meet them at cross roads third i of VAUCHELLES LES AUTHIE at 11.15 am to conduct company to LOUVENCOURT

FROM C.R.E.

PLACE & TIME 10.45 pm.

R J Hart Lieut.

* This line should be erased if not required.

W.2384—583. 30,000 Pads - 8/14. S. B. Ltd.- Forms/C.2123.

"A" Form.

Army Form C. 2121.

MESSAGES AND SIGNALS.

No. of Message

Prefix ____ Code* ____ m.	Words	Charge	This message is on a/c of:	Recd. at ____ m.
Office of Origin and Service Instructions.	Sent		____ Service.	Date
	At ____ m.			From
	To			
	By		(Signature of "Franking Officer.")	By

TO: O.C. 202nd Fd Co. R.E.

Sender's Number.	Day of Month	In reply to Number	AAA
* R. 120	1st		

Following message from 30th DIV. to VII Corps is forwarded for your information:— Begins AAA As 48th DIV. are putting 202nd Fd. Co. COUIN night 5th – 6th PUCHEVILLERS rather out of their way AAA would your arrangements be affected if 202nd Fd Co marched direct from CANDAS to COUIN on 5th instead of spending night 4th – 5th at PUCHEVILLERS AAA ends.

From: C.R.E.

Place

Time

The above may be forwarded as now corrected.

Censor.

(Z) R. J. Stone Lieut

Signature of Addressor or person authorised to telegraph in his name.

* This line should be erased if not required.

(774-5) —McC. & Co. Ltd., London.— W 1789/1602. 150,000. 8/15. Forms C2121/10.

app! 2. Vol 2.

Operation Orders No. (cont)

The Company will be accomodated at ~~Gezaincourt~~ Couin on the night of 5-6. December 1915. On 6th December 1915, Headquarters + Nos. 1 and 2 Sections will proceed to Hebuterne and Nos. 3+4 Sections will proceed to Fonquevillers. The 144th and 143rd Infantry Brigades will arrange for their accomodation in Hebuterne and Fonquevillers respectively

3-12-1915

H. O. W. [illegible]

Major R.E.

O/C 202nd Field Co. R.E.

app. Vol 2

202ND FIELD CO. R.E.

OPERATION ORDER NO. FOR MARCH ON 5-12-1915.

MAP REFERENCE:- AMIENS. SHEET 12 1/80,000

---

1. TRANSPORT AND SUPPLY. Copy of supply & transport arrangements attached.
The following vehicles only will accompany the Company:-
Bicycles.
G.S. Wagon.
~~Cart. Light Spring.~~ Tool
Cooks Limber Wagon.
One R.E. Limber Wagon per Section Water Cart
Supply Wagons (attached)
The transport not accompanying the 202nd. Field Co R.E. will be left in charge of Section of 200th Field Co R.E. at Candas.

2. TIME
Breakfast 5.45 a.m.
Parade 6.45 a.m.
March off 7.0. a.m.

3. ROUTE. DOULENS - SARTON - MARIEUX - AUTHIE - ~~QUIN~~ COUIN.
The C.R.E. 48th Division will detail an Officer to meet the Company at Cross Roads point 141 on Marieux - Authie road at 11.15 a.m. 5-12-15.

4. DRESS. Marching Order. Great coats on pack. Ground sheet carried on the man for use if wet. Blankets will be carried on the blanket wagon

App. Vol 2

EXTRACT FROM SUPPLY AND TRANSPORT ARRANGEMENTS ISSUED IN ACCORDANCE WITH 30TH DIVISION OPERATION ORDER NO.4 DATED 2ND DECEMBER 1915.

90TH BRIGADE.

The undermentioned additional Transport for the conveyance of blankets will be issued as under:-

Headquarters 90th Brigade	1 G.S. Wagon.
202nd Field Coy. R.E.	1 G.S. Wagon.
Each Infantry Battalion.	4 G.S. Wagons.

Units will send a N.C.O. to the O.C. Headquarter Company Divisional Train at BERNEUIL to take over these wagons at 11-0am on the day prior to moving from their present area.

Supply and Baggage Wagons will be provided by the O.C. No.3 Company Divisional Train and sent to Units on the evening of the day previous to departure.

All Train Transport allotted to the Units of the 90th Infantry Brigade and the 202nd Field Company R.E. will remain with the Units until their return to the 30th Divisional Area when they will at once be returned to the Train Companies concerned.

Units will draw rations on the day of arrival in the new area from the Division to which they are attached for consumption on the following day under arrangements to be made by the Divisions concerned.

Units attached to the 4th Division will remain under the 30th Division for Rations.

Units marching East to the trenches will carry with them 2 days rations. 1 day's rations will be issued at the same time as usual on the morning previous to the march, and these will be carried in the Cookers. The other days rations will be issued in the evening of the same day at a time to be fixed by the Formation Supply Officer, and will remain in the Supply Wagons. At the end of the first days march, the rations in the Cookers will be issued to the men and the rations in the Supply Wagons will be transferred to the Cookers.

Units will forward ration indents (including A.S.C. personnel and Heavy Draught Horses attached) for requirements for the first 3 days that they will be attached to either the 37th or 48th Divisions to their Formation Supply Officer at once.

2-12-15.

(Sd) L.Hume-Spry, Lt-Col.
A.A. & Q.M.G. 30th Division.

Vol 2

App i

COPY.

48th Divn.
G.x.604.

ATTACHMENT OF 202ND FIELD COY. R.E., 30TH DIVISION TO 48TH DIVISION.

1. The 202nd Field Coy. R.E. will be attached to the Division for a period of about 14 days.

2. The Company will arrive in the Divisional Area on 5th December, and will be accommodated at COUIN on the night of 5th/6th December.

3. The following transport only will accompany it to the 48th Divnl. Area:-

Bicycles and waggons for supplies, baggage and cooking.

4. The C.R.E. will detail an Officer to meet the Company on its entry into the 48th Divnl. Area and conduct it to COUIN. The time and place of meeting will be notified later.

5. On 6th December, H.Q. & 2 Sections will proceed to HEBUTERNE and 2 Sections to FONQUEVILLERS, under instructions that will be issued to them by the C.R.E., in consultation with the G.O.C's 144th and 143rd Infantry Brigades.

6. The 144th and 143rd Inf: Bdes. will arrange for their accommodation in HEBUTERNE & FONQUEVILLERS respectively.

7. The C.R.E. will forward a programme of proposed course of instruction for approval of the G.O.C., to reach this office by 12noon, 4th instant.

(Sd) R.H.Livesay, Capt.
for Lieut-Col.
General Staff, 48th Division.

2nd Dec., 1915.

NOTE.

1. Reference para: 4 of above the Company will be met at Cross Roads Point 141 on MARIEUX AUTHIE Road at 11-15am, 5th December.

2. Reference para 3 Transport not accompanying 202nd Field Co.R.E. will be left in charge of Section of 200th Field Co.R.E. which arrived at CANDAS to-day.

R Patone Lieut
Adjt RE

3/12/15

App 1

Vol 2

Copy No. 2

SECRET.

MARCH TABLE ISSUED WITH C.R.E. OPERATION ORDER NO.2.

	Date. Decr.	From	To	Approx distance in miles.	Route	Time of starting.	Remarks.	Date Decr.	To.	Approx. distance in miles.	Route.	Time of start-ing.	Remarks
202nd Field Co. R. E.	5th	CANDAS	COUIN	16	DOULLENS-SARTON-MARIEUX-AUTHIE-COUIN-	7.15 am	will be met by officer of 48th DIV. at 11.15 am at pt. 141 on AUTHIE—MARIEUX road.	6th	48th Divn. Area	— under instructions of C.R.E. 48th DIV.			—

App 1. Vol 2.

SECRET. Copy No. 2

C.R.E's Operation Order No.2.

Reference 1/80,000 - Sheet 12.

3rd December 1915.

1. The 202nd Field Coy. R.E. will be attached to the 7th Corps for trench training.

2. The Company will move in accordance with the attached March Table.

3. Extract from Supply and Transport Arrangements issued in accordance with 30th Division Operation Order No.4 dated 2nd December 1915 attached.

4. Copy of instructions issued by G.S. 48th Division attached.

Lieut. R.E.
Adjutant, 30th Divisional Engineers.

No.1 Copy filed.

No.2 Copy issued to O.C.202nd Field Coy. R.E.

Vol 2.

Instructions regarding War Diaries and Intelligence Summaries are contained in F. S. Regs., Part II. and the Staff Manual respectively. Title pages will be prepared in manuscript.

WAR DIARY
or
INTELLIGENCE SUMMARY.

202nd Field Co. RE (Erase heading not required.)

Army Form C. 2118.

Place	Date	Hour	Summary of Events and Information	Remarks and references to Appendices
CANDAS	5/12/15	7.0am	Proceeded to LOUVENCOURT into 48th Divn. Area for training. Left Pontoon Wagons and Tool carts at CANDAS in charge of Section of 200th Field Co. RE. Handed over stores and Workshop at CANDAS to Officer in Charge No. 2 Section, 200th Field Co.	App 1
		12.15 pm	Arrived LOUVENCOURT. Wind EAST, cold and dry. Company billeted. Horses picketed in open.	
LOUVENCOURT	6/12/15	9.0am	Left LOUVENCOURT via BUS – SAILLY. Detached Nos. 3 and 4 Sections in charge of Lieut G RAYNER, RE & 2nd Lieut BUCKLEY RE respectively to proceed to FONQUEVILLERS	App 2.
		1.0pm	Headquarters and Nos 1 & 2 Sections proceeded HEBUTERNE.	
HEBUTERNE	7/12/15 to 17/12/15 incl.		Attached to 7th Corps for trench training under CRE 48th Division. Head Quarters & Nos. 1 & 2 sections attached to 3rd South Midland Field Co. for instruction at HEBUTERNE and Nos. 3 & 4 Sections to 2nd South Midland Field Co. at FONQUEVILLERS. Sections worked with parties of the S.M. Field Cos. for first 2 days and afterwards carried out work independently in conjunction with Infantry in Trenches. No casualties during the period. Wagons parked at ROSSIGNOL.	
HEBUTERNE	18/12/15	8.0am	Marched to LOUVENCOURT. Hd Qtrs and 1 & 2 Sections from HEBUTERNE, Nos. 3 & 4 Sections independently from FONQUEVILLERS to LOUVENCOURT.	App 3
LOUVENCOURT	20/12/15	9.30am	Marched to CANDAS and took over R.E. 30th Divisional Workshop from 201st Field Co. RE.	
CANDAS	21/12/15 to		Work done:- collection, storage and distribution of timber and other material for hutting scheme, Buying of material, Reconnaisance of woods. Manufacture	

H.O.W.

Vol 2.

Instructions regarding War Diaries and Intelligence Summaries are contained in F. S. Regs., Part II. and the Staff Manual respectively. Title pages will be prepared in manuscript.

WAR DIARY
or
~~INTELLIGENCE SUMMARY.~~
(Erase heading not required.)

Army Form C. 2118.

Page 2.

202nd Field Co. R.E.

Place	Date	Hour	Summary of Events and Information	Remarks and references to Appendices
			cont^d	
CANDAS	26/12/15 to 27/12/15		manufacture of samples and material and issue of same to units. On Dec 25 2nd Lieut Buckley ~~thrown~~ (officer i/c No 4 Section) thrown off horse and dislocated shoulder. attended in billet by 97th F.A.	
	27/12/15.		Sent No 1 Section under Lieut Ellis RE to BERNEUIL, No 2 under 2nd Lt STANIAR to OUTREBOIS, No 3 under Lieut RAYNER to BERNAVILLE, to assist Brigades in connection with hutting & billeting scheme. Capt HULTON RE, appointed officer in Sub charge, NORTH CANDAS. area.	App 4
	28/12/15.		2nd Lieut P.B. BUCKLEY. R.E. sent to C.C.S. by 97th FA (see date 25/12/15).	
	30/12/15.		Capt HULTON R.E. proceeded CHIPILLY to be attached 5th Division preliminary to move of Company and to take over from 1/2 Home Counties Field Co. RE.	App 5.

H. W. Wraith [?]
Major R.E.

O.C. 202ND FIELD CO. R.E.
(COUNTY PALATINE) R.E.

2353 Wt. W2544/1454 700,000 5/15 D. D. & L. A.D.S.S./Forms/C. 2118.

/ App 2

Vol 2.

O.C.,

202nd Field Company, R.E.

Please arrange to march tomorrow via BUS-BAYENCOURT Road so as to reach SAILLY at 11 a.m.

The half Company for FONQUEVILLERS will branch off at the junction of the BUS-BAYENCOURT Road and the COIGNEUX-SAILLY Road, J.10.c.3.7.

The party for HEBUTERNE will march as follows:-

Men by LARREY Communication trench.
Carts by SAILLY-HEBUTERNE Road at 100 yards interval.

The party for FONQUEVILLERS will march as follows:-

Men via BAYENCOURT-LA HAIE-Sunken Road-SAILLY ROAD trench.
Carts via BAYENCOURT-SOUASTRE to FONQUEVILLERS. From one mile east of SOUASTRE carts will proceed to FONQUEVILLERS at 100 yards interval.

O.C., 2nd Field Company will arrange for two guides to report to O.C., 202nd Field Co. at LOUVENCOURT at 9 am to guide parties to FONQUEVILLERS.

O.C., 3rd Field Company will arrange for one guide to report to O.C., 202nd Field Co. at LOUVENCOURT at 9 am to guide party to HEBUTERNE.

The party proceeding via LARREY will leave the trench at the RAMPS on the roadworks and get on to the road.

[signature]
Major R.E.
for C.R.E. 48th Div

5th December 1915.

app 3

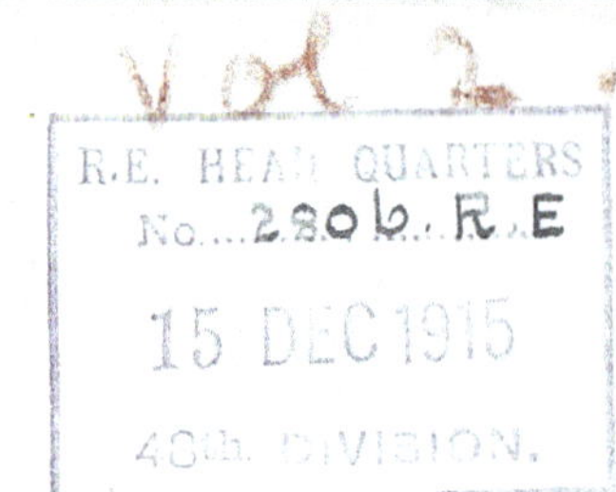

1st
O.C., 2nd Field Co.
202nd

The 202nd Field Company will leave the Divisional area on the 19th inst.

There will be no work for this Company on the night of the 17/18; the Company will march on the 18th inst., at an hour to be fixed after arrangement with the Brigades, to LOUVENCOURT where billeting arrangements will have been made by O.C., Div. Train.

O.C., 202nd Company will send forward a billeting party to take over the billets so as to reach LOUVENCOURT three hours before the arrival of the Company.

15th December 1915.

Major R.E.
for C.R.E. 48th Div

"C" Form (Duplicate). Army

App 4 Vol 2

MESSAGES AND SIGNALS. No. of Message..........

Service Instructions.	Charges to Pay £ s. d.	Office Stamp.

Handed in at the.......... Office, at..........m. Received here at..........m.

TO 202 Field Coy R E

Sender's Number	Day of Month.	In reply to Number.	AAA
BR 176	21st		

26/12 AOS

Following amalgamation of 202 Field Co for work on new building scheme will be effected tomorrow under arrangements to be made by O C 202 Field Coy aaa Headquarters and one section remain at CANDAS aaa One section to BERNAVILLE aaa One section to OUTREBOIS aaa Addressed 202 Field Coy Repeated 89 Brigade Pioneers cyclists and CE

FROM CE

PLACE 30 Division

TIME

GALE & POLDEN, LTD. PRINTERS, ALDERSHOT.
(69,017). Wt. 7981—443. 40,000 Pads. 4/18. W.

APP 4 Vol 2.

"C" Form (Quadruplicate). Army Form C. 2123 A.

MESSAGES AND SIGNALS. No. of Message..................

	Charges to Pay £ s. d.	Office Stamp.
1C Z 26		KLR 26.12.15
Service Instructions.		

Handed in at the 91st Bde Office, at 4.45 P.m. Received here at 4.56 P.m.

TO 202 Field Coy R E

Sender's Number	Day of Month.	In reply to Number.	AAA
R 36	26th	QM192	

Fourth section go to BERNEUIL aaa This information was sent you by Headquarters 30th Division

FROM
PLACE C R E 30th Division
TIME

GALE & POLDEN, LTD. PRINTERS, ALDERSHOT.
(69,017). Wt. 7981—443. 40,000 Pads. 4/13. W.

"A" Form. Army Form C. 2121.

app 5 Vol 2

MESSAGES AND SIGNALS.

No. of Message 20.

Prefix SM Code CD m. | Words 76 | Charge

Office of Origin and Service Instructions.

YCZ 8

repeated at request of sender YCZ

Sent At m. To By

This message is on a/c of: Service.

(Signature of "Franking Officer.")

29 DEC 1915

Recd. at 6-0 pm.

Date 28/12/15

From 2H

By W Pearce

SIGNALS 18 K.L.R.

TO 202nd Fd Co RE

Sender's Number	Day of Month	In reply to Number	AAA
* 250	29th		

following are arrangements for bus tomorrow aaa bus calls HALLOY at 8.30 am to pick up CAPT HEBDEN and batman aaa then proceeds to LANCHES for CAPT IRWIN and batman aaa then to HQ RE at LE-MEILLARD aaa then to CANDAS for CAPT HILTON and batman aaa thence to CHIPILLY aaa Officers concerned to look out for bus and instruct driver as to meet place of call

From CRE 30th DIV

Place

Time

(Repeated message)

The above may be forwarded as now corrected. (Z)

Censor. Signature of Addressor or person authorised to telegraph in his name.

* This line should be erased if not required.

23146—W. & S. Ltd., London.—W 1789/1202—100,000—7/15 Forms C 2121/10.

App5 Vol 2

"A" Form.

Army Form C. 2121.

MESSAGES AND SIGNALS.

No. of Message 18

Prefix SM Code CK m. Words 76 Charge

Office of Origin and Service Instructions.

CYCZ

This message is on a/c of: ....Service.

(Signature of "Franking Officer.")

Sent At ......m. To ...... By ......

Recd. at 3.45 p m.

Date 29/12/15

From CYZ

By Pearce

TO 202nd Fd Coy RE

Sender's Number	Day of Month	In reply to Number	AAA
* E 50	29		

following are arrangments for bus tomorrow aaa bus calls HALLOY at 8.30 am to pick up capt HEBDEN and batman aaa then to HQ RE at LE MEILLARD aaa then to CANDAS for CAPT hutton and batman aaa thence to CHIPILLY aaa officers concerned to look out for bus and instruct driver as to next place of call

Capt Hutton

From CRE 30th DIVN

Place

Time

The above may be forwarded as now corrected.

Censor.

(Z)

Signature of Addressor or person authorised to telegraph in his name.

* This line should be erased if not required.

23146—W. & S. Ltd., London.—W 1787/1402—150,000—7/15 Forms C 2121 10.

Confidential

War Diary
of
202nd Field Compy. R.E.

Month of:- January 1916
Volume 3

Vol 3.

Instructions regarding War Diaries and Intelligence Summaries are contained in F. S. Regs., Part II. and the Staff Manual respectively. Title pages will be prepared in manuscript.

WAR DIARY
or
INTELLIGENCE SUMMARY.

202nd Field Co. R.E. *(Erase heading not required.)*

Army Form C. 2118.

Page 1

Place	Date	Hour	Summary of Events and Information	Remarks and references to Appendices
CANDAS	3/1/16		Company marched as part of No. 2 Column (30th Div. Operation Order No. 6) under command of Lt. Col. E W Trotter (O C 18th K Liverpool Regt) to WARGNIES via MONTRELET and CANAPLES. Billeted for the night. Transport insufficient to carry stores. Some tools, 2 oxy-acetylene searchlights, and a few details left behind at CANDAS on authority given by A.A. & QMG 30th Div.	App 1
WARGNIES	4/1/16		Resumed march via TALMAS, MOLLIENS au BOIS – ST GRATIEN – QUERRIEUX to PONT-NOYELLE. Billeted over night. East Wind. Entered 10th Corps area, 5th Division.	
PONT-NOYELLES	5/1/16.		Resumed march via CORBIE, points 102, 108, 105 to BRAY sur SOMME. Out-spanned from 1.0 pm to 4.30 pm near point 105 so as to reach BRAY at 6.30 pm. No men fell out on march from CANDAS to BRAY.	
BRAY sur SOMME	6/1/16		Took over from 1/2nd Home Counties Field Co. RE on 30th Divn. taking over from 5th Div.	
	8/1/16		Commenced increasing Dug outs at L 16 C. 2 I N COs & men in front line trenches, billeted at CARNOY. Rest of Company at Work in BRAY & Surroundings. Notification received from CRE that 2nd Lieut Buckley evacuated to England on 1/1/16.	
	11/1/16		Casualties O.R. one wounded, one wounded (serious). The organisation and control of work carried out is found to be difficult. Two officers and 21 men detailed for trenches, leaving 1 Captain & 1 Subaltern for BRAY & district beside the O C, one Subaltern being in hospital. 2 Subalterns per Section could with advantage be employed.	
	12/1/16		2nd Lieut P.F. CAMPBELL joined in place of 2nd Lt. BUCKLEY, and took command No. 4 Section.	
	13/1/16		Casualties. O R one reported wounded (serious) on 11th, since reported died.	

H.O.W.

2353 Wt. W2514/1454 700,000 5/15 D. D. & L. A.D.S.S./Forms/C. 2118.

Vol 3.

Instructions regarding War Diaries and Intelligence Summaries are contained in F. S. Regs., Part II. and the Staff Manual respectively. Title pages will be prepared in manuscript.

WAR DIARY
or
INTELLIGENCE SUMMARY.
(Erase heading not required.)

Army Form C. 2118.

Page 2

202nd Field Co. RE

Place	Date	Hour	Summary of Events and Information	Remarks and references to Appendices
BRAY SUR SOMME	15/1/16		Received C.R.E's order No. 77 of 15/1/16 to report on stores.	App 2.
	16/1/16		Reported on C.R.E's No. 77 of 15/1/16.	
"	23/1/16.		Received C.R.E's letter No. R556 referring to bad state of BRONFAY-CARNOY Road and giving instructions as to its repair. No road metal available, except bricks from ruined buildings. The local chalk is useless.	
"	25/1/16		FROISSY QUAY shelled. Casualties O.R. one, slight remained at duty.	
"	25/1/16.		Work commenced under Lieut RAYNER on new No. 3 Surrey Post.	
"	27/1/16		KAISER's birthday. Day passed quietly, but heavy shelling of BRONFAY FARM and towards SUZANNE took place during the night. About 5 p.m. 2nd Lieut BILLINGTON of 200th Fld Co. R.E., while examining parts of live shell he had brought to 202nd Co's workshop, had his foot blown off by portion dropping on floor. Lieut GIBBONS of 200th Co. also injured with splinters in back. Our casualties O.R. wounded one, wounded slightly one, remained at duty.	
"	28/1/16		Enemy Shelling continued. Very heavy on B & A sectors and on SUZANNE. Lachrymatory shell used and was quite perceptible in streets of BRAY during night of 27/28th. Attack delivered by Enemy on FRISE during the day. Orders received from 21st BRIGADE for men to sleep in boots & puttees, ready to move. Received also orders from H.Q. 30th Dvn as to disposal of transport in case of bombardment of BRAY. GAS alarm received at 7. a.m. and cancelled shortly after. It probably arose from use of lachrymatory shell by enemy. Infantry relief could not take place on night of 28/29th. H.O.W.	App 3.

Army Form C. 2118.

Instructions regarding War Diaries and Intelligence Summaries are contained in F. S. Regs., Part II. and the Staff Manual respectively. Title pages will be prepared in manuscript.

VOL. 3.

WAR DIARY
or
INTELLIGENCE SUMMARY.
(Erase heading not required.)

Page 3

Place	Date	Hour	Summary of Events and Information	Remarks and references to Appendices
BRAY SUR SOMME	29/1/16	~~10.0 a.m.~~	Heavy shelling to E and NE continued during the night of the 28/29 and during the 29th. At 10 AM proceeded with the CRE 30th Divn and Major HOLLAND, GSO of 30th Divn to lay out barbed wire from a point about L27C.0.8 down marshes of SOMME river to CAPPY BRIDGE L.30.a. Detailed Lieut Ellis RE and men to commence work. Gas alarm at 11.0 p.m. Warned men to be prepared. Details of Nos 1 & 3 Sections relieved details of Nos 2 and 4 in trenches.	HOW
"	30/1/16		Shelling to E & N.E. continued, 8 shells (heavy) fell on outskirts of BRAY, North East of Railway Station about 11.30 am. GAS alarm at 2.30 pm, cancelled at 2.50 pm. Detailed 2nd Lieut STANIAR on barbed wire at CAPPY Bridge.	HOW
"	31/1/16.		Blew down tall chimney at FROISSY under orders of ~~[illegible]~~ G.O.C. 30th Divn, as it formed a ranging mark for the enemy. Shelling continued to E & N.E. through the day.	

HOWSmith
Major RE
1/2/16.

March Orders for Jany 3rd, 4th & 5th 1916.

App I Vol 3

1. Map Reference Amiens Sheet 12. 1/80.000

2. First Day Jany 3rd 1916.

Blankets & Leather Jackets to be in baggage wagons by 7-0 a.m.

Breakfast 7-30 a.m.
Parade 8-30 a.m.
March 9-5 a.m.

Route MONTRELET – CANAPLES – HAVERNAS – WARGNIES

3. Second Day Jany 4th 1916

Blankets & Leather Jackets to be in baggage wagons by 7-0 am.

Breakfast. 7-30 am
Parade 8-30 a.m.
March 9-5 am.

Route. NAOURS – TALMAS – SEPTENVILLE – PIERREGOT – MOLLIENS-AU-BOIS – ST. GRATIEN – QUERRIEUX – PONT-NOYELLES.

Third Day Jany 5th 1916

Blankets & Leather Jackets to be in baggage wagons by 7-0 a.m.

Breakfast 7-30 a.m.
Parade 8-20 a.m.
March 8-50 a.m.

No 2.

Route. CORBIE – via point 102, 108, 105 upper road. – BRAY.

Dress. No great coats to be worn. Waterproof sheets to be carried on the man.

Supply & Transport. Baggage wagon must be returned to O.C. Divisional Train at ETINEHEM the day following arrival, with 1 day's supplies for men & horses.

Reports. Units will report their arrival and position of Headquarters to the H.Q. of the 18th Battn Kings Liverpool Regt daily.

On Jany 3rd 1916. at TALMAS
" " 4th " " LAHOUSSOYE
" " 5th " " SAILLY-LORETTE

Billet Parties. Lt Rayner & Section 3 Cyclists will go ahead each day to take over billets at destination

H. O. Wraith. Major R.E.
O/C 202nd Fld Co R.E.

2/1/16.

Copy No 2

Operation Order No. 1.
By Lieut Col. G. H. Trotter, D.S.O.
Commanding No. 2 Column.

Reference 1/100,000 map Sheet 11 (LENS) + 17 (AMIENS) & 1/40,000 ALBERT Combined sheet.

1. The 30th Division will march commencing Sunday January 2nd to relieve the 5th Division (less 1 Brigade) of the 10th Corps.
The Division will take over the line from River SOMME about ECLUSIER to a point about F.12.C.1/7.
The 5th (or 6th) Division of the French 3rd Corps will be on our right S. of the River SOMME.

2 The Division is to be attached to the 10th Corps and the troops enter the 10th Corps area on their second days march (PONT NOYELLES – LA HOUSSOYE.
The relief will be carried out under the orders of the G.O.C. 5th Division, in whose area the troops will arrive on their third day's march (VAUX – SAILLY LAURETTE – ETINEHAM).

3 (i) Moves will be in accordance with the attached march table

(ii) Route :- TALMAS – SEPTENVILLE – PIERREGOT – MOLLIENS AU BOIS – ST. GRATIEN – CORBIE – thence by lower river road. The troops of the 5th Division will use the upper road to CORBIE via Point 108.

(iii) Movements on the fourth day and afterwards will take place after dark, and will be under orders of the 5th Division, who may also issue special orders as regards moves on the third day into their area.

(iv) Units will report their arrival at their destinations and the position of their Headquarters to the Headquarters of the 18th Ser Bn. King's Liverpool Regt daily :- on 4th January at TALMAS 5th January – LA HOUSSOYE; 6th January – SAILLY LAURETTE.
Orderlies will await the arrival of the 18th Ser. Bn. King's Liverpool Regt. if they have not arrived at those places.
Information should be sent as quickly as possible as it has to be transmitted.

(v) Baggage Section of the train will accompany troops on the march

4. The billeting accommodation is approximately as follows:-

1st Day. TALMAS 1 Battalion
NAOURS 1 Battalion – more could be obtained
WARGNIES ½ Battalion.

2nd day. LA HOUSSOYE 1 Battalion
PONT NOYELLES 1500 & more could be obtained on application to H.Q. 10th Corps

3rd day. SAILLY LAURETTE 2 Battalions
VAUX SUR SOMME 1 Battalion

This area will be in occupation by 5th and 30th Division troops simultaneously throughout the relief, and billeting in it will be arranged by 5th Division
Units will send forward billeting party daily to arrange for their own billets.

5. The scheme of distribution in the trenches is being communicated separately to all concerned.

6. Every man on entering the trenches will carry with him 120 rounds of ammunition.
Arrangements are being made by 5th Division to allow, one Officer and 1 N.C.O. per Company and 1 N.C.O. per platoon besides representatives of Bde. and Battalion Headquarters, visiting the trenches before relief, as well as taking over by daylight trench stores, trench ammunition, and grenades.

7. Divisional Headquarters will remain open at LE MEILLARD until 4 pm 8th January, when they will close and re-open at DAOURS, 3 miles S. of QUERRIEUX. Communications with Dvl H.Q after this time will be via 10th Corps Signal Office.
G.O.C. 30th Division will take over the line at 12 noon on 12th January.

8. No. 2. Column Troops:-
202 Field Company R.E
18th Ser. Bn. King's Liverpool Regt
19th Ser. Bn Manchester Regt

9. In all cases Units vacating billets must leave same clean and billet stores left correct and not carried away.

[signature]

Copy No 1. 18th K L R
Copy No 2 202 Co RE
Copy No 3 19th ~~K L R~~ Manchester

MARCH TABLE

1st Day. Jany 3rd 1916

	From	To	Time of march
202nd Field Co. R.E	CANDAS	WARGNIES	9.15 am
19th Bn. Manchester Regt.	BOIS BERGUES	NAOURS	9.15 am
18th Bn. Liverpool Regt	CANDAS	TALMAS	9.15 am.

2nd Day. Jany 4th 1916

	From	To	Time of march
202nd Field Co. R.E.	WARGNIES	PONT NOYELLE	Resume march at 9.15 am
19th Bn. Manchester Regt.	NAOURS	PONT NOYELLE	" " " 9.15 am
18th Bn. Liverpool Regt	TALMAS	LA HOUSSOYE.	" " " 9.15 am

VIA :- TALMAS – SEPTENVILLE – PIERRECOT – MOLLIENS-AU BOIS – ST. GRATIEN. 202nd Co. R.E 19th Bn. Manchester Regt } QUERRIEU billeted PONT NOYELLE. 18th Sr. Bn. K.L.R FREHENCOURT billeted LA HOUSSOYE.

3rd Day – January 5th 1916

	From	To	Time of march
202 Field Co. R.E.	PONT NOYELLE	BRAY SUR SOMME	Resume march at 9 am
19th Bn. Manchester Regt	PONT NOYELLE	VAUX SUR SOMME	" " " 9.45 am
18th Bn. Liverpool Regt	LA HOUSSAYE	SAILLY LAURETTE	" " " 9 am.

202nd FIELD CO. R.E. after CORBIE via Points 102, 108, 105 Upper road
19th Manchesters & 18th Liverpools via NEUVILLE – CORBIE – LOWER RIVER ROAD

4th Day. January 6th 1916.

18th Bn Liverpool Regt. – to BRONFAY
19th Bn. Manchester Regt – to BRAY

Note :- Move to these places will take place after dark and will be under orders of the 5th Division.

G 794 30th Decr 1915.

Communication during Move.

1. According to Operation Order No. 6. para 3 (iv) (a) a motor cyclist was to accompany each column Commander on the first day of the march and bring back to Divisional H.Q the arrival report.
It is intended however to extend the LE MEILLARD - CANAPLES wire to TALMAS and to keep a small office there until the evening of the 7th January, so that communication may be maintained between the Columns and Divl. H.Q. If this is found feasible the location of the office will be notified and no motor cyclist will accompany the column on the march.

2. From the Div. Ammn. Column Office at LA HOUSSOYE a line runs to the 10th Corps at QUERRIEUX, whence a communication can be obtained with Div. H.Q.

3. From SAILLY LAURETTE, SAILLY LE SEC, CHIPILLY there are lines running to 5th Divisional Office at ETINEHAM.

4. From 4 pm the 8th January Divl. H.Q. will be at DAOURS whence a line runs to the 10th Corps at QUERRIEUX until G.O.C. 30th Division takes over the line on the 12th January.

sequill (Sd) W.H.F. Weber, Lieut Colonel.
General Staff.

30th Divn.

Transport and Supply arrangement issued with Operation Order No. 6 dated 29th December 1915

(a) TRANSPORT ARRANGEMENTS.

All Infantry Battalions will be issued with two motor lorries or 5 G.S. Wagons for the conveyance of blankets and additional authorised stores.

2. Infantry Brigade Headquarters and Field Co. R.E. will be issued with 1 additional G.S. Wagon for the conveyance of blankets, etc.

The above additional Transport and the baggage wagons as per War Establishment will be issued to Units by 2 pm on the day previous to the commencement of the march and will accompany Units as far as the 1st Line transport billets in the 5th Divisional area. The contents will be unloaded as soon as possible and the lorries returned to their Units.
The baggage wagons and additional G.S. Wagons will be withdrawn on the day following day of arrival under instructions which will be issued to Units by the O.C. 30th Divisional Train. Similarly after arrival at final destination Supply wagons will return to the Divisional Train as soon as possible after Supplies have been issued.

(b) SUPPLY ARRANGEMENTS.

Each Unit will draw 2 days Supplies on the day previous to the commencement of their march; 1 days supplies will be carried in the Cookers, the other in Supply Wagons.

2. 2 days supplies will be issued at PONT NOYELLES to all troops billeted on the evening of the 2nd days march in the PONT NOYELLES – LA HOUSSOYE area. The Supply Officer will post a man outside the main door of the Church at PONT NOYELLES to direct Units to the Refilling Point.

3. On the evening of the 4th days march Units will draw rations from the 5th Divisional Refilling Point under instructions which will be issued by the Senior Supply Officer 30th Division as soon as Units arrive in billets at the end of the 3rd days march.

4. All Train Transport and personnel will be rationed by the Unit to which they are attached. They will require rations from and including the 1st days march of the Unit.

5. All Troops billeting at DAOURS on the 2nd days march will be issued with rations at DAOURS, 2 days rations being issued the day before leaving the present area. The Refilling point at DAOURS will be notified later to all the troops concerned.

30/12/1915

signed L. Hume Spry, Lieut Colonel
A.A. + Q.M.G, 30th Division

Copy No. 9

21st INFANTRY BRIGADE OPERATION ORDERS No.100.

~~2nd~~ 3rd January 1916.

Reference 1:80,000 Map AMIENS.
1:40,000 " ALBERT, Combined Sheet.

1. The 30th Division will march, commencing Sunday, Jany. 2nd, to relieve the 5th Division (less 1 Brigade) of the 10th Corps.
The Division will take over the line from River SOMME about ECLUSIER to a point about F.12.c.1/7.
The 5th (or 6th) Division of the French 3rd Corps will be on our right S. of the River SOMME. The 15th Brigade will continue to hold the left (Northern or "C") sector of the present 5th Division line on our left, and will come under G.O.C. 30th Division when he takes over command.

2. The Division is to be attached to the 10th Corps and the troops enter the 10th Corps area on their second day's march (PONT NOYELLES - LA HOUSSOYE).
The relief will be carried out under the orders of the G.O.C. 5th Division in whose area the troops will arrive on their third day's march (VAUX - SAILLY LAURETTE - ETINEHEM).

3. (a) The Brigade (with 19th Bn. Liverpools attached) will take over the Centre (B) Sector of the line
B.1. 2nd Bn. Wiltshire Regiment and will find its own relief.
B.2. 18th Kings (Liverpool) Regiment.
B.3. 19th Bn. Manchester Regiment.
The 2nd Bn. Yorkshire Regiment will relieve the 18th Kings (Liverpool) Regiment and the 19th Liverpools will relieve the 19th Manchester Regiment.

(b) The 90th Infantry Brigade will be on our right and the 15th Infantry Brigade, 5th Division on our left.

4. Moves will be in accordance with attached March Table. The 18th Kings (Liverpool) Regt. and 19th Bn. Manchester Regt. will march under Lieut. Col. E.H. TROTTER, D.S.O. to whom separate instructions have been issued.

5. 1st Line Transport will march in rear of Battalions. Train Transport will march in rear of the Column in the same order as Battalions.

6. Billeting parties will be sent ahead of the Column each day. Where two units are billeted in the same place the Staff Captain will allot the billets.

7. Medical arrangements. Appendix "A".

8. Transport and Supply arrangements. Appendix "B".

9/

Operation Order No.106 continued.

9. Battalion Commanders are to ensure that Billets are left clean and that billet stores are left correct and not taken away.

10. Battalions will report each day when billets have been taken over, giving the exact position of their Headquarters and the number of men who have fallen out on the march.

[signature] Major,

Brigade Major, 91st Infantry Brigade.

Issued to Signal Section at

Copy No.1 Retained.
2 18th Kings (Liverpool) Regt.
3 2nd Bn.Yorkshire Regiment.
4 2nd Bn.Wiltshire Regiment.
5 19th Bn.Manchester Regiment.
6 30th Division.
7 8th Division.
8 Supply Officer.
9 202nd Field Company R.E.
10. 11th S Lancs Regt

March Table

Date	Unit	Starting Point	Hour	Route	To	Remarks
Jan. 5	2nd Bn Yorkshire Regiment	Eastern Road Junction in FIENVILLERS	9 a.m.	CANDAS – Cross Roads 1/4 mile N of VERT-GALAND FERME.	TALMAS	
	2nd Bn Wiltshire Regiment	Cross Roads at H of AUTHEUX	9 a.m.	FIENVILLERS – MONTRELET – CANAPLES	WARGNIES	
	11th Bn South Lancashire Regt.	PERNOIS		via CANAPLES	NAOURS	To be clear of CANAPLES by 11 a.m.
Jan 6	2nd Yorks Regt	Road Junction 1 mile ESE of "S" in TALMAS	9 a.m.	SEPTENVILLE – PIERREGOT – MOLLIENS AU BOIS – ST GRATIEN – PONT NOYELLES	LA HOUSSOYE	
	11th S. Lancs Regt	do	9. 6 a.m.	do	PONT NOYELLES	
	2nd Wilts Regt	do	9. 12 a.m.	do	PONT NOYELLES	

March Table (Cont.)

Date	Unit	Starting Point	Hour	Route	To	Remarks
Jan. 7	2nd Bn Yorkshire Regt	Road Junction in S.W. Corner of LA HOUSSOYE	9 a.m.	via LA VEUVILLE	SAILLY LORETTE	To be clear of Road Jn. N of VEUVILLE by 9.45 a.m.
	11th Bn S. Lancashire Regt	Cross Roads ½ mile S of P in PONT.	9 a.m.	LA VEUVILLE and CORBIE	ETINEHEM and CHIPILLY	
	2nd Bn Wiltshire Regt	do	9.6 a.m.	do	VAUX SUR SOMME	
Jan. 8	11th Bn S. Lancashire Regt	ETINEHEM	To be notified		BRAY	BRAY may be changed to FROISSY for a few days
Jan. 9	2nd Bn Yorkshire Regt	SAILLY LORETTE	To be notified	CHIPILLY – ETINEHEM – BRAY	BRONFAY	
	2nd Bn Wiltshire Regt	VAUX SUR SOMME	To be notified	SAILLY LORETTE & ETINEHEM	BRAY	Trenches Sector B1 on 10th

Notes.

1. After CORBIE all troops will move by the Lower River Road.
2. Halts will commence at 10 minutes to (and finish at) every clock hour.
3. The rate of marching is not to exceed 2½ miles per hour.
4. On going into the trenches troops will carry 120 rounds on the man.

Operation Order No 2

S E C R E T.

C.R.E's Instructions to Field Companies R.E.
Supplementary to Div. Operation Order No.6.

Decr. 30th 1915.

Reference 1/100,000 Map, Sheet 11 (LENS).
17 (AMIENS) and 1/40,000 ALBERT combined sheet.

1. The 30th Division march, commencing Sunday, Jany 2nd to relieve the 5th Division (less 1 Bde) of 10th Corps.

The Division will take over the line from River SOMME about ECLUSIER to a point about F.12.c. 1/7.

The 5th (or 6th) Division of the French 3rd Corps will be on our right S. of the River SOMME. The 15th Bde will continueto hold the left (Northern or "C") sector of the present 5th Division line on our left and will come under G.O.C. 30th Division when he takes over command.

2. The Division is to be attached to 10th Corps and the troops enter the 10th Corps area on their second days march (PONT NOYELLES - LA HOUSSOYE).

The relief will be carried out under the orders of the G.O.C. 5th Division in whose area the troops will arrive on their third days march (VAUX - SAILLY LAURETTE - ETINEHEM).

3. 200th, 201st & 202nd Field Cos. R.E. will move in accordance with the attached extracts from March tables under orders issued by the respective Column Commanders.

4. Baggage section of the Train will accompany troops on the march.

5. Arrangements for extra transport and supplies - See Table A. which will be forwarded later.

6. Div. H.Q. will remain open at LE MEILLARD until 4-0pm 8th Jany, 1916 when they will close and reopen at ~~XXXXX~~ DAOURS 3 miles S. of QUERRIEUX. Communication with DIV. H.Q. after this time will be via 10th Corps.Signal Office.

Sheet 2.

G.O.C., 30th. Div. will take over the line at 12 noon on the 12th. January, 1916. Exact hour at which H.Q. will close at [illegible] and re-open at ETINEHEM on that date will be published later.

H.Q.R.E., will be at CHIPILLY.

R J Stone Capt
for Lieut-Col. R.E.,
C.R.E., 30th. Division.

To : Headquarters, 30th. Div.
90th. Brigade.
Lieut.Col. [illegible] Potter, D.S.O., 18th. Lpool Regt.
Lieut.Col. [illegible] Walsh, 2nd. R.Scots.Fusiliers.
200th. Field Coy. R.E.,
201st. Field Coy. R.E.,
202nd. Field Coy. R.E.,

Table B. 1.

No. 1 Column. Commander Brig: General G. J. Steavenson.

1.	2.	3.	4.	5.	6	7.
Troops.	2nd. Jany:	3rd. Jany:	4th.Jany:	5th.Jany:	6th.Jany:	Remarks.
201st.Coy. R.E.	WARGNIES.	PONT NOYELLES.	SAILLY LAURETTE	SUZANNE		

Table [illegible].

No. 2 Column Commander Lt.Col. [illegible].Trotter,[illegible], 18th.L'pool R.

1.	2.	3.	4.	5.	6.	7.
Troops.	3rd.Jany:	4th.Jany:	5th. Jany:	6th.Jany:	7th.Jany:	Remarks.
202nd.Field Co.R.E.	WARGNIES.	PONT NOYELLES.	BRAY.			Via Upper Road (pts.1[illegible]2-106-105.)

Table 8.3.

No. 3 Column. Commander Lt. Col. M. K. Welch, 2nd. R. Scots.Fus.

1.	2.	3.	4.	5.	6.	7.
Troops.	4th. Jany:	5th. Jany:	6th. Jany:	7th.Jany.	8th.Jany:	Remarks .
200th. Field Co.R.E.	[illegible]ECHONIKS.	PONT NOYELLES.	QUAY.			Via Upper Road. (pts. 1[illegible]-108-105.)

TRANSPORT AND SUPPLY ARRANGEMENT ISSUED WITH OPERATION ORDER NO. 6, dated 29th December 1915.

(a). <u>TRANSPORT ARRANGEMENTS.</u>

All Infantry Battalions will be issued with two motor lorries or 45 G.S. Wagons for the conveyance of blankets and additional authorised stores.

2. Infantry Brigade Headquarters and Field Company R.E. will be issued with 1 additional G.S. Wagon for the conveyance of blankets etc.

The above additional Transport and the Baggage Wagons as per War Establishment will be issued to Units by 3 pm. on the day previous to the commencement of the march and will accompany Units as far as the 1st Line Transport billets in the 5th Divisional Area. The contents will be unloaded as soon as possible and the lorries returned to their units.

The Baggage Wagons and additional G.S. Wagons will be withdrawn on the day following day of arrival under instructions which will be issued to units by the O.C. 30th Divisional Train. Similarly after arrival at final destination Supply Wagons will return to the Divisional Train as soon as possible after Supplies have been issued.

(b). <u>SUPPLY ARRANGEMENTS.</u>

Each Unit will draw 2 day's Supplies on the day previous to the commencement of their march; 1 day's supplies will be carried in the Cookers, the other in Supply Wagons.

2. 2 Day's supplies will be issued at PONT NOYELLES to all troops billeted on the evening of the 2nd day's march in the PONT NOYELLES - LA HOUSSOYE area. The Supply Officer will post a man outside the main door of the Church at PONT NOYELLES to direct Units to the Refilling Point.

3. On the evening of the 4th day's march Units will draw rations from the 5th Divisional Refilling Point, under instructions which will be issued by the Senior Supply Officer 30th Division as soon as Units arrive in billets at the end of the 3rd day's march.

4. All Train Transport and personnel will be rationed by the Unit to which they are attached. They will require rations from and including the 1st day's march of the Unit.

5. All troops billeting at DAOURS on the 2nd day's march will be issued with rations at DAOURS, 2 day's rations being issued the day before leaving the present area.

The Refilling Point at DAOURS will be notified later to all troops concerned.

30/12/1915.

L. Hume-Spry, Lieut. Colonel.
A.A. & Q.M.G., 30th Division.

Supplementary table of Moves – (Issued in connection with 5th Div O.O. 9)

Unit	Date	Route	Time	Remarks
202nd Field Coy R.E	5th	Main CORBIE - BRAY ROAD	Pass Road Junction L.15.c.3/7 at 6.30. p.m	Billeting party to report to Town Major BRAY at 1. p.m
19th Manchester Regt	6th	ETINEHEM - L.20.a - BRAY	Pass Cross Roads L.15.c.3/7 at 5.40. p.m	13th I Bde will provide guides at Cross Roads L.15.c.3/7
18th Liverpool Regt	6th	SAILLY LORETTE - ETINEHEM L.20.a	Pass Cross Roads L.16.c.3/7 at 6.15. p.m	Billeting party to report to Staff Captain 13th Infy Bde at BRAY at 1. p.m
4/1/16			F.G. Hobson Lieut. for Major Brigade Major 2nd Infy Bde	

COPY App 2. Vol 3

Q. 4608.
No 77
15th Jan. 1916.

C.R.E.

Please report as soon as possible for the information of the G.O.C. the amount of
Reserve Rations
Grenades.
S.A.A.
Water.
supposed to be in various places and the amount actually taken over from the 5th Division. A plan should accompany this report showing where the various stores of the above mentioned articles are situated.

Please treat this report as URGENT.

All stores will be properly marked by a notice board and a report rendered to this office as soon as it has been done.

(sd.) F.A. CORFIELD, Major.
14/1/16. D.A.Q.M.G., 30th Division.

2.

O.C. 202nd Field Company, R.E.

For information and early report.

R.G. STONE
Captain R.E.
15/1/16. Adjt. 30th Divisional Engineers.

Certified true copy
17/1/16. [signature] Major R.E.

"A" Form. Army Form C. 2121.

MESSAGES AND SIGNALS.

No. of Message

Prefix Code m. | Words | Charge

Office of Origin and Service Instructions.

5 APP 3

Sent

At m.

To

By

This message is on a/c of:

Vol 3

Service.

(Signature of "Franking Officer")

Recd. at m.

Date

From

By

TO Officer Commanding 202nd Field Coy R.E.

Sender's Number.	Day of Month	In reply to Number	AAA
* BM 107	28th		

Troops should sleep with boots and puttees on tonight and all arms and equipment alongside them.

From 21st Infy Bde

Place

Time

The above may be forwarded as now corrected.

(Z) [signature]

Censor.

Signature of Addressor or person authorised to telegraph in his name.

BM

* This line should be erased if not required.

(774-5) —McC. & Co. Ltd., London.— W 1789/1402. 150,000. 8/15. Forms C 2121/10.

202ND FIELD

1/2/16 — 29/2/16

Vol 4

CONFIDENTIAL

WAR DIARY

OF

202ND FIELD COY. R.E.

FROM. 1/2/16 TO. 29/2/16.

(VOLUME No 4).

Instructions regarding War Diaries and Intelligence Summaries are contained in F. S. Regs., Part II. and the Staff Manual respectively. Title pages will be prepared in manuscript.

Vol. 4.

WAR DIARY
or
INTELLIGENCE SUMMARY.
(*Erase heading not required.*)

Army Form C. 2118.

Page 1.

Place	Date	Hour	Summary of Events and Information	Remarks and references to Appendices
BRAY SUR SOMME	1/2/16		Intermittent shelling during day heard to E and N E.	HOW
"	2/2/16		Intermittent shelling during day to E & N E. About 4.30 pm. about 16 shells fell round BRAY station & just East of BRAY & about 10 in BRAY.	
"	3/2/16		Handed over wiring South of BRAY to 200th Field Co RE (Major E. BLUNN) 2 shells fell in BRAY about 5 pm.	HOW
"	4/2/16		60 shells fell in BRAY about 3.30 pm. and about 8 about 3.55 pm.	
"	6/2/16	7.45 pm	While was at mess of 200th Field Co RE, Rue CORBIE, 2nd Lt BICKLE of that Co shot himself in the foot in his bedroom in same house. with his revolver. He was taken to F A.	
"	7/2/16		About 50 shells fell into BRAY about 2.30 p.m.	HOW
		7.30 pm	Attended Court of Inquiry at Office of 200th Field Co RE on injury sustained by 2Lt BICKLE. RE (see 6/2/16). President Major Lunn RE. Gave evidence.	
"	9/2/16		Wire entanglement from CAPPY Bridge to point L.22.b.2.2. completed.	HOW
"	10/2/16	1. am	About 30 shells fired into BRAY from a direction about 30° E of North. This is the first time since 6/1/16 that shells have come into BRAY from that direction. Firing lasted about 45 mins. A large proportion (probably 50%) were blind. Office was hit by a blind shell. Casualties O.R. 1 slightly wounded, still at duty.	
"	12/2/16		Selected M G positions with Brigade M.G officer at 4 points in reserve line & put in hand	HOW
	13/2/16		Casualties O.R. 1 slightly wounded, still at duty.	

Army Form C. 2118.

Instructions regarding War Diaries and Intelligence Summaries are contained in F. S. Regs., Part II. and the Staff Manual respectively. Title pages will be prepared in manuscript.

Vol 4.

WAR DIARY
or
INTELLIGENCE SUMMARY.
(*Erase heading not required.*)

Page 2.

Place	Date	Hour	Summary of Events and Information	Remarks and references to Appendices
BRAY SUR SOMME	14/2/16		CRE 30th Divn inspected portion of front trenches, BERWICK AVENUE, trenches 51-61 and FRANCIS AVENUE, also CARNOY & PERONNE avenues, point 104 etc.	HOW
"	15/2/16		Little artillery fire. Order received that 1/2 Highland Field Co. RE would take over on relief of Division	APP 1.
"	16/2/16		Heavy firing heard to SOUTH.	
"	17/2/16	7.0pm	Lieut Gordon RE of 1/2 Highland Field Co RE arrived to take over, Major MITCHELL, RE (O.C.) being ill.	HOW
"	18/2/16		Took Lieut GORDON RE over BRAY & works in vicinity of BRAY, Workshops, Billets, handed over maps and papers in connection with water supply of sector, No 3 Post etc. Received march orders for 24th inst (CRE's No 516 of 17/2/16).	
"	18/2/16	11.0pm	CRE's wire R207 of 18/2/16 cancels orders for relief. Lieut ~~Go~~ GORDON RE ordered to rejoin unit.	HOW APP 2.
"	23/2/16		Bought ~~at~~ a quantity of sawn timber at yard of Leconte-Vignon. Capt Hulton RE left on leave to England.	
"	24/2/16		Commenced to cart timber to workshop from Leconte-Vignon. Arranged extension of Divnl Baths at BRAY with CRE ~~30~~ 30th Divn. 2nd Lt MacFadyen temporarily attached from 51st Divn	
"	26/2/16	8.0pm	About 15 shells fell at top end of BRAY.	
"	27/2/16	8.0pm	2nd Lt Buckley RE reported at BRAY for duty with Coy.	
	29/2/16		Started pump at SUZANNE to pump to BRONFAY. 4 breaks found in pipe line due to shell bursts. Pumping stopped to repair these. 2nd Lt MacFADYEN returned to 51st Divn	

HOWarth Major R.E.
O.C. 202ND FIELD CO.,
(COUNTY PALATINE) R.E.

APPENDIX 2

8

"C" Form (Duplicate).

Army Form C. 2123

MESSAGES AND SIGNALS.

No. of Message

Charges to Pay. £ s. d.

Office Stamp. Z 13. 11. 16. U 208

Service Instructions.

Handed in at .... Office ....m. Received ....m.

TO 202nd Fd Co RE

Sender's Number	Day of Month	In reply to Number	AAA
R 207	18th	—	

My 516 of 18th cancelled

FROM CRE 30th Div

PLACE & TIME

(B 5004) Wt. w. 12550—4108 37,500 Pads 12/15 H & S Forms/C.2123.

202 Fob Coy
12 E

APPENDIX 1

"C" Form (Duplicate). Army Form C. 2123.

MESSAGES AND SIGNALS.

No. of Message

8

Charges to Pay. £ s. d.

Office Stamp.

Service Instructions. CRE 30th Divn

Handed in at ... Office 7.33p m. Received 8 54p m.

TO 202nd Field Coy R E

Sender's Number	Day of Month	In reply to Number	AAA
R 109	15th		

Major MITCHELL 1/2 Highland Field Coy will be attached to your Coy from Thursday Feb 17th inst Please arrange for billet

FROM CRE 30th Divn

PLACE & TIME

(B 5004) Wt. w. 12750–4108 37,500 Pads 12/15 H & S Forms/C.2123.

202nd Fd CoR

202 FIELD COY

1/3/16 — 31/3/16

Vol 5

CONFIDENTIAL

30

202 F.C.R.
Vol 5

WAR DIARY OF
202ND FIELD COY. ROYAL ENGINEERS
FROM MARCH 1ST 1916 TO MARCH 31ST 1916

VOL. 5

Instructions regarding War Diaries and Intelligence Summaries are contained in F. S. Regs., Part II. and the Staff Manual respectively. Title pages will be prepared in manuscript.

Vol 5.

WAR DIARY
or
~~INTELLIGENCE SUMMARY~~.
(Erase heading not required.)

Page 1,

Army Form C. 2118.

Place	Date	Hour	Summary of Events and Information	Remarks and references to Appendices
BRAY	3/3/16		Pumped Water tanks at ~~Bron~~ BRONFAY from ~~SUZANN~~ SUZANNE and pumping daily thereafter.	
			Capt HULTON RE returned after leave.	
	6/3/16		Company stores park commenced instead of Divisional RE PARK.	
"	7/3/16	11. AM	21st Brigade relieved by 54th Brigade in A Sector.	[illegible]
"	8/3/16		2Lt BREMNER, 79th Field Co RE. reported and attached to Company in commencement of the 79th Co taking over from 202nd Co.	
			Screen erected along PERONNE Road, point 104 to U Works.	
"	11/3/16		Major DONE RE, O.C. 80th Field Co RE attached for rations.	
"	12/3/16		Permanent Working party withdrawn by 21st Brigade.	[illegible]
	13/3/16		Received verbal instructions from CRE (30th Divn) to put 2 sections onto Corps Work on Rangée d'ABREES under Major DONE, and to hand over to the 80th Field Co RE on 30th Divn moving out of the area.	
	14/3/16		Enemy aeroplane passed over BRAY about 8.50 pm going South. It or another passed over again going NW & dropped 2 or 3 bombs on N side of the town.	[illegible]
	15/3/16		Handed over plans maps & programme to Capt CHAMBERS, OC the 80th Field Co RE.	[illegible]
	17/3/16		Received verbal orders from CRE 30th DW to hand over all ~~works~~ works to 80th Field Co RE	
	18/3/16		2 Sections at work on Rangée d'ABREES defensive works.	[illegible]
	19/3/16		Verbal orders from CE 13th Corps to take over 13th Corps Dump at BRAY	
	20/3/16		Took over 13th Corps Dump at BRAY.	
	21/3/16		Casualties O.R. one killed, one wounded.	

2353 Wt. W2544/1454 700,000 5/15 D. D. & L. A.D.S.S./Forms/C. 2118.

Instructions regarding War Diaries and Intelligence Summaries are contained in F. S. Regs., Part II. and the Staff Manual respectively. Title pages will be prepared in manuscript.

WAR DIARY

or

~~INTELLIGENCE SUMMARY.~~

(Erase heading not required.)

Army Form C. 2118.

VOL 5 PAGE 2

Place	Date	Hour	Summary of Events and Information	Remarks and references to Appendices
BRAY	22/3/16		Major Wraith on leave leaving Capt Hulton acting OC The whole company working on Rangée d'Arbres with 400 men of 16th Manchester battalion as permanent working party	ARH
	24/3/16		Took over RE dump at FROISSY QUAY from 2/4th AT Coy for 13th Corps	ARH
	25/3/16		2nd Lieut ~~[illegible]~~ STANIAR left at 10 am. for Divisional School. Corbie, & was attached to the 201st Fld Coy. RE	ARH
	27/3/16		17th Battalion Manchester took over fatigues on the Rangée d'Arbres Information received that the 200th Coy would relieve the 202 Coy R.E. early in April: A wire barb found in oat sack & handed to A.D.V.S. 18th Division. Sack was marked app I	App I ARH
	28/3/16		20th Batt. Liverpools relieved 17th Manchesters on RANGÉE d'ARBRES fatigue. Germans registered RANGÉE d'ARBRES with field and 21cc guns mostly on the Southern end	ARH

2353 Wt. W2514/1454 700,000 5/15 D. D. & L. A.D.S.S./Forms/C. 2118.

Army Form C. 2118.

Instructions regarding War Diaries and Intelligence Summaries are contained in F. S. Regs., Part II. and the Staff Manual respectively. Title pages will be prepared in manuscript.

WAR DIARY
or
~~INTELLIGENCE SUMMARY.~~

(Erase heading not required.)

Vol 5

Page 3

Place	Date	Hour	Summary of Events and Information	Remarks and references to Appendices
BRAY	30/3/16		Received instructions that on relief to hand over 13 Corps RE dumps at BRAY + FROISSY to 214th AT Coy RE ARH	
	31/3/16		2nd Batt Bedfords took over Corps fatigues on the RANGÉE d'ARBRES	
			Orders received for one officer to take over work from the 200th Coy RE at FRECHENCOURT ARH	

ARHulton Capt RE
202 Fld Coy

2353 Wt. W2544/1454 700,000 5/15 D. D. & L. A.D.S.S./Forms/C. 2118.

202 FIELD COY

1/4/16 — 30/4/16

Vol 6

202 FCRE
Vol 6

XXX

Confidential

War Diary
of
202nd Field Company Royal Engineers
From April 1st 1916 to April 30th 1916.

Volume 6

Instructions regarding War Diaries and Intelligence Summaries are contained in F. S. Regs., Part II. and the Staff Manual respectively. Title pages will be prepared in manuscript.

Army Form C. 2118.

WAR DIARY
or
INTELLIGENCE SUMMARY.
(*Erase heading not required.*)

Vol 6

Page I

Place	Date	Hour	Summary of Events and Information	Remarks and references to Appendices
BRAY	1/4/16	10am	Lieut RAYNER left for FRECHENCOURT in accordance with orders to take over work from the 200th Coy RE	ARH
"	2/4/16		The forward defenses of the RANGEE d'ARBRES line were pointed out by the CE. 13 Corps & work started on them	ARH
			Lieut Ellis left on Leave to England till the 13th April	
"	3/4/16		Lieut Ellis leave altered from the 5th to the 14th April	ARH
			Major H.O. Wraith returned to duty & took over command of the Company	ARH
"	4/4/16	7.0pm	H.Q & 1 Section of 200th Field Co RE arrived BRAY to take over from 202nd Company.	H.O.W.
"	5/4/16		Proceeded ~~with~~ handing over work on RANGEE d'ABRES works ~~to OC~~ 200th Field Co RE. No 3 section marched BRAY to FRECHENCOURT.	
"	6/4/16		Withdrew all men of 202nd Coy from RANGEE d'ABRES works on it being taken over by 200th Field Co RE	
"	7/4/16	3.30am	HQ & 3 Sections marched out from BRAY. Halted at CORBIE and detached No 2 Section there to work under 2nd Lieut Stanier at 30th Divisional School. Detached No 1 Section at QUERRIEUX for work at 4th Army HQ with No 3 Section under Lieut RAYNER. ~~Arrived~~ HQ & No 4 Section arrived Frechencourt 1.0pm	

2353 Wt. W25H/1454 700,000 5/15 D. D. & L. A.D.S.S./Forms/C. 2118.

Instructions regarding War Diaries and Intelligence Summaries are contained in F. S. Regs., Part II. and the Staff Manual respectively. Title pages will be prepared in manuscript.

Vol 6.

WAR DIARY
or
INTELLIGENCE SUMMARY.
(Erase heading not required.)

Army Form C. 2118.

Page 2.

Place	Date	Hour	Summary of Events and Information	Remarks and references to Appendices
FRECHENCOURT	8/4/16		Visited QUERRIEUX to see work of Sections 1 & 3. Reported to Chief Engineer 4th Army & CE 13th Corps. who instructed me ~~that~~ HQ & Section 4 would move in a day or two as ~~that~~ village had been handed over to the 3rd Army Corp.	H.O.W.
"	10/4/16		Visited CORBIE ~~to~~ inspect work of Section 2 at 30th Divn. School.	
"	11/4/16		Received orders to move HQ & No 4 Section to BERTANGLES to undertake improvement of billeds.	H.O.W.
BERTANGLES	12/4/16	10.am	HQ & No 4 Section marched to BERTANGLES. Snow, Rain Wind	
	13/4/16		With CRE 30th Divn to POULANVILLE Station & received instructions as to flagging out ~~training~~ ground. Timber arrived for bunks etc at BERTANGLES.	
	14/4/16		Commenced work flagging POULANVILLE ~~training~~ ground, and building bunks etc to increase billet accomodation at BERTANGLES.	H.O.W.
	17/4/16.		With O C 3rd Wing R F C to arrange work for increasing Officers accomodation at aerodrome. Finished flagging training ground at POULANVILLE.	H.O.W.
	~~18/4/16~~		Visited CARDONETTE ~~with Capt~~ PIERCE R.A.M.C to inspect wells ~~with~~ a view to fitting pump vide C R E's order received 16/4/16.	
	18/4/16.		Training ground inspected by CRE. digging of trenches commenced by C Coy, 2nd Wilts Regt. Received orders as to inspection on 20/4/16 by G.O.C. 13th Corps.	H.O.W.
	20 ~~19~~/4/16 H.O.W.		HQ & No 4 Section inspected by G.O.C. 13th Corps. 11.45 am. Lt Ellis to QUERRIEUX to take charge Sections I & III at 4th army HQ. Lt RAYNER proceeded on leave.	

2353 Wt. W2514/1454 700,000 5/15 D. D. & L. A.D.S.S./Forms/C. 2118.

Instructions regarding War Diaries and Intelligence Summaries are contained in F. S. Regs., Part II. and the Staff Manual respectively. Title pages will be prepared in manuscript.

Vol 6

WAR DIARY
or
INTELLIGENCE SUMMARY.
(*Erase heading not required.*)

Page 3.

Army Form C. 2118.

Place	Date	Hour	Summary of Events and Information	Remarks and references to Appendices
BERTANGLES	21/4/16		2nd Lt BUCKLEY rejoined from 201st Field Co RE. ~~Lt ELLIS to CARDONETTE to take charge of pump~~ H.O.W. 2nd Lt Buckley to QUERRIEUX to take over Sections I & III at 4th ARMY H.Q.	
	22/4/16		Lt Ellis proceeded to CARDONETTE to take charge of well pump erection. H.O.W.	
	23/4/16		I inspected pump at CARDONETTE. Received orders to proceed with company to BRAY on 29th.	
	24/4/16		Capt Hulton RE went to hospital at AMIENS.	
	25/4/16		Inspection of transport by C.R.E.	
	26/4/16.		2nd Lieut BUCKLEY went to BRAY in advance to take over from 80th Fld Co.	
CORBIE	28/4/16		Company marched to CORBIE picking up Sections I & III at QUERRIEUX.	
	29/4/16		Marched with whole company to BRAY.	
	30/4/16		Commenced taking over from 80th Field Co RE.	
			H O W [signature] Major RE OC 202nd Field Co R.E.	

2353 Wt. W2514/1454 700,000 5/15 D. D. & L. A.D.S.S./Forms/C. 2118.

CONFIDENTIAL

WAR DIARY
OF
202ND FIELD COY. ROYAL ENGRS.

FROM MAY 1ST 1916 TO. MAY 31ST 1916

VOLUME Y.

Army Form C. 2118.

Instructions regarding War Diaries and Intelligence Summaries are contained in F. S. Regs., Part II. and the Staff Manual respectively. Title pages will be prepared in manuscript.

Vol 7

WAR DIARY
or
INTELLIGENCE SUMMARY.
(*Erase heading not required.*)

Page 1

Place	Date	Hour	Summary of Events and Information	Remarks and references to Appendices
BRAY SUR SOMME	1/5/16		Taking over from ~~[illegible]~~ 80th Field Co. R E. No 1 Section proceeded to trenches HOW.	
	2/5/16		Lt. Rayner returned from leave.	
	4/5/16		Section 4 proceeded to trenches	
	5/5/16		Completed taking over from 80th Fld Co. RE HOW	
	6/5/16		Sections 2 & 3 proceeded to trenches	
	7/5/16		Major H.O. WRAITH, R.E (T.C) was admitted into Hospital, Lieut N.I. ELLIS, R.E (T.C). assumed command of Company	
	10/5/16		Major H.E.F. RATHBONE, R.E. joined Company and took over Command from Lieut. Ellis. 2nd Lieut. J.G.N. CLIFT joined in place of II Lieut. STANIAR, & took command of Section 2.	
	12/5/16		Lieut. G. RAYNER wounded by bullet night 11/12. when marking out new works.	
	15/5/16		II Lieut. C.H. COTTEW, R.E (T.C) joined Company in place of Lieut RAYNER and took Command of Section 3. Lieuts. CAMPBELL, CLIFT and BUCKLEY took up quarters in the trenches.	
	19/5/16		II Lieut COTTEW took up quarters in the trenches. Casualties O.R wounded one; 2 mules killed.	
	20/5/16		About 50 enemy shells dropped around Divisional Dump. Our Canteen was destroyed by shell.	
	24/5/16		Casualties O.R. Killed one by shell	
	24/5/16		Traced out new trench in No Man's land. Casualties O.R. Wounded Four.	
	28/5/16		Superintended Infantry working parties digging new trench. (see attached)	App 1

[signature] Lieut R.E.
O.C. 202ND FIELD CO., (COUNTY PALATINE) R.E.

2353 Wt. W2514/1454 700,000 5/15 D. D. & L. A.D.S.S./Forms/C. 2118.

App 1

Copy

Officer Commanding
202nd Field Co R.E.

I want to congratulate you, your officers, N.C.O's and men on the work they performed last night and the previous night.

The preparations which you carried out and the detail in which the tasks for the infantry were marked out, made the work not only possible, but undoubtedly assisted materially in reducing the casualties incurred to what they were.

It is most gratifying that the first operation of your Company in conjunction with the Infantry of the 21st Brigade should be so successful.

Sd. C. SACKVILLE WEST.
Brigadier General
Cdg. 21st Infantry Brigade

2

Copy of telegram received from H.Q. 30th Division 29.5.16
C.R.E.

Senders No. G.30 Day of month 29th
Please thank Major Rathbone and all the R.E. employed on last two nights in connection with the trench dug by 21st Brigade for the good work that they have done

Sd. J SHEA M.G.

3.

O.C. 202nd. Field C R.E.
R.11. 29th.
In forwarding copy of G.O.C's. message, the C.R.E. wishes to add his own thanks and express his high appreciation of the splendid work done by the Company.

From C.R.E. 30th Divn.

Sd R.G. Stone Capt R.E.
for C.R.E. 30th Division

Jane
202 FeRE
XXX Vol 8

<u>Confidential.</u>

War Diary

of

202nd Field Coy. Royal Engineers

Volume 8.

<u>From</u> June 1st 1916 <u>To</u> June 30th 1916

Instructions regarding War Diaries and Intelligence Summaries are contained in F. S. Regs., Part II. and the Staff Manual respectively. Title pages will be prepared in manuscript.

202nd Field Coy R.E.

Vol. 8.

WAR DIARY
or
~~INTELLIGENCE SUMMARY.~~

(*Erase heading not required.*)

Page 1

Army Form C. 2118.

Place	Date	Hour	Summary of Events and Information	Remarks and references to Appendices
BRAY SUR SOMME	1/6/16		Lieut. BUCKLEY P.B. R.E. proceeded to BRIQUESNIEL upon C.R.E.'s Authority to supervise digging of training trenches	
	2/6/16		Our Artillery active night 2/3rd June. Casualties O.R. Wounded one.	
	3/6/16		Heavy shelling heard N.E. of BRAY night of 3/4 June	
	4/6/16		ii Lieut. P.F. CAMPBELL proceeded on leave to United Kingdom. Leave granted from 5/6/16 to 14/6/16.	
	5/6/16		Lieut. N.T. ELLIS, R.E. proceeded to AMIENS to purchase stores for Dumpete. Heavy Artillery bombardment heard direction of ALBERT, about 9-0 P.M.	
	7/6/16		ii Lieut. J.G.N. CLIFT, R.E. was wounded in jaw by bullet. Evacuated C.C.S. 8/6/16.	
	13/6/16		ii Lieut. F.K.O. MOYNAN, R.E. (T.C.) joined Company for duty. Artillery bombardment heard direction of MARICOURT about 11-0 p.m.	
	14/6/16		Casualties, 2nd Wilts attached 202nd Fld Co R.E., Wounded O.R. one	
	"	11-0 P.M.	Time advanced 60 minutes in accordance with XIII Corps orders, & 11-0 P.M. became 12-midnight.	
	14/6/16		ii Lieut. P.F. CAMPBELL, R.E. rejoined from leave in United Kingdom	
	16/6/16		Major H.E.F. RATHBONE, R.E. and Lieut. N.T. ELLIS R.E. together with 2 N.C.O's proceeded to OISSY re Divisional Trench training scheme.	
	22/6/16		On the night 22/23rd June ii Lieut. P.F. Campbell was slightly wounded in the hand by shrapnel. He remained at duty. A Sapper was wounded by a bullet in the arm on 22/6/16	
	24/6/16		Sections 1, 2, 3 & 4 came out of the trenches for a "rest"	
	25/6/16 to 30/6/16		Heavy bombardment of enemy positions by our Artillery	
	30/6/16		Headquarters & all sections went into the trenches, only Drivers & a few details were left behind	

H Rathbone Major R.E.
O/C 202nd Field Coy R.E.

2353 Wt. W2544/1454 700,000 5/15 D. D. & L. A.D.S.S./Forms/C. 2118.

30/July
202 FCRE
Vol 9

CONFIDENTIAL.

WAR DIARY

OF

202ND FIELD COMPANY, ROYAL ENGINEERS

FROM:- JULY 1ST 1916 TO:- JULY 31ST 1916

VOLUME 9.

202nd Field Co RE.

Instructions regarding War Diaries and Intelligence Summaries are contained in F. S. Regs., Part II. and the Staff Manual respectively. Title pages will be prepared in manuscript.

Vol. 9

WAR DIARY
or
~~INTELLIGENCE SUMMARY.~~
(Erase heading not required.)

Page One

Army Form C. 2118.

Place	Date	Hour	Summary of Events and Information	Remarks and references to Appendices
BRAY	1-7-16		Intensive Bombardment: attack launched 7-30 am	
Trenches		9.0 am	No1 section to GLATZ Redoubt from assembly trenches, began 1st Strong Point.	
	2-7-16		Nos 2.3. sections from TRIGGER WOOD to ~~[struck]~~ MONTAUBAN to form Strong Point under OC 201 Fd Co.	
			No 4 section to TALUS BOISE in reserve. No 2+3 section withdrawn from MONTAUBAN to TALUS BOISE	
		7.5pm	No 4 section relieved No1 in GLATZ redoubt.	
	3-7-16	4.0pm	1.2.&3 sections from TALUS BOISE to GLATZ Redoubt on Strong Points 1.2a.3 &4.	
	4-7-16		All 4 sections working on Strong Point 1.2.2a.3.4.5.6.7 till 9pm.	
BRAY	5-7-16	1.0 am	Co arrived at BRAY dump for rest.	
		9.0pm	Co ordered back to trenches, 2 sections No2 and 4 leaving late at night, to TALUS BOISE	
Trenches	6-7-16		Remt 2 sections to trenches, bivouacing in TALUS BOISE	
			OC to Bde HQ TRAIN ALLEY. Bde HQ shelled out in evening, went to fresh shelter	
	7-7-16		also in TRAIN ALLEY. Capt Reece temporarily attached to Coy	
			Sections 2 attached to 2nd Yorks, and Section 4 to 2nd Wilts; many casualties while waiting with Bn supports.	
	8-7-16		Section 4 formed & cleared well in BRIQUETERIE; party from No1 to BRIQUETERIE to clear out dugouts	
			Sections 1 and 3 in reserve in TALUS BOISE. Secs 2&4 withdrawn to NORD ALLEY, then GLATZ	
			Redoubt; then concentrated all 4 sections at No3 Strong Point GLATZ Redoubt.	
	9-7-16	Night & afternoon	No 2 Section on repairs to 2 bridges on MARICOURT-MONTAUBAN Road, & F. Bridge over NORD ALLEY	
			and at night unloading RE. Wagon carrying	
			Nos 1.2&3. Sections, reinforced by 2 sections of 201st Fd Co RE, and 3 coys 1st S. Lancs Pioneers	
			dug trench from S.E. of BERNAFAY WOOD to Sunken Road & first-tapped Sunken Road towards	
			CHIMPANZEE trench, & put out wire in front of above. i de MOYNAN - Shell Short -	
			to BRAY, evacuated.	
	10-7-16	3.0 am	Work described above ceased at dawn.	
		2.30pm	Coy ordered back from trenches to camp F, on relief by 205th Fd Co RE. Casualties since 1-7-16: Killed O.R. 6; Wounded Officer 1 (Shell Shock); Wounded O.R. 19; Injured O.R. 3	
BRAY	11-7-16		Coy returned to Coy HQ BRAY for rest.	
Do	12/7/16 – 14		Coy at BRAY overhauling Mob equipt, packing tool carts etc	
VAUX	15-7-16		Coy marched to VAUX-sur-SOMME, into bivouac.	
	16-7-16		Route march in afternoon (13½ miles)	
	17-7-16		" " " morning (15½ miles)	
	18-7-16		" " " (7½ ...)	

202nd Field Co R.E.

Instructions regarding War Diaries and Intelligence Summaries are contained in F. S. Regs., Part II. and the Staff Manual respectively. Title pages will be prepared in manuscript.

Vol. 9

WAR DIARY
or
~~INTELLIGENCE SUMMARY.~~
(Erase heading not required.)

Page Two

Army Form C. 2118.

Place	Date	Hour	Summary of Events and Information	Remarks and references to Appendices
VAUX	19-7-16	10.45	C.R.E.'s inspection parade of transport. Received order to proceed to BOIS CAFTET area	
			Coy marched off in rear of 89th Infantry Brigade	
		2.30 6.45	arrived BRAY; ordered to form bivouac for the night	
BRAY	20-7-16		awaiting orders till 4 pm: then ordered to join 21st Inf Bde in BOIS CAFTET – MANSEL COPSE area: reached bivouac site 6.30 pm. F.16.	
F.16.	21-7-16		Reconnaissance: self to Bde H.Q. & to see Lt COTTEW to TRONES WOOD or R.E. then to BERNAFAY, thence to C.R.E. BILLON FARM: then to BRAY re transport of tools to F.16: Lt BUCKLEY to TRONES WOOD etc to see if lanes cut thro' wood for operations.	
SILESIA TRENCH	22-7-16		2 sections (No 3 and No 4) to TRONES WOOD to cut lanes: found work nearly done & returned to BRICK POINT, where Secs No 1 & 2 arrived 6.30 pm. R.E. etc to Bde H.Q. TRAIN ALLEY.	
			Sections 1.2.3.4 awaiting orders during attack of GUILLEMONT by 21st Bde	
do	23-7-16		Recd order to return to BRAY.	
		5 pm 6 pm	Section marched off, arriving BRAY 7.30 pm, leaving party of 8 men & more men at Bde H.Q. TRAIN ALLEY to improve dugout.	
			2. Lt FROST R.E. joined Coy	
			overhauling tool carts etc. TRAIN ALLEY Bde H.Q. party rejoined Coy.	
BRAY	24-7-16		Constructing 10 dugouts for Divisional Head Quarters near BILLON FARM.	
"	25-7-16			
"	26-7-16			
"	27-7-16			
"	28-7-16		25 men completing Divl dugouts. remainder fatigue, repairing & cleaning transport vehicles: afternoon resting	
"	29-7-16			
CAFTET Wd	30-7-16	3.0 am	4 Sections to CAFTET WOOD, in Divisional Reserve	
	do	7.0 pm	Sections ordered back to BRAY.	
BRAY	31-7-16		Completing tool carts, loading pontoon & trestle wagons, drill, & preparing to move.	

H Rathbone
Maj RE
OC. 202nd Fd Coy RE

2353 Wt. W2544/1454 700,000 5/15 D. D. & L. A.D.S.S./Forms/C. 2118.

30th Divisional Engineers

202nd FIELD COMPANY R. E.

AUGUST 1 9 1 6

202nd Field Co RE

Instructions regarding War Diaries and Intelligence Summaries are contained in F. S. Regs., Part II. and the Staff Manual respectively. Title pages will be prepared in manuscript.

Vol. 10

WAR DIARY
or
~~INTELLIGENCE~~ SUMMARY.

(Erase heading not required.)

Page One.

Army Form C. 2118.

Place	Date	Hour	Summary of Events and Information	Remarks and references to Appendices
BRAY-SUR-SOMME	1/8/16	10-0am	Transport left BRAY-SUR-SOMME.	
		9-45pm	Dismounted troops marched to MERICOURT L'ABBÉ.	
MERICOURT L'ABBE	2-8-16	1-30am	Dismounted troops arrived – slept in field. Left at 10-a.m. by train. Detrained LONGPRÉ at 1-0pm. Left about 3-0pm destination HOCQUINCOURT by road, and arrived at 6-30pm. Transport joined at 7-0pm. Erected bivouacs.	
HOCQUINCOURT	3.8.16		Squad Drill etc.	
"	4.8.16		Squad Drill. Left at 9-30pm on march to PONT REMY	
	5.8.16		Arrived PONT REMY 2-0a.m. At 3-0a.m. commenced entraining. All transport loaded by 5-0a.m. Men entrained 6-0a.m. Arrived MERVILLE about 12-0-noon. Detrained and marched at 3-30pm to ROBECQ – arrived 6-0pm. Erected bivouacs and horse lines etc.	
ROBECQ	6.8.16		DRILL etc. BATHS	
"	7.8.16		Major RATHBONE, RE., 4 officers + 12 men proceeded to GORRE to take over from 234th Field Co RE and inspect the line.	
"	8.8.16		Physical drill etc. Baths.	
"	9.8.16		Drill etc. Kit inspection	
GORRE	10.8.16		Company left ROBECQ 5-30am to march to GORRE. Upon arrival proceeded to clean up billets.	
"	11.8.16	–	Major RATHBONE, Section Officers and all N.C.O's made tour of trenches. Company employed upon whitewashing and thoroughly cleaning up billet which was in a very insanitary condition. Carpenters erected shelters for attached men.	

2353 Wt. W2514/1454 700,000 5/15 D. D. & L. A.D.S.S./Forms/C. 2118.

202nd Field Co R.E.

Instructions regarding War Diaries and Intelligence Summaries are contained in F. S. Regs., Part II. and the Staff Manual respectively. Title pages will be prepared in manuscript.

VOL 10

WAR DIARY
or
~~INTELLIGENCE~~ SUMMARY.
(Erase heading not required.)

Page 2

Army Form C. 2118.

Place	Date	Hour	Summary of Events and Information	Remarks and references to Appendices
GORRE	12.8.16		Company employed on erection of shelter, petrol store, Armstrong Hut, and whitewashing billet etc.	
"	13.8.16		Company, with 200 Infantry employed in trenches, fire stepping, revetting, widening etc.	
"	14.8.16		Ditto: attached Co. of S. Lancs Pioneers commenced work on Communication trenches.	
"	15/8/16		Continued repairs & maintenance of Givenchy trench system & consolidation of crater lips. CRE goes on leave.	
"	16.8.16		No 2 Section sent up to Givenchy Village Line under orders from B.G. 21st Bde, [illegible] to provide an emergency [illegible] party. Showed enemy blow a mine. Showery. Lt Campbell invalided.	
"	17.8.16		Weather showery. Repairs to trench system continued.	
"	18.8.16		[illegible] + H.T.K. in hand. Spr Kelsey mortally wounded 21st, died	
"	19 20 21 22 23		Consolidation of lips at Red Dragon, on 23rd.	
"	24		CRE returned from leave.	Trench maintenance work as above continued
"	25		Visit to Co H.Q. by CRE	
"	26		CRE sick & to No 7 Stationary Hospital Boulogne	
"	27		21st Bde relieved by 89th Bde in GIVENCHY Sector	
"	28		Round sector with B.G. comd. 89th Bde	
"	29		To LA GORGUE in pm with Adj. In evening with G.O.C. Div. (1½ hours) Visited O.C. 201 F. Co. at Le Touret.	r. wet wet
"	30		Lt Buckley goes on 7 days leave to England.	
"	31		Usual work carried on in trenches	

[illegible] Lieut. R.E.
O.C. 202ND FIELD CO.,
(COUNTY PALATINE) R.E.

2353 Wt. W2544/1454 700,000 5/15 D. D. & L. A.D.S.S./Forms/C. 2118.

202 FIELD COY

1/10/16 — 31/10/16

VOL 12

Vol 11

SECRET

War Diary
of
202nd Field Company R. E.
For the month of
SEPTEMBER 1916

Volume 11

202nd Field Co R.E.

Instructions regarding War Diaries and Intelligence Summaries are contained in F. S. Regs., Part II. and the Staff Manual respectively. Title pages will be prepared in manuscript.

WAR DIARY
or
INTELLIGENCE SUMMARY.
(*Erase heading not required.*)

Army Form C. 2118.

VOL 11

Page One

Place	Date	Hour	Summary of Events and Information	Remarks and references to Appendices
GORRE	Sept 2		Reinforcements O.R. one	
	" 3		Major RATHBONE, R.E. proceeded to H.Q. R.E. as Acting C.R.E. Lieut N.T. ELLIS. R.E. assumed Command of Company. 1 NCO + 2 men attached to 61st Division for instruction in "pipe-pushing" II Lieut. GORMAN, 11th S. Lancs Regt. temporarily attached to Company.	
	" 4		Reinforcements O.R. one	
	" 7		Lieut. P.B. BUCKLEY, R.E. returned from special leave to U.K.	
	" 8		II Lieut. C.H. COTTEW, R.E. proceeded on 7 days special leave to U.K. 1 NCO + 2 men returned from "pipe pushing" class.	
	" 10		II Lieut. GORMAN returned to his Unit (11th S. Lancs. Regt) 11th S. Lancs left area	
	" 11		II Lieut A. SEARLE joined Company as reinforcement, also 1 O.R. Company took over work of 201st Field Co R.E. Section 2, in GIVENCHY SECTOR. 200th Field Co R.E. left area	
	12		Usual work in trenches. Weather fine.	
	14			
	15		II Lt C.H. Cottew returned from Special Leave to UK	
	17		Section 3 came down from trenches at GIVENCHY	
	18	10-0pm	Company left GORRE at 10.0 pm and marched to FOUQUEREUIL	
	19		Entrained at FOUQUEREUIL. Detrained at DOULLENS and marched to AMPLIER	
	21		Company marched from AMPLIER to WARGNIES	
WARGNIES	22		Sections employed on rifle drill, physical drill etc	
	23		Reconnaissance and route march by Sections	
	24		Manoeuvres + training with Infy Brigade	
	25		ditto	
	27		Company marched from WARGNIES to ALLONVILLE	

2353 Wt. W2541/1454 700,000 5/15 D. D. & L. A.D.S.S./Forms/C. 2118.

202nd Field Co RE

Instructions regarding War Diaries and Intelligence Summaries are contained in F. S. Regs., Part II. and the Staff Manual respectively. Title pages will be prepared in manuscript.

Army Form C. 2118.

WAR DIARY
or
INTELLIGENCE SUMMARY.
(Erase heading not required.)

Vol 11.

Page 2

Place	Date	Hour	Summary of Events and Information	Remarks and references to Appendices
	Sept 28th		Company marched from ALLONVILLE to Hutments near DERNANCOURT	
	29		Company marched to MONTAUBAN	
MONTAUBAN	30		Sections 1, 2, 3 & 4 employed on repairing & clearing road at BAZENTIN-LE-GRAND	

P.B. Buckley Lieut. RE
for Actg O/C 202nd Field Co RE

2353 Wt. W2544/1454 700,000 5/15 D. D. & L. A.D.S.S./Forms/C. 2118.

Vol 12

SECRET.

War Diary

of

202nd Field Company R.E.

for the month of

OCTOBER 1916

VOLUME 12

202nd Field Co R.E.

Instructions regarding War Diaries and Intelligence Summaries are contained in F. S. Regs., Part II. and the Staff Manual respectively. Title pages will be prepared in manuscript.

WAR DIARY or ~~INTELLIGENCE SUMMARY~~.

(Erase heading not required.)

Army Form C. 2118.

VOL 12. Page One

Place	Date	Hour	Summary of Events and Information	Remarks and references to Appendices
MONTAUBAN	Oct 1		Sections 1, 2, 3 & 4 employed on repairing and clearing road at BAZENTIN-LE-GRAND	
"	2		ditto ditto ditto	
"	3		ditto ditto. Major RATHBONE granted leave to U.K	
"	4/6		ditto ditto	
"	7		ditto ditto Casualties Wounded O.R one	
"	8		ditto ditto Major RATHBONE rejoined Coy from leave to U.K.	
"	9		ditto ditto	
"	10		ditto ditto until 12 0 noon. Coy moved and encamped near BAZENTIN-LE-GRAND (S21 d 8.8).	
	11/12		Completed undug portion of TURK TRENCH to GOOSE ALLEY etc. Casualties Killed O.R five Wounded O.R. three	
	13		Sections employed on front line work.	
	14		Straightened original front line & reconnoitred front line trench. Casualties, Gassed O.R. 4	
	15/16		Sections employed on preparation of assembly trenches for proposed attack on 18th.	
	17		Ditto Ditto, also preparing & erecting trench sign plates	
	18th		Sections 1 & 2 ~~extended~~ dug new trench on Brigades left from M24a 2.7 to M18c 05/30, and extended TURK LANE to the new trench. Maintenance of TURK LANE & drainage of trenches. In several places between FLERS TRENCH and FLERS-EAUCOURT Road mud was knee deep. Casualties Wounded O.R. two. Lieut. N.T. ELLIS proceeded on leave (special) to U.K.	
	19		Constructed strong point on left on new Brigade front line. Enemy's artillery active. Weather extremely bad.	
	20		Major H.E.F. RATHBONE. R.E (O.C. Company) admitted to Hospital (sick) leaving Lieut P.B. BUCKLEY acting O.C. Company.	
	21		Preparation for move.	

2353 Wt. W2544/1454 700,000 5/15 D. D. & L. A.D.S.S./Forms/C. 2118.

212th Field Co R.E.

Instructions regarding War Diaries and Intelligence Summaries are contained in F. S. Regs., Part II. and the Staff Manual respectively. Title pages will be prepared in manuscript.

Vol 12.

WAR DIARY
or
~~INTELLIGENCE SUMMARY.~~
(Erase heading not required.)

Page Two

Army Form C. 2118.

Place	Date October	Hour	Summary of Events and Information	Remarks and references to Appendices
	22		Company moved from S21 A8.8 to POMMIERS REDOUBT, after handing over to Australian R.E.	
POMMIERS RDT.	23		Men employed on cleaning equipment & clothing etc.	
"	24		Company marched to DERNANCOURT	
	25		Transport moved with 21st Brigade Transport to TALMAS. DERNANCOURT heavily shelled by enemy artillery.	
	26		Transport moved with 21st Brigade Transport from TALMAS to LUCHEUX. Dismounted portion of Company proceed by 'bus from DERNANCOURT to LUCHEUX	
LUCHEUX	27		Repairing & washing wagons etc. Lieut. BUCKLEY proceeded to BAILLEULMONT to take over from 1/2 N. Midland Field Co R.E.	
do	28		Repairing & washing wagons etc. Section 1 proceeded to BERLES-AU-BOIS	
do.	29		Preparing and standing by for move.	
	30		Sections 2, 3, 4 & HQ. marched from LUCHEUX to BAILLEULMONT, where H.Q. & Section 3 remained. Sections 2 & 4 then marched to BERLES-AU-BOIS.	
BAILLEULMONT	31		H.Q. & Section 3 employed on cleaning up Camp, & in workshops. Sects. 1, 2 & 4 working in the line.	

P.B. Buckley Lieut. R.E.
Actg O/C 202nd Field Co R.E.

Secret.

Vol 13

War Diary

of

202nd Field Coy. RE

For month of

November 1916.

VOL: 13.

202nd Field Co RE

Instructions regarding War Diaries and Intelligence Summaries are contained in F. S. Regs., Part II. and the Staff Manual respectively. Title pages will be prepared in manuscript.

VOL. 13.

WAR DIARY
or
~~INTELLIGENCE SUMMARY.~~
(Erase heading not required.)

Army Form C. 2118.

Page One

Place	Date NOV	Hour	Summary of Events and Information	Remarks and references to Appendices
H.Q. BAILLEULMONT Sections at BERLES-AU-BOIS	1		H.Q. & Sect 3 in workshops etc. Sections 1, 2 & 4 in trenches, clearing front line trenches, revetting firesteps front line (at night) and general maintenance of trenches.	
	2		Cutting firesteps and clearing front line, repairing gun pits, repairing Recreation room &c.	
	3		Clearing front line trenches, C.T.s, and blocks. Workshops etc.	
	4		" " " " ", revetting, dugouts, outposts, workshops, etc.	
	5		" " " " ", " , " , " , repairing gunpits, workshops &c	
	6.		" " " " " " " making sumps etc. clay very wet and hard to work. Lieut. N. T. ELLIS returned from leave to U.K.	
	7		Clearing blocks & revetting trenches in front line, making O.P. Clearing trench and emptying ~~trenches~~ sandbags, dugouts and outposts, repairing gunpits. Trenches falling in owing to wet weather.	MR
	8		Trenches in parts fallen in during the night. Clearing ~~&~~ ~~settling~~ revetting front line trenches. Emptying sandbags. Repairing gunpits. Clearing blocks & pumping water.	MR
	9/10		Clearing front line trenches, stripping M.G.E. of concrete, revetting etc. On night of 10/11 we demolished a German M.G.E.	MR
	11		Clearing & revetting front line; repairing dugouts etc.	MR
	12		Revetting & trimming off etc; excavating, covering M.G.E.; converting baths into drying room for gumboots; clearing front line; preparation for light railway.	MR
	13/15		Clearing trenches, making drain trench (night), repairing gunpits, revetting front line. Half of Sect 1 came down to BAILLEULMONT. Wiring back revetment and instructing Infantry	
	16		Excavating and revetting, clearing, dugouts, drying room.	
	17		Making Stokes Gun dugout, clearing and revetting & wiring back. collecting trolleys etc.	

2353 Wt. W2544/1454 700,000 5/15 D. D. & L. A.D.S.S./Forms/C. 2118.

202nd Field Co R.E.

Instructions regarding War Diaries and Intelligence Summaries are contained in F. S. Regs., Part II. and the Staff Manual respectively. Title pages will be prepared in manuscript.

WAR DIARY
or
~~INTELLIGENCE SUMMARY.~~
(Erase heading not required.)

Army Form C. 2118.

VOL. 13

Page Two

Place	Date 1916	Hour	Summary of Events and Information	Remarks and references to Appendices
BAILLEULMONT. Sections at BELLACOURT and BERLES	Nov. 18		Sections re-arranged as follows. Remaining half of Sect. 1 to BAILLEULMONT, Sections 2 and 3 to BELLACOURT, Section 4 remains at BERLES. Laying rails for DECAUVILLE track. repairing dugouts, wiring back revetments.	
	19		Making bunks and repairing billets, clearing & revetting, drying room, dugouts, laying rails, erecting canvas screen for railway (~~[illegible]~~)	
	20		Fixing billets & erecting bunks, revetting & excavating, blocking trench with wire, drying room, laying rails etc., repairing trench pumps, clearing blocks in fire trench.	
	21/22		Clearing berm & trench, and widening for 'V' frames, revetting, drying room, repairing Hospital, BELLACOURT, laying rails and making screen. Repairing billets; cutting through & framing drain.	
	23		Ditto ditto. Stokes Mortar Emplacement.	
	24		Clearing & revetting trenches; repairing billets; drying room; laying rails and making screen; workshops	
	25.		Erecting 2 huts; Instructing Infantry in revetting etc.; clearing berm & picketting back revetting & clearing; laying rails & making screen	
	26 } 27 }		Clearing & revetting trenches; clearing blocks; laying tramway etc; inspecting dugouts &c instructing Infantry; clearing falls of earth in front line trenches; Stokes Mortar Emplacement; making screen,	
	28/29		Erecting Huts; clearing pumping & excavating etc; revetting F.L. trenches; laying rails etc & making screen; fixing 'V' frames; instructing re "AMMONAL" tube.	
	30		Demonstration (practice) of Bangalore torpedo; revetting & excavating, dugouts; preparing for mined dugouts; making sign boards etc; laying rails etc.	

S.W. T[illegible] Major R.E.

O.C. 202ND FIELD CO., (COUNTY PALATINE) R.E.

2353 Wt. W2544/1454 700,000 5/15 D. D. & L. A.D.S.S./Forms/C. 2118.

SECRET

Vol 14

War Diary

of

202nd Field Coy, Royal Engineers

for the month of

DECEMBER 1916

VOLUME 14.

202nd Field Co R.E.

Instructions regarding War Diaries and Intelligence Summaries are contained in F. S. Regs., Part II. and the Staff Manual respectively. Title pages will be prepared in manuscript.

WAR DIARY
or
~~INTELLIGENCE SUMMARY~~.
(Erase heading not required.)

Army Form C. 2118.

Vol. 14

Page One

Place	1916 Date DEC.	Hour	Summary of Events and Information	Remarks and references to Appendices
H.Q. BAILLEULMONT Sections at BELLACOURT & BERLES-AU-BOIS	1/3		Clearing and revetting trenches, bunking billets, Instructing Infantry in revetting, erecting huts, dugouts, laying tramways, making level crossings, instructing in Bangalore torpedoes, officers' class, drying room, salvaging materials.	
	4/6		Cleaning berm & trenches, revetting, dugouts, erecting huts, repairing billets, and erecting bunks, glazing, repairing roads, mined dugouts, drying room, laying rails, making level crossing, wireless station, Infantry Officers class in revetting, repairing well.	
	7/9		Clearing and revetting trenches, repairing pumps, revetting class for Infantry N.C.O's, repairs to wells, rifle range, new baths, Infantry officers class in revetting, mined dugouts, wireless station, laying rails, revetting embankment, bending rails & racking line, making level crossing, coupling rails etc., making new Orderly Room at Left Bn. HQ.	
	10/12		Anchoring pickets, clearing and revetting trenches, dugouts, repairing billets and erecting bunks, new baths, repairing theatre, repairing wells, making new Orderly Room, preparing timber (trimming) searching Brigade area for rails, rifle range, Regl Aid post.	
	13/15		Clearing trench & berm & revetting, dugouts, repairing pumps, repairing billets and erecting bunks, making alterations to theatre, rifle range, repairing wells, new baths, Regl Aid post, preparing Ammonal tubes, making barricade, repairing buffers, salving trench boards & timber, digging trench Mortar emplacement.	
	16		Clearing & revetting trenches etc., mined & tubular dugouts, rifle range, Canteen and theatre, new baths, repairing billets and erecting bunks, preparing logs, Regl Aid post, drying room, preparing track — coupling & bending rails, packing line for engine, digging emplacements.	
			Two NCO's & 4 sappers took part in two raids conducted by 21st Bde against enemy trenches on night 16-17. The R.E. were responsible for clearing gaps in enemy wire with ammonal torpedos & fulfilled their mission successfully earning the thanks of O.C. raid for their services.	App 1

2353 Wt. W25-4/1454 700,000 5/15 D. D. & L. A.D.S.S./Forms/C. 2118.

202nd Field Co R.E.

Instructions regarding War Diaries and Intelligence Summaries are contained in F. S. Regs., Part II. and the Staff Manual respectively. Title pages will be prepared in manuscript.

WAR DIARY
or
~~INTELLIGENCE SUMMARY.~~
(Erase heading not required.)

Army Form C. 2118.

VOL. 14

Page Two

Place	1916 Date DEC.	Hour	Summary of Events and Information	Remarks and references to Appendices
H.Q. BAILLEULMONT Sections at Bellacourt Berles-au-Bois	17/20		Repairs to mined dugouts; drying room; clearing track & coupling rails; repairing rails blown up by shell fire; making miniature rifle range; new baths; erecting bunks, dugouts; Coy. Workshops; clearing and revetting trenches; erecting new huts; making mine frames; repairing wells; repairs to Lt. Batt. Orderly Room; Regl Aid post; making trench stools; salving timber; fitting up theatre; arranging and fitting electric alarm to trip wire; clearing berm; repairing pumps; squaring timbers etc; excavating and widening bomb store.	
	21/24		Erecting bunks and wiring; repairing wells; bomb store; clearing and revetting trenches and pumping out water; making mine frames; repairing & making dugouts mined & tubular; building ovens; Coy. workshops and dumps; making wheelbarrows; preparing track and coupling; digging and fixing emplacements; clearing berm; Regl Aid Post; repairing billets; repairing tool cart; wiring back pickets; overhauling motor pump; new chimney fixed Bde. H.Q. 21/12/16. No 81940 Sgt. Kenyon awarded Military Medal in connection with raid.	
	25.		Company dinner, followed by Concert; both greatly enjoyed by the troops.	
	26/28		Erecting new huts, erecting bomb store; making mine frames; preparing trench stools; repairing wells and pumps; drying room; working on theatre; repairing billets and bunking; repairing and making dugouts; Regl Aid post; preparing track and coupling rails; squaring timbers; digging and fixing emplacements; recovering timber; Coy. workshops & dumps; erecting fire-steps for flank defences; rifle range; taking down and clearing Canteen.	
	29/31		Tubular bomb stores; preparing props; dugouts; making trench stools and loophole boxes; excavations for mined dugouts; rifle range; new baths; Canteen & theatre; repairing wells; Regl Aid post; excavating & preparing track; coupling etc; making level crossings; fixing and wiring bunks; Coy. workshops and dumps; repairing pumps; preparing and fixing emplacements; fixing bridge; laying trench boards, fixing petrol pump.	

O. Wellis Capt. R.E.
O/C 202nd Field Coy R.E.

Report on Raids night of 16/17 Nov. 1916.

C.R.E. 30th Division

(1) I have to report that 202nd Field Coy. R.E. provided the ammonal tube parties for destroying enemy wire in two raids conducted in 21st Brigade area night of 16/17 November 1916.
Both raids were successful and there was no hitch in the R.E. work on which the success of the right raiding party entirely depended, as the wire was found intact and the artillery bombardment was directed on the enemy trenches only at this point of entry. The 'O/C raids' congratulated the R.E. on their work.

(2) The following points are of R.E. interest:-

Right raiding party:- Sgt. KENYON, S.
Spr. NEWHAM, J.R.
Spr. McNICHOLAS. F.

Left raiding party: 2nd Cpl. WILLIAMS J.
Spr. HOUGHTON G.
Spr. BLACK. L.

formed the Ammonal tube parties. Each party carried an ammonal tube 18 foot long, 50 lbs. ammonal, weight with torpedo wood case about 65 lbs. The method of detonating being as sketch A attached — detonators with both time (2 minutes) and instantaneous (50 yards) being fixed through a wood plug at end of ammonal tube in a dry g.c. primer in close contact with the ammonal. The detonators and fuzes joined up, but carried separately till the torpedo is under the wire. The torpedo had to be fired ½ minute after zero. — the time fuze being first lighted and the instantaneous being ready in case of failure. The fuzes were ignited by 'friction ignitors.' An Infantryman was detailed to hold the instantaneous fuze drum 50 yards from

enemy

enemy wire while the R.E. Sergeant went forwarded with the torpedo to the wire reeling off the fuze as he went.
A tape previously placed on the ground by an Infantry reconnoitering party to the point of entry at enemy wire was the torpedo-party's guide — the night was so dark that the tape had to be followed by hand. Two more infantry were detailed to carry a spare torpedo in case of an unexpected thickness of wire, or failure.

(3) The whole procedure had been carefully rehearsed beforehand on trenches reproduced by our aerial photos of the German lines at point of entry and careful reconnaissance made of the actual ground — but what actually occurred indicates possible causes of failure if attention is not paid to the following points:-

(a) It was found that owing to visibility given on rising ground by enemy Very lights, the right R.E. party had to crawl on all fours for the last 120 yards, with the result that by the time the torpedo was shoved under the wire it was zero less three minutes — a very small margin of safety. Iwith the two sappers, one pulling and the other pushing the torpedo (slings had been provided) were quite exhausted and could not have gone a yard further without a rest.
Inference — more time should have been allowed — a relief carrying Sapper advisable.

(b.) Only one torpedo arrived on the site – the spare torpedo was broken by Infantry in transit – and the one actually in use had a narrow escape as the party fell into a shell crater.
The necessity for two torpedoes at least clearly indicated.
(c) The enemy threw up about four lights which made crawling necessary – the R.E. Sgt. saw a man standing up at least 50 yards away during the illumination – he attributes this to the fact that they were going up hill. The left raiding party were on the level and stood up during the lights without detection.
(d.) In the case of right raiding party R.E. Sergt. in charge states the time fuze did not splutter or make a light and went off at the right time, so no instantaneous was necessary. In the case of the left raiding party the time fuze made a noise, and our own trench mortar fire was so inaccurate that the R.E. Corpl. was compelled to detonate the torpedo by instantaneous fuze ½ minute before the stipulated time. This shows the necessity for a double method of firing charge
(e) In each case it took the united efforts of the N.C.O. and two sappers to force the full length of the torpedo under the wire – and some noise was created thereby – I therefore consider the plough tip to casing of torpedo very advisable

and consider 18 ft. long about the maximum practical length.
(f.) The friction ignitor is the most satisfactory way of lighting fuze, as I have not known a failure and no light is given.
(g) The right raiding party found intact two apron fences with thick concertina wire between total depth 17 ft. of obstacle.

a.

A clear gap some fifteen foot wide was made by the torpedo, only one loose strand being left on the enemy side.
The left, being only a feint raid on three belts of wire some 40ˣ deep, no useful result was intended or expected.

(h) It is found that men can lie down from 40 to 50 yards from the Ammonal tube, and on the occasion in question, the right raid Artillery bombardment was so accurate on enemy trench that men lay down at less than that distance after the torpedo was detonated.

(i) In conclusion I consider the N.C.O.s and sappers concerned did very well, and desire to specially mention Sgt. KENYON, R.E. for keeping his party to time under difficult circumstances.

18/12/16

[illegible] Maj R.E.
O/C 202 Fd Coy

Vol 15

War Diary

of

202nd Field Company, Royal Engineers

For the month of January 1917

Volume 15

202nd Field Co RE

Instructions regarding War Diaries and Intelligence Summaries are contained in F. S. Regs., Part II. and the Staff Manual respectively. Title pages will be prepared in manuscript.

WAR DIARY
or
~~INTELLIGENCE SUMMARY.~~
(Erase heading not required.)

VOL 15.

Army Form C. 2118.

Page One

Place	Date 1917	Hour	Summary of Events and Information	Remarks and references to Appendices
BAILLEUL-MONT.	Jany 1/7		Preparing props and mining frames, Tubular Bomb Stores, repairing billets and bunking, Rifle range, new Baths, Testing petrol pumps, Mined and tubular dugouts, Regl Aid Post, Laying Decauville track, coupling rails and preparing track. On 5th inst. Section 4 moved by 'bus to LE SOUICH	NB
	8		Company less Section 4 marched from BAILLEULMONT. Sections distributed in the following places, LE SOUICH, BREVILLERS, MONDICOURT, LE GROS TISON FARM, Headquarters & transport at BREVILLERS	NB
BRÉVILLERS	9/10		Company employed on increasing billeting accommodation by close bunking, also erecting NISSEN Huts for Officers Billets and Rest Camp etc.	NB
	11/14		Company employed as above. Major McKECHNIE D, R.E. to R.E. School, LE PARCQ for course on 11th inst	NB
	15/22		Company employed as detailed for Jany 9/10, also water schemes. Capt N.T. ELLIS, R.E. to Hospital (sick) on 15th inst. Major D. McKECHNIE, R.E. rejoined Company on 20th inst.	NB
	23/27		Company employed as detailed Jany 15/22. ~~Jany 24th Capt N.T. ELLIS, R.E. rejoined from Hospital~~. Major D. McKECHNIE, R.E. to Hospital 24th inst. Jany 27th Capt. N.T. ELLIS, R.E. rejoined Company and assumed Command of Company during O.C.s absence in Hospital	NB
	28th		Lieut J.B. FROST, RE. with Section 2 attached to 200th Field Co RE for work &c and proceeded by 'bus to the line. Transport by road. Lieut P.B. BUCKLEY, R.E. took over work of 200th & 201st Field Coys RE and arrangements made to carry on with their work.	NB

2353 Wt. W2544/1454 700,000 5/15 D. D. & L. A.D.S.S./Forms/C. 2118.

202nd Field Co R.E.

Instructions regarding War Diaries and Intelligence Summaries are contained in F. S. Regs., Part II. and the Staff Manual respectively. Title pages will be prepared in manuscript.

WAR DIARY
or
~~INTELLIGENCE~~ SUMMARY.

(Erase heading not required.)

Army Form C. 2118.

Vol. 15. Page Two.

Place	Date	Hour	Summary of Events and Information	Remarks and references to Appendices
	1917			
BREVILLERS	Jany 29		Lieut A. SEARLE, R.E. proceeded with Section 4 to REBREUVIETTE for purpose of erecting huts and accessory buildings.	[initials]
			Remainder of company employed on bunking, hutting & water supply &c.	[initials]
	30/31		Company employed as detailed in Jany 29th entry	

[signature] Ellis Capt. R.E.
O/C 202nd Field Coy R.E.

2353 Wt. W2544/1454 700,000 5/15 D. D. & L. A.D.S.S./Forms/C. 2118.

Vol 16

SECRET.

WAR DIARY
OF
202ND FIELD COY. ROYAL ENGINEERS
FROM 1ST FEBRUARY 1917
TO. 28TH FEBRUARY 1917.

VOLUME No 16.

202nd Field Co R.E.

Instructions regarding War Diaries and Intelligence Summaries are contained in F. S. Regs., Part II. and the Staff Manual respectively. Title pages will be prepared in manuscript.

WAR DIARY
or
~~INTELLIGENCE SUMMARY.~~
(Erase heading not required.)

Army Form C. 2118.

Vol. 16 Page One.

Place	Date	Hour	Summary of Events and Information	Remarks and references to Appendices
RÉVILLERS	1917 Feby. 1/4		Company employed on bunking, erecting NISSEN and VII Corps Huts, provision of accessory building repairing wells and erecting water troughs, and water supply scheme.	
	5/6		Company employed on work as detailed for Feby 1/4. Orders received to be prepared to move on Feby 8th.	
	7		Preparing for move on 8th inst, and handing over work etc to 503rd Field Coy. R.E.	
	8		H.Q., Sect 1 and transport marched to BEAUMETZ, and were joined on the march by Sections 3+4. Rested at BEAUMETZ for the night.	
	9		H.Q., Sects 1, 3+4 marched to ACHICOURT, while transport and a few details moved to SIMENCOURT. Company took over work and billets from 200th Field Coy. R.E. Section 2, stationed at ACHICOURT since Jany 28th — joined Company.	
ACHICOURT	10		Company employed on improvements to Billets. Officers and all N.C.O.s made a reconnaissance of the trenches.	
	11		Company mainly employed on Trench Mortar Emplacements (Medium and Heavy) also making and repairing dugouts, etc. Capt. J.E. CHIPPINDALL, R.E. joined Company and assumed Command. Lieut. P.F. CAMPBELL, R.E. (T.C.) joined Coy. as supernumerary Officer	
	12		Company employed on same work as detailed for Feby 11th 1917.	

Date	HQ and Workshops	Section 1	Section 2	Section 3	Section 4	Remarks
13	Making + writing Notice Boards, making mining frames; Machine Gun Mountings, and Rocket Stands	Medium T.M.s 87 Emplacements G.6 d + H. 17	Heavy T.M.s – 11 J – T.	Brigade H.Q. 2 Aid Posts + workshops	2 Bn. H.Q.s	Only 60 Infy available.
14		Ditto	Ditto	Making Dugouts 2 Aid Posts	Making dugouts Bde. Bomb Store First Aid Post	No Infy. available for day – 100 at night emptying sandbags.
15		Ditto	Ditto	Ditto	Ditto	No Infy. again available for Medium T.M.s

202nd Field Co RE

Instructions regarding War Diaries and Intelligence Summaries are contained in F. S. Regs., Part II. and the Staff Manual respectively. Title pages will be prepared in manuscript.

WAR DIARY
or
~~INTELLIGENCE~~ SUMMARY.
(Erase heading not required.)

VOLUME 16 — Page Two

Army Form C. 2118.

Place	Date 1917	Hour	H.Q. & Workshops.	Section 1	Section 2	Section 3	Section 4	Remarks.	Remarks and references to Appendices
	Feby.								
ACHICOURT	16		Making & writing notice Boards; making Mining frames; ~~[illegible]~~ and Machine Gun Mountings etc.	Medium T.M.s	Heavy T.M.s	Dugouts 2 First Aid Posts Blasting	Dugouts Bde. Bomb Store Aid Posts	Owing to shortage of Inf. parties, work on T.M.Es has been very much delayed.	
	17			Ditto	Ditto	Ditto	As above also Bn. Bomb Store		
	18		Ditto	Ditto	Ditto	Ditto	Ditto		
	19		Ditto	Ditto	Ditto	Ditto	Ditto		
	20		Ditto	Ditto	Ditto	As above also Remaking Bridge	Ditto		
	21		No Infantry working parties available. Inspection of Company during morning after which the NCOs & men were given the day off. II Lieut. C.C. LINDSAY joined Company for duty as supernumerary officer						
	22		2/Lieut A SEARLE RE proceeded on leave to UK. Leave granted from 22.2.17 to 3.3.17						
			Notice Boards, mining frames, Rocket stands, Machine Gun Mountings etc.	Medium T.M.s	Heavy T.M.s	Dugouts ~~[illegible]~~ 2 Aid Posts ~~[illegible]~~ Remaking Bridge	Dugouts Bde. Bomb Store Aid Post.	Total Infantry party for day 47. No night party.	
	23.		Ditto	Ditto	Ditto	Ditto	Ditto		
	24		Ditto	Ditto	Ditto	Ditto	as above also Bn Bomb Store	Total Inf. party 269	
	25		Ditto	Ditto	Ditto	Ditto	Ditto	Total Inf. parties 294	
	26		Ditto	Ditto	Ditto	Ditto	Ditto	Total Inf. parties 167	
			Company moved at night to AGNY and took over billets at AGNY CHATEAU. II Lieut C.C. LINDSAY RE proceeded to 3rd Divisional Dump, LARBRET for duty						

2353 Wt. W2544/1454 700,000 5/15 D. D. & L. A.D.S.S./Forms/C. 2118.

202nd Field Co RE

Instructions regarding War Diaries and Intelligence Summaries are contained in F. S. Regs., Part II. and the Staff Manual respectively. Title pages will be prepared in manuscript.

WAR DIARY
or
INTELLIGENCE SUMMARY.
(Erase heading not required.)

VOLUME 16.

Page Three

Army Form C. 2118.

Place	Date	Hour	Summary of Events and Information						Remarks and references to Appendices
	1917 FEB.		HQ & WORKSHOPS	SECTION 1.	SECTION 2.	SECTION 3	SECTION 4.	REMARKS	
AGNY.	27.		Company to billets	employed on repairing and improvements					
				night work emptying sandbags	night work emptying sandbags	night work emptying sandbags	night work, emptying sandbags.	No Infy parties either day or night	
	28.		Making mining frames, step ladders etc.	Medium TMs.	Heavy TMs.	Dugouts. B and Posts Remaking bridge	Dugouts Bde & Bn. Bomb Stores	Local Infy parties 203	
			Company moved back to ACHICOURT at night, upon receipt of orders from 21st Brigade and took over previous billets						

[illegible]

Capt RE

O/C 202nd Field Co RE

SECRET.

Vol 17

War Diary

of

202nd Field Coy R.E.

from March 1st to March 31st 1917.

Volume 17

202nd Field Co R.E.

Instructions regarding War Diaries and Intelligence Summaries are contained in F. S. Regs., Part II. and the Staff Manual respectively. Title pages will be prepared in manuscript.

WAR DIARY
or
~~INTELLIGENCE SUMMARY~~.
(Erase heading not required.)

Army Form C. 2118.

VOLUME 17.

Page One.

Place	Date 1917.	Hour	Summary of Events and Information						Remarks and references to Appendices
	MARCH		H.Q. & Workshops	SECTION 1	SECTION 2	SECTION 3	SECTION 4	REMARKS	
ACHICOURT	1		Making Mining frames, notice boards, pickets, stairstringers etc.	Medium T.M.E's Excavating Dugouts	Heavy T.M.E's	2 Aid Posts	2 Bn. HQ's 2 Bomb Stores First Aid Post.	Infy. Working Parties = 238	
	2		do.	do.	do	do	do.	do do = 243 Casualties, Wounded O.R. 1 Spr Say [illegible]	
	3		do.	do.	do.	do.	do.	Infantry Parties NIL	
			About 5.30 p.m. 3/3/17 during enemy shelling, Section 1 Billet was struck and five men were wounded, four of whom remained at duty and one evacuated to Hospital (Spr. A. S. Porter)						
	4		Making Mining frames, notice boards, pickets, stairstringers etc.	Medium T.M.E's Excavating Dugouts.	Heavy T.M.E's	2 Aid Posts	2 Bn. HQ's 2 Bomb Stores First Aid Post	Infantry Parties 216	
	5		do	do.	do.	do. Working on Bridge 16	do.	do do. 206	
	6		do	do	do	do	do	do do. 204	
	7		do	do Revetting Bomb Store	do.	do.	do	do do. 274.	
	8		do	do.	do.	do.	do 2 Heavy T.M.E's	do do. 238	
	9		do	do.	do	do	do.	do do 40	
	10		do	do	do	do	2 Heavy T.M.E's	do do 20	
	11		do	Medium T.M.E's Strutting &c D.O.	do.	Aid Post Working on Bridge 16	do 2 Bn. HQ. 2 Bomb Stores First Aid Post.	do do 230	

2353 Wt. W2544/1454 700,000 5/15 D. D. & L. A.D.S.S./Forms/C. 2118.

202nd Field Co R.E.

*Instructions regarding War Diaries and Intelligence Summaries are contained in F. S. Regs., Part II. and the Staff Manual respectively. Title pages will be prepared in manuscript.

WAR DIARY
or
~~INTELLIGENCE SUMMARY.~~
(*Erase heading not required.*)

Army Form C. 2118.

VOLUME 17. Page Two

Place	Date 1917	Hour	HQ & Workshops	Section 1	Section 2	Section 3	Section 4	Remarks	Remarks and references to Appendices
ACHICOURT	MARCH 12		Making Mining frames, notice boards, pickets, stair stringers, etc.	Medium T.M.E.s	Heavy T.M.E.s	2 First Aid Posts Working on bridge 16	2 Bn H.Q. 2 Bomb Stores First Aid Post 2 Heavy T.M.E.s	Infantry Parties 150	
	13		ditto	ditto	ditto	First Aid Post Working on bridge 16	3 Bn. HQ. 1 Bde. Bomb Store 2 First Aid Posts 2 Heavy T.M.E.s	No Infantry Parties	
	14		ditto	ditto	ditto	ditto	2 Bn. HQ. 2 First Aid Posts	No Infantry Parties	
			Company moved to AGNY at night, by order of C.R.E. and went into Billets in CHATEAU.						
AGNY	15		Making Mining frames, pickets, petrol tin carriers etc.	Medium T.M.E.s	Heavy T.M.E.s	First Aid Post Working on Bridge 16	2 Bn. HQ. 2 First Aid Posts	No Infantry Parties	
	16		ditto	ditto	ditto	ditto	ditto	No Infantry Parties	
			Handed over Medium T.M.E.s Nos 34 to 50 and heavy T.M.E.s O.P.Q.R.S.T.U. to 513th Field Company R.E.						
	17		as 16th	as 16th	as 16th	as 16th	as 16th	No Infantry Parties	
	18		Sections to the usual work as detailed in entry of 17th inst.						
		10-0am	All sections recalled from work and 'standing to' as enemy had evacuated his lines						
		12-0noon	Men recalled from Workshops to 'stand to'						
		2-15pm	Instructions received from C.R.E. 30th Division that Company would work under orders of 89th Brigade. Under instructions from Brigadier 89th Brigade, Lieut. P.B. BUCKLEY, R.E. and Section 1 together with two platoons 21st Bde. Pioneer Coy. were sent up to form two strong points at M15 d 7.6 and M16 a 6.2.						
		6.0pm	Sections 3 & 4 carrying stores from Company Dump to form a forward R.E. Dump at M15 b 5.8. Section 4 returned to Billet about 9-0 pm.						
	19	1-15am	Section 3 returned from carrying stores						
		2-0am	Section 1 returned to Billet — strong points completed but not wired						
		9-0am	Section 4 to M15 d 7.6 and M16 a 6.2 to wire the strong points. Returned to Billet about 2.30pm.						
		1-0pm	Section 2 and 25 Pioneers of 21st Bde Pioneer Coy. went out to make Advanced Battalion H.Q.s Right Batt. HQs at M28 c 4.3 and M28 c 85.45. Left Bn HQ about M22 b 30.50.						

2353 Wt. W2544/1454 700,000 5/15 D. D. & L. A.D.S.S./Forms/C. 2118.

(Continued)

202nd Field Coy, RE

*Instructions regarding War Diaries and Intelligence Summaries are contained in F. S. Regs., Part II. and the Staff Manual respectively. Title pages will be prepared in manuscript.

WAR DIARY
or
~~INTELLIGENCE SUMMARY.~~
(Erase heading not required.)

Army Form C. 2118.

VOLUME 17 — Page Three

Place	Date 1917	Hour	Summary of Events and Information	Remarks and references to Appendices
AGNY	MARCH 19th (Continued)		Major J.E. CHIPPINDALL, R.E. made reconnaissance of part of ground evacuated by enemy. The following are the chief points:- ARRAS-BUCQUOY road blocked at M21c 65.40 and blown up at M27a 30.25. Very great damage to surface of road at latter point. Railway damaged at M27a 65.10 — big crater. All rails and sleepers removed along whole railway as far as visible. Road from M27a 35.25 running East to MERCATEL blown up in two places between railway and M27d 90.70	
	20th	6-0 a.m.	Party of 1 NCO., 4 RE. & 10 Pioneers of 21st Bde Pioneer Coy proceeded to M22b 30.50 to complete Batt. HQ. Returned to Billet at 5.0 p.m.	
		8-0 am	Sections 1 & 3 proceeded to commence work on Bridge at M21c 65.35. Only able to work on West side owing to enemy shelling. 10 yards of road cleared.	
		4-0 pm	Section 4 proceeded to Bridge to relieve Sections 1 & 3	
	21st	6-0 am	Section 2 went out to work on Bridge at M21c 65.35	
		10-30 am	Telegram received from C.R.E. to stop work on Bridge. Section 2 recalled. Company ordered to be prepared to move at one hours notice. Sections employed cleaning and oiling tool carts, sacking up tools, etc.	
		11-0 am	Lieut P.B. BUCKLEY. RE. and Lieut C.H. COTTEW, R.E. on a reconnaissance of BRETENCOURT — BLAIREVILLE — FICHEUX roads. Report rendered to C.R.E.	
	22nd	6-0 am	II Lieut. A. SEARLE, R.E. on a reconnaissance of MERCATEL — BOISLEUX ST. MARC road.	
		12-30 pm	Order received from C.R.E. to continue work on Bridge at M21c 6.3	
		2-0 pm	Section 3 to work on bridge " 4 to fill in crater in MERCATEL — BOISLEUX-ST-MARC road O.C. and Lieut. CAMPBELL, RE. to BLAIREVILLE to look for Billets.	
		10-0 p.m.	Sect 1 to work on Bridge	
BLAIREVILLE	23rd	7-0 a.m.	Sect 2 left to start work on new Billets. Sects 3 & 4 moved from AGNY to BLAIREVILLE, and transport with details from MONCHIET to BLAIREVILLE. Sect. 1 marched to BLAIREVILLE after working on Bridge.	
	24th	8-0 a.m.	Section 1 working on billets and lines. Sect. 4 started work on road	
		3-0 pm	Sect. 2 proceeded to relieve No 4 Section on road. Sect 3 proceeded to Bridge on ARRAS-BUCQUOY road but found Tunnelling Coy. working there. Section returned to Billets & continued work there.	
	25th	8-0 a.m.	No 4 Sect to new road. Diversion over railway completed. Road can now be used for wheeled traffic	
		4-30 p.m.	Sect 2 relieved Sect 4	
		4-0 pm	Nos 1 & 3 Sections proceeded to work on BOISLEUX-ST-MARC — MERCATEL road O.C. accompanied G.O.C. 21st Brigade on minor reconnaissance. Bn. Hqs. and Assembly trenches selected	

2353 Wt. W2544/1454 700,000 5/15 D. D. & L. A.D.S.S./Forms/C. 2118.

202nd Field Co. R.E.

Instructions regarding War Diaries and Intelligence Summaries are contained in F. S. Regs., Part II. and the Staff Manual respectively. Title pages will be prepared in manuscript.

VOLUME 17

WAR DIARY
or
~~INTELLIGENCE SUMMARY.~~
(Erase heading not required.)

Page Four

Army Form C. 2118.

Place	Date	Hour	Summary of Events and Information	Remarks and references to Appendices
[B]LAIREVILLE	1917 MARCH 26th	9.0 am	Sect. 4 proceeded to work on road.	
		2.0 PM	Nos 1 & 3 to relieve Sect 4	
		4.0 PM	Sect 2, with 4 limbered wagons and one G.S. wagon, to collect bricks	
	27	8.0 AM	No 4 Section continued work on road.	
		~~2.0pm~~	~~No 1 & 3 Sect. to relieve Sect 4~~	
		~~4.0pm~~		
		12-0 noon	No 2 Section relieved No 4	
		5-0 p.m.	Nos 1 & 3 " " " 2	
			Deviation round big crater completed for single track. Filling in other craters	
	28th		Company employed on road	
	29th		Work on road continued. Six posts taped out for night digging.	
	30th		Corduroying and filling in continued on road. Also work on Bn HQs.	
	31st		Company employed on posts on Railway Support Line; also three Bn HQrs.	

J.R. [signature] Major R.E.
O/C 202nd Field Coy. R.E.

2353 Wt. W2544/1454 700,000 5/15 D. D. & L. A.D.S.S./Forms/C. 2118.

30

Vol 18

SECRET

War Diary
of
202nd Field Company R.E.
From:- April 1st 1917
To :- April 30th 1917

VOLUME 18.

202nd Field Co RE

Instructions regarding War Diaries and Intelligence Summaries are contained in F. S. Regs., Part II. and the Staff Manual respectively. Title pages will be prepared in manuscript.

VOLUME 18

WAR DIARY
or
~~INTELLIGENCE SUMMARY.~~

(Erase heading not required.)

Army Form C. 2118.

Page One

Place	Date 1917	Hour	Summary of Events and Information	Remarks and references to Appendices
BLAIREVILLE	APRIL 1st.		Digging completed on railway Support Line. Working in three shifts on Bn. HQs. Commenced work on collecting station at N35 a 20.55	
	2nd		Wiring posts in Railway Support Line. Working on Bn. HQs – good progress made. Excavation continued for collecting Station. 2 Sections in HENIN making strong points. All work is being seriously delayed through having no Infantry working parties.	
	3rd		2 Sections in HENIN making strong points. Working on Bn. H.Qs. + collecting Station. No Infantry parties	
	4th		5 points completed on railway Support Line. Working on Bn. HQs; Coy + Bde Dumps and Collecting Station.	
	5/6th		Working on Bn. HQrs; Coy + Bde Dump and Collecting Station. Trestle bridge erected BOIRY-BECQUERELLE.	

Date	Section 1	Section 2	Section 3	Section 4	Remarks
7th	Employed cleaning toolcarts, packing etc.	As Section 1	As Section 1. 50' Water Troughing erected	As Section 1 50' Water Troughing erected	Supervising erection of 2 Nissen Huts.
8th	Preparing for operations	As Section 1	As Section 1	As Section 1	3 Platoons 17th Manchesters attached
9th/10th	In Reserve	9/4/17 3.0p.m. No. 2 Sect. ordered forward to make strong points at N24b2.1 and N18d 4.1. Owing to Brigade failing to get objectives and 3 Platoons (Working Party) halted	9/4/17 3.0p.m. No 3 Sect. ordered forward to commence on water supply of WANCOURT.	9/4/17 3.0pm No. 4 Sect. ordered forward to start defence of WANCOURT. The 3 Sections RE at RE forward Dump	10-15pm. Orders to O.C. from CRE to go to DON for orders. 11-0pm. arrived DON + ordered to dig trench 100 yards behind (Contd)

2353 Wt. W2544/1454 700,000 5/15 D. D. & L. A.D.S.S./Forms/C. 2118.

202nd Field Coy R.E.

Instructions regarding War Diaries and Intelligence Summaries are contained in F. S. Regs., Part II. and the Staff Manual respectively. Title pages will be prepared in manuscript.

VOLUME 18

WAR DIARY
or
~~INTELLIGENCE SUMMARY.~~
(Erase heading not required.)

Page Two

Army Form C. 2118.

Place	Date 1917	Hour	Section 1	Section 2	Section 3	Section 4	Remarks	Remarks and references to Appendices
BLAIREVILLE	APRIL 9/10 (Contd).		5.30 p.m. 10/4/17 Sect 1 proceeded to fill in mine craters & shell holes in HENIN-SUR-COJEUL – ST MARTIN-SUR-COJEUL road. Returned to Billets at 4-0 a.m. 11th.	Same as Sect 1.	Same as Sect 1	Same as Sect 1.	(Contd) NEUVILLE VITASSE – ST MARC road, touching road at N20c 7.1 and N26 Central. 12-0 midnt. Arrived Dump & collected Party. 1.35 a.m. Arrived at N26 a 7.7 & commenced work. 4.30 a.m. Parties returned to Billets – 520 yards of trench dug. The 3 Platoons 17th Manchesters did very good work.	
	11th						Company standing to in readiness to move.	
BAILLEULMONT	12th						Company moved from BLAIREVILLE to BAILLEULMONT	
MONCHY-AU-BOIS	13th						Company moved from BAILLEULMONT to HANNESCAMPS, and there received orders to proceed to MONCHY-AU-BOIS.	
	14th						Company employed on repairing roads etc.	
POMMIER	15th						Company marched from MONCHY-AU-BOIS to POMMIER 9.30 a.m.	
	16th		Squad Drill Knotting & Lashing Weldon Trestle etc.	Pontooning Knotting & Lashing Squad Drill	Pontooning Knotting & Lashing Squad Drill	Collecting stores etc.		

2353 Wt. W2544/1454 700,000 5/15 D. D. & L. A.D.S.S./Forms/C. 2118.

202nd Field Co RE

Instructions regarding War Diaries and Intelligence Summaries are contained in F. S. Regs., Part II. and the Staff Manual respectively. Title pages will be prepared in manuscript.

WAR DIARY
or
INTELLIGENCE SUMMARY.
(Erase heading not required.)

VOLUME 18 — Page Three

Army Form C. 2118.

Place	Date 1917	Hour	Section 1	Section 2	Section 3	Section 4	Remarks	Remarks and references to Appendices
POMMIER	APRIL 17		Squad Drill Baths Pontooning Rifle Exercises Knotting & Lashing	Sheers & Derricks Squad Drill Baths Pontooning Knotting & Lashing Rifle Exercises	Pontooning Baths Sheers & Derricks Trestling	Pontooning Sheers & Derricks Baths Trestling		
	18		Squad Drill Lecture by Section Officer Pontooning Rifle Exercises Knotting & Lashing	Sheers & Derricks Squad Drill Lecture by Section Officer Pontooning Knotting & Lashing Rifle Exercises	Pontooning Lecture by Section Officer Sheers & Derricks Trestling	Pontooning Lecture by Section Officer Sheers & Derricks Trestling	Orders received to be prepared to move at short notice.	
BEAURAINS	19						Company, less Transport & details, moved at 9.30 a.m. from POMMIER to BEAURAINS. Transport & details moved from POMMIER to ACHICOURT	
	20		Making shelters for bivouacs, and clearing ground for parade ground.	Making shelters for bivouacs etc.	Repairing roads on HENIN-HENINEL road.	Repairing roads on HENIN-HENINEL road		
	21		8-0 a.m Repairing roads on HENIN-HENINEL road.	As Sect 1.	Unloading and checking sections of NISSEN Huts	Unloading & checking sections of NISSENS Huts		
	22		7.30 p.m. Proceeded to work on strong points near HENINEL (Corps Defensive Line) returned to Billet 2.30 a.m. 23/4/17	Standing to for operations	Erecting 8 NISSEN Huts for Div! H.Q. near NEUVILLE VITASSE	Standing to for operations		

M

2353 Wt. W2544/1454 700,000 5/15 D. D. & L. A.D.S.S./Forms/C. 2118.

202nd Field Co R.E.

Instructions regarding War Diaries and Intelligence Summaries are contained in F. S. Regs., Part II. and the Staff Manual respectively. Title pages will be prepared in manuscript.

WAR DIARY
or
~~INTELLIGENCE SUMMARY.~~

(Erase heading not required.)

VOLUME 18

Page Four

Army Form C. 2118.

Place	Date 1917	Hour	Summary of Events and Information: Section 1	Section 2	Section 3	Section 4	Remarks	Remarks and references to Appendices
BEAURAINS	APRIL 23rd		7.0am. 8 OR. with Infantry party working on Corps Defensive Line	12.30AM. Proceeded to SUNKEN ROAD W. of HENINEL. Lieut. P.F. CAMPBELL. RE. with Spr. BLACK & Spr. KELLY reported to 'C' Coy. 16th Manchesters in Support Line. At 6.0am. Spr. KELLY returned with orders from Lieut. CAMPBELL for section to proceed to Cemetery, where they remained until 8.0 p.m. same day. Section 'stood to' to repel expected German attack. Relieved 8.0pm. by section of 200th Field Co RE. From 6.0am. no news whatever received of Lt. CAMPBELL beyond that he went over with the Infantry. Spr. BLACK wounded in thigh by M.G. Bullet. Lieut. CAMPBELL posted as missing.	Erecting 8 NISSEN Huts for Divl HQs	12.30 am. 2/Lt. A. SEARLE RE + Sect 4 proceeded to Assembly place in SUNKEN Rd W. of HENINEL — arrived 3.0am. 2/Lt. SEARLE Corpl MALKIN & Sapper INGRAM left at 3.45 am. to report to Infy Bn. HQ in Support Line. Lt. SEARLE and the 2 O.Rs went over with the Infy. to reconnoitre the proposed objective. About 6.15am Sp. INGRAM returned to SUNKEN RD. & reported that Lt. SEARLE had been killed by M.G. Bullet and Cpl. MALKIN wounded. A runner was sent to the O.C. with this report. O.C. immediately proceeded to SUNKEN RD. and instructed section to stand by for further orders. 8.0pm order received to return to BEAURAINS — arrived 10.15 PM		
	24		7.0am. Employed on same work as 23rd inst.	Report on reconnaissance received from Lt. Campbell at 8.45pm. He was in Hospital (wounded in 4 places). He was left on the Battlefield for 30 hours before being ~~brought~~ carried in	As above.			
	25/26		Working on roads & cleaning wagons.	Employed on roads near HENINEL	As above	Employed on roads near HENINEL		

2353 Wt. W2544/1454 700,000 5/15 D. D. & L. A.D.S.S./Forms/C. 2118.

202nd Field Co R.E.

Instructions regarding War Diaries and Intelligence Summaries are contained in F. S. Regs., Part II. and the Staff Manual respectively. Title pages will be prepared in manuscript.

VOLUME 18

WAR DIARY
or
~~INTELLIGENCE SUMMARY.~~
(Erase heading not required.)

Page Five

Army Form C. 2118.

Place	Date 1917 APRIL	Hour	Summary of Events and Information					Remarks and references to Appendices
			Section 1	Section 2	Section 3	Section 4	Remarks	
BEAURAINS	27th		Employed on roads near NEUVILLE VITASSE	As sect 1.	As sect 1.	As sect 1		
OCOCHE	28						Sections 1, 2, 3 + 4 marched to ARRAS and entrained. Detrained at PETIT HOUVAIN and marched to OCOCHE. Transport + cyclists moved by road to Gouy en ARTOIS.	
	29		Cleaning up Making bivouaks	Cleaning up Making bivouacs	Cleaning up Making bivouacs	Cleaning up Making bivouaks	Transport + cyclists move to OCOCHE	
	30		Squad Drill Washing web equipment Musketry	Squad Drill Washing web equipment Musketry	Squad Drill Washing web equipment Musketry	Squad Drill Washing web equipment Musketry		

[signature] Major R.E.
O/C 202nd Field Co R.E.

202 FIELD COY

1/MAY/16 — 31/MAY/16

VOL 19

Vol 19

SECRET.

WAR DIARY

of

202nd Field Coy, Royal Engineers

from MAY 1st 1917 to MAY 31st 1917

Volume No 19.

202nd Field Co R.E.

Instructions regarding War Diaries and Intelligence Summaries are contained in F. S. Regs., Part II. and the Staff Manual respectively. Title pages will be prepared in manuscript.

VOLUME 19

WAR DIARY
or
~~INTELLIGENCE SUMMARY.~~

(Erase heading not required.)

Army Form C. 2118.

Page One

Place	Date 1917 MAY	Hour	Section 1	Section 2	Section 3	Section 4	Remarks	Remarks and references to Appendices
OCOCHE	1		Squad Drill Knotting & Lashing Musketry Horse Trough erecting.	As No 1 Sect.	Physical Drill Musketry Squad Drill	Physical Drill Squad Drill Musketry		
	2		Physical Drill Knotting & Lashing Squad Drill Extended Order	as No 1 Sect.	Pontooning	Pontooning	Orders received to be prepared to move.	
TEULETTE	3						Company with transport moved by road from OCOCHE to TIEULETTE. Erected bivouacs for Drivers etc.	
	4.		Squad Drill Extended order Musketry	Squad Drill Extended Order Musketry	Extended Order Erecting latrines etc. for Division	Squad Drill Physical Drill Fatigues Overhauling Toolcart		
	5		Squad drill & musketry Afternoon off duty	Squad drill & musketry As No 1 Sect.	Erecting latrines etc for Division As No 1 Sect.	Squad drill & musketry As No 1 Sect.		
	6		Day off	As No 1 Sec	As No 1 Sec	As No 1 Sec		
	7		Pontooning	Pontooning	Physical drill Strong Points Musketry.	Physical Drill Musketry Strong Points		
	8		Squad drill bombing musketry	Squad drill Rapid wiring Strong points	Rifle exercises. Scheme of strong points	Rifle exercises Rapid wiring Lecture on Sanitation		

Army Form C. 2118.

Instructions regarding War Diaries and Intelligence Summaries are contained in F. S. Regs., Part II. and the Staff Manual respectively. Title pages will be prepared in manuscript.

WAR DIARY
or
INTELLIGENCE SUMMARY.
(Erase heading not required.)

VOLUME 19

Page two

Place	Date	Hour	Summary of Events and Information					Remarks and references to Appendices
	1917 MAY		SECTION 1	SECTION 2	SECTION 3	SECTION 4	REMARKS	
	9		Physical drill Scheme for strong points Rapid wiring (at night)	Lecture on Sanitation Bombing Musketry Rapid wiring (at night)	Bombing Visual Training Rapid wiring Strong points (at night)	Bombing Physical drill Scheme for strong points Strong points (at night)		
	10		Musketry Drill Rapid wiring	Phys. drill Scheme for strong points Strong points (at night)	Pontooning Rapid wiring (at night)	Pontooning		
	11		Rifle exercises Squad drill Explosives Knotting lashing Strong points (at night)	Squad drill Explosives Bombing Rapid wiring	Squad drill Bombing Musketry	Squad drill Rifle exercises Semaphore Explosives Rapid wiring (at night)		
	12		Semaphore Musketry Physical drill Rapid wiring	Rifle exercises Bombing Knotting lashing Musketry	Squad drill Knotting lashing Lecture on Sanitation Bombing	Bomb throwing Knotting lashing Rapid wiring Squad drill		
	13		Gas drill for one hour & rest of day off duty	Same as No 1	Same as No 1	Same as No 1		
	14		Company drill Physical drill Bombing Stokes Guns & [illegible]	Physical drill Company drill Explosives Bombing Musketry	Bayonet Fighting Company drill Musketry Lecture Knotting lashing	Physical drill Company [illegible] Bombing Semaphore Knotting lashing		

2353 Wt. W2544/1454 700,000 5/15 D. D. & L. A.D.S.S./Forms/C. 2118.

Instructions regarding War Diaries and Intelligence Summaries are contained in F. S. Regs., Part II. and the Staff Manual respectively. Title pages will be prepared in manuscript.

WAR DIARY
or
INTELLIGENCE SUMMARY.
(Erase heading not required.)

Army Form C. 2118.

VOLUME 19.

Page three

Place	Date	Hour	Summary of Events and Information					Remarks and references to Appendices
	1917 MAY.		Section 1	Section 2	Section. 3.	Section 4	Remarks.	
NEULETTE	15		Bayonet Fighting Company Drill Bombing Semaphore Musketry	Bayonet Fighting Company Drill Rapid Wiring Semaphore Knots & Lashings.	Physical Drill Company Drill Bombing Semaphore Musketry	Bayonet Fighting Company Drill Shears & Derricks		
	16		Pontooning Rapid Wiring	Pontooning	Bayonet Fighting Physical Drill Semaphore Rapid Wiring Shears & Derricks	Physical Drill Semaphore Weldon Trestle		
	17		Bayonet Fighting Explosives Bombing Knots & Lashings Musketry.	Bayonet Fighting Bombing Lecture on Sanitary arrangements Shears & Derricks Rapid Wiring.	Pontooning	Pontooning Rapid Wiring		
	18.		Physical Drill Coy. Drill Rapid Wiring Semaphore	Physical Drill Lecture: Grenades & Bombs Semaphore Compy Drill Musketry	Bayonet Fighting Compy Drill Semaphore. Explosives Rapid Wiring	Physical Drill Compy Drill Bombing Musketry		
	19		Bayonet Fighting Physical Drill Compy Drill Semaphore Shears & Derricks	Bayonet Fighting Compy Drill Semaphore Bridging Lecture Musketry	Physical Drill Compy Drill Bombing Rapid Wiring Explosives	Bayonet Fighting Compy Drill Semaphore Explosives Rifle Exercises		

2353 Wt. W2544/1454 700,000 5/15 D. D. & L. A.D.S.S./Forms/C. 2118.

WAR DIARY
or
INTELLIGENCE SUMMARY.
(Erase heading not required.)

Army Form C. 2118.

Instructions regarding War Diaries and Intelligence Summaries are contained in F. S. Regs., Part II. and the Staff Manual respectively. Title pages will be prepared in manuscript.

VOLUME 19. Page four

Place	Date 1917 MAY	Hour	Section 1	Section 2	Section 3	Section 4	Remarks	Remarks and references to Appendices
NEULETTE	20.						Coy moved from NEULETTE to GAUCHIN. Capt Ellis & Lieut Botton granted leave to U.K.	
GAUCHIN	21.						Coy moved from GAUCHIN to EQUIRRE.	
EQUIRRE	22						Coy moved from EQUIRRE to FLECHINELLE.	
FLECHINELLE	23.		Baths Cleaning Wagons and Harness	Baths Same as No 1	Baths Same as No 1	Baths Same as No 1		
"	24.						Coy moved from FLECHINELLE to LES CISEAUX	
LES CISEAUX	25						Coy moved from LES CISEAX to LE BREARDE	
LE BREARDE	26.						Coy moved from LE BREARDE to WINNEZEELE.	
WINNEZEELE	29						Coy moved from WINNEZEELE to BRANDHOEK	
BRANDHOEK	30						Coy moved from BRANDHOEK to YPRES. Arrived at YPRES. 2·45. a.m.	

2353 Wt. W2544/1454 700,000 5/15 D. D. & L. A.D.S.S./Forms/C. 2118.

Army Form C. 2118.

WAR DIARY
or
INTELLIGENCE SUMMARY.
(*Erase heading not required.*)

Instructions regarding War Diaries and Intelligence Summaries are contained in F. S. Regs., Part II. and the Staff Manual respectively. Title pages will be prepared in manuscript.

VOLUME 19. Page five.

Place	Date	Hour	Summary of Events and Information	Remarks and references to Appendices
	1917 MAY		Section 1. Section 2. Section 3. Section 4 Remarks.	
YPRES	31.		Nos 1 & 3 Sections engaged on Wiring of BORDER LANE NORTH. Heavy shelling by enemy of Western side of town. Company Water Cart pierced in two places by fragments of shell. about 11-45 pm.	

[illegible]

202 FIELD COY

1/JUNE/1917 – 30/JUNE/17

VOL 20

SECRET.

Vol 20

War Diary

of

202nd Field Company R.E.

from :- June 1st 1917.

to :- June 30th 1917.

Volume 20.

20 2nd Field Coy. R.E.

Army Form C. 2118.

WAR DIARY
or
INTELLIGENCE SUMMARY.

(Erase heading not required.)

Instructions regarding War Diaries and Intelligence Summaries are contained in F. S. Regs., Part II. and the Staff Manual respectively. Title pages will be prepared in manuscript.

VOLUME 20 — Sheet One

Place	Date	Hour	Section 1	Section 2	Section 3	Section 4	Remarks	Remarks and references to Appendices
YPRES	1917 JUNE 1st		Wiring BORDER LANE trench	Preparing Wire entanglements & General fatigues. Wire drill	Wiring BORDER LANE trench	Carrying stores to forward dump	Intermittent enemy shelling at intervals	
	2nd		Moving stores from GASWORKS DUMP to SANCTUARY WOOD DUMP	Preparing Wire entanglements. Wire drill. Carrying stores from ZILLEBEKE DUMP to FRONT LINE	Moving stores from GASWORKS DUMP to SANCTUARY WOOD DUMP.	Preparing stores for night wiring. Wire drill	Frequent enemy shelling of gun positions around BARRACKS	
	3rd		Sections proceeded at night to put wire entanglement outside SANCTUARY WOOD		Spr. JAMES reported as Missing on arrival back at Billet. Spr. SMITHSON gassed.	Wire drill. Carrying wiring stores to front line	Heavy shelling all day. Heavy Gas Shell bombardment by enemy commenced about 10 pm & lasted till about 4-30 am on morning of 4th.	
	4th		3 N.C.O's & men completing wire entanglement	6 N.C.O's & men completing wire entanglement S. SIDE of BORDER LANE to HILL ST. Cleaning billets		3 men completing wire entanglement	Frequent shelling by enemy during day. A few gas shells were fired into YPRES about 9 pm.	

2353 Wt. W2544/1454 700,000 5/15 D. D. & L. A.D.S.S./Forms/C. 2118.

202nd Field Coy R.E.

Instructions regarding War Diaries and Intelligence Summaries are contained in F. S. Regs., Part II. and the Staff Manual respectively. Title pages will be prepared in manuscript.

WAR DIARY
or
~~INTELLIGENCE SUMMARY.~~

(Erase heading not required.)

Army Form C. 2118.

Volume 20. Page two

Place	Date	Hour	Summary of Events and Information					Remarks and references to Appendices
	1917 JUNE		Section 1.	Section 2.	Section 3.	Section 4.	Remarks.	
YPRES.	5th		Company "Standing to"				Enemy artillery fairly active	
	6th.		Commenced work on Medium Trench Mortar Emplacement at VIGO ST and HILL ST.	Loading wagons with R.E. stores at GASWORKS DUMP and unloading at HELLBLAST CORNER			Violent explosion heard from the direction of HILL 60 immediately followed by intense bombardment by our artillery about 3.0 a.m. Attack launched by Corps on right of Divisional front. Frequent shelling by enemy during day. Corpl Chapman struck on head by falling debris. Capt Ellis & Lieut [illegible] returned from leave.	
	7th.		Unloading stores at KRUISSTRAAT DUMP.	Loading stores at KRUISSTRAAT DUMP.		Commenced work on Water Supply replacing breaks in pipes & cleaning pumps.	Enemy artillery again very active during day. 2nd Lt Prestwich & Spr Stalland wounded	

2353 Wt. W2544/1454 700,000 5/15 D. D. & L. A.D.S.S./Forms/C. 2118.

202nd Field Co R.E.

Instructions regarding War Diaries and Intelligence Summaries are contained in F. S. Regs., Part II. and the Staff Manual respectively. Title pages will be prepared in manuscript.

Volume 20.

WAR DIARY
or
~~INTELLIGENCE SUMMARY.~~
(Erase heading not required.)

Page three

Army Form C. 2118.

Place	Date 1917 JUNE	Hour	Summary of Events and Information: Section 1.	Section 2	Section 3	Section 4	Remarks.	Remarks and references to Appendices
YPRES	8th		Medium Trench Mortar Emplacement VIGO ST and HILL ST.	Repairing bridges at MOAT GRANGE ROAD. Carrying stores at KRUISSTRAAT DUMP.		Water supply system.	Enemy artillery fairly quiet all day. Occasional shelling. Our guns in neighbourhood of barracks very active all day. Enemy fired a few gas shells into the town.	
	9th		Medium Trench Mortar emplacement VIGO ST & HILL ST	Carrying stores from KRUISSTRAAT DUMP to SANCTUARY DUMP. Removing timber from Lby dump to COW HOME FARM		Water supply system.	Enemy artillery again very active all day & night. Spr Richardson slightly wounded in arm whilst on guard. Drvrs Keighley & Pugh wounded at KRUISSTRAAT DUMP at night also 2 mules killed by enemy fire	
	10th		Medium Trench Mortar Emplacement HILL ST. Making concertina wire				Enemy bombarded town & ZILLEBEKE district with gas shells. Spr Davidson gassed & evacuated Sprs Hughes, Kelly & Lange gassed, but remained at duty	

2353 Wt. W2544/1454 700,000 5/15 D. D. & L. A.D.S.S./Forms/C. 2118.

202nd Field CRE

Instructions regarding War Diaries and Intelligence Summaries are contained in F. S. Regs., Part II. and the Staff Manual respectively. Title pages will be prepared in manuscript.

WAR DIARY
or
~~INTELLIGENCE SUMMARY.~~

(Erase heading not required.)

Volume 20 — Page four

Army Form C. 2118.

Place	Date 1917	Hour	Section 1.	Section 2	Section 3	Section 4	Remarks	Remarks and references to Appendices
YPRES	JUNE 11th		Medium Trench Mortar Emp. VIGO ST. Repairing trenches VINCE ST, DORMY HOUSE, VNr. HELLBLAST CORNER.			Water supply system	Enemy artillery fairly active during day.	
	12th			Opening disused trench CROSS ST. Repairing bridge at SALLY PORTE No1. Preparing timber for bridge.	Repairing trench boards VINCE ST. Burying mules	Water supply system	Enemy artillery fairly active. Cpl. Chapman wounded in arm. L/Cpl Bentley wounded in leg whilst on guard. Received order from CRE to be prepared to move to ZILLEBEKE BUND.	
			C.S.M. Moore & advanced party proceeded to ZILLEBEKE to take over billets					
	13th		Dressing station MAPLE ST and [illegible] frames. Improving billets at ZILLEBEKE.	Cleaning old trench CROSS ST. Repairing & improving dugouts. Working party of 30 Infantry.	Repairing trench boards VINCE ST. Burying mules. Revetting dugouts	Repairing & improving dugouts. Water supply system	Received orders from CRE to move to ZILLEKE BUND. Move completed about 10.30 pm. Enemy artillery very quiet whilst move was in progress.	

2353 Wt. W2544/1454 700,000 5/15 D. D. & L. A.D.S.S./Forms/C. 2118.

202nd Field Coy R.E.

Instructions regarding War Diaries and Intelligence Summaries are contained in F. S. Regs., Part II. and the Staff Manual respectively. Title pages will be prepared in manuscript.

Volume 20

Army Form C. 2118.

WAR DIARY
or
~~INTELLIGENCE SUMMARY.~~
(Erase heading not required.)

Page five

Place	Date	Hour	Section 1	Section 2	Section 3	Section 4	Remarks	Remarks and references to Appendices
YPRES	14th		Dressing Station MAPLE ST. and Preparing tracks	Clearing trench CROSS ST. Repairing dugout ZILLEBEKE BUND Working party of 3d Infantry	Excavating for dugout DORMY HOUSE Unloading party GASWORKS DUMP Repairing trench boards Repairing dugouts	Carrying stores Making dugouts Water supply	Enemy artillery fairly quiet in region of ZILLEBEKE BUND only a few shells being fired at the batteries in the district.	
	15th		Dressing station MAPLE ST. Fatigue at Billets	Cleaning and repairing billets	Excavating for dugout DORMY HOUSE Repairing trench boards VINCE ST Preparing frames for tubular dugouts	Repairing dugouts	Enemy shelling of batteries continuous all day.	
	16th		Dressing station MAPLE ST. Repairing trench boards ZILLEBEKE ST. Fatigue at Billets	Order received from CRE at 11.45 pm that a leakage was reported in the ZILLEBEKE LAKE. Lieut RAINE with No 2 Sect. proceeded but no break found.	Preparing rills & props. Making concertina wire entanglement Repairing trench boards VINCE ST. Excavating for dugout RITZ ST Working party 20 RAMC		Enemy artillery very active all day. Spr Attwood wounded in leg by piece of shell. Our artillery opened out with an intense bombardment about 7.25 pm.	

2353 Wt. W2544/1454 700,000 5/15 D. D. & L. A.D.S.S./Forms/C. 2118.

202nd Field Co RE

Instructions regarding War Diaries and Intelligence Summaries are contained in F. S. Regs., Part II. and the Staff Manual respectively. Title pages will be prepared in manuscript.

WAR DIARY
or
~~INTELLIGENCE~~ SUMMARY.

(Erase heading not required.)

Army Form C. 2118.

Volume 20 Page six

Place	Date	Hour	Summary of Events and Information					Remarks and references to Appendices
	1917		Section 1	Section 2	Section 3	Section 4	Remarks	
YPRES.	JUNE 17th.		Dressing station MAPLE ST. Clearing trench repairing T. boards ZILLEBEKE ST. Covering dugouts at ZILLEBEKE BUND		Preparing timber for tubular dugout Concertina wire entanglements Excavating for dugout. RITZ ST. Repairing trench boards VINCE ST.		Enemy artillery very active all day. A great number of shells being fired all round company dugouts. Our artillery very quiet	
	18th		Dressing station MAPLE ST Clearing trench & repairing boards ZILLEBEKE ST. Clearing trees etc. from LILLE Rd.		Preparing framework for tubular dugout Making concertina wire entanglements Excavating for dugout RITZ ST		Enemy artillery again very active Our artillery very quiet 4 NCOs & men to 5th Army Rest Camp (10 days) 1 Off (Lt. RAINE) & 3 O.R. transferred to II Corps School	
	19th		Dressing Station Clearing trenches Repairing T boards Clearing trees from Roads	Repairing Trench Boards Revetting trenches Preparing timber for D.O. RAMC Shelter	Preparing framework for tubular D.O. Making Concertina Wire Repairing Trench Boards Excavation for D.O.	Repairing trenches Improving D.O.		

2353 Wt. W2544/1454 700,000 5/15 D. D. & L. A.D.S.S./Forms/C. 2118.

202nd Field Co R.E.

Instructions regarding War Diaries and Intelligence Summaries are contained in F. S. Regs., Part II. and the Staff Manual respectively. Title pages will be prepared in manuscript.

VOLUME 20

WAR DIARY
or
~~INTELLIGENCE SUMMARY~~.
(Erase heading not required.)

Page Seven

Army Form C. 2118.

Place	Date 1917	Hour	Summary of Events and Information					Remarks and references to Appendices
	JUNE		SECTION 1	Section 2	Section 3	Section 4	Remarks	
YPRES	20th		Dressing Station Clearing trenches Constructing Wire fence	RAMC Shelter Repairing trench Boards Reveting trenches	Excav. for Dressing Stn. Making Concertina Wire Repairing trench Boards	Clearing trenches Clearing trees from Road		
	21st		Clearing trenches	Repairing trench Boards Clearing trenches.	Repairing trench Boards	Clearing trenches	Coy. was relieved by 200th Field Co R.E. and moved to Camp in Area A. Heavy shelling during move, but only one casualty — Sapper TEAGUE slight wound face, remains at duty. 2 O.R. leave to U.K.	
	22nd		Cleaning up Camp Fatigues	As No 1	As No 1	As No 1	Lt. McCallum & 12 O.R. to 90th Bde HQ. to make Picture Ground: Lt. Buckley + 10 O.R. to Fifth Army Rest Camp	
	23rd		Corps Picture Ground Workshops. Making Water Carriers	Making Water Carriers & trestles Corps Picture Ground Camp Fatigues	Lt. Cotten to Chateau Segard re Observation Tower Workshops	Workshops Fatigues		
	24th		Corps Picture Ground Workshops Making Water Carriers	As No 1.	Workshops Fatigues	Building 'Prisoners Cage'		
	25th		Corps Picture Ground. Workshops Camp Fatigues	As No 1.	Workshops Camp Fatigues Superstructure for O.P	ditto Camp Fatigues Workshops		
	26th		ditto	ditto	ditto	ditto		
	27th		ditto Washing Wagons.	ditto Washing Wagons	ditto	ditto	Sgt. Rogers to England (Cadet School) for Comm in R.F.A.	
	28th		Erecting Stage. Camp Fatigues Workshops Corps Picture Ground	As No 1	ditto	ditto		

2353 Wt. W2544/1454 700,000 5/15 D. D. & L. A.D.S.S./Forms/C. 2118.

202nd Field Co R.E.

Instructions regarding War Diaries and Intelligence Summaries are contained in F. S. Regs., Part II. and the Staff Manual respectively. Title pages will be prepared in manuscript.

WAR DIARY
or
~~INTELLIGENCE SUMMARY.~~
(Erase heading not required.)

VOLUME 20

Army Form C. 2118.

Page Eight

Place	Date 1917	Hour	Section 1	Section 2	Section 3	Section 4	Remarks	Remarks and references to Appendices
YPRES	JUNE							
	29th		Cleaning & painting Wagons Corps Picture Ground	Erecting Stage	Workshops Preparing & Erecting D.P at CHATEAU SEGARD	Workshops Camp Fatigues	Divisional Entertainers – 'BLUEBIRDS' – gave performance at Camp.	
	30.		Ditto	Cleaning & Painting wagons	Ditto	Ditto		

[illegible signature]
Major R.E.
O.C. 202ND FIELD CO.
(COUNTY PALATINE) R.E.

2353 Wt. W2544/1454 700,000 5/15 D. D. & L. A.D.S.S./Forms/C. 2118.

202 FIELD COY

1/JULY/17 — 31/JULY/17

VOL 21

SECRET

Vol 21

War Diary

of

202nd Field Co R.E.

From July 1st 1917

To :- July 31st 1917

Volume 21

202nd Field Co R.E.

WAR DIARY
or
~~INTELLIGENCE SUMMARY.~~
(Erase heading not required.)

Army Form C. 2118.

Instructions regarding War Diaries and Intelligence Summaries are contained in F. S. Regs., Part II. and the Staff Manual respectively. Title pages will be prepared in manuscript.

VOLUME 21

Page One

Place	Date 1917	Hour	Section 1	Section 2	Section 3	Section 4	Remarks.	Remarks and references to Appendices
YPRES Area H26b3.7	July 1st		Making 'Prisoners Cage' Corps Picture Ground Workshops	Corps Picture Ground Workshops Fatigues	Observation Post Workshops	Workshops Fatigues etc		
	2nd		ditto	ditto	ditto Baths	Making latrines for Prisoners Cage Workshops etc Baths		
	3rd		Camp Drainage Corps Picture Ground Workshops Washing wagons	ditto Washing Wagons	Observation Post Workshops Washing wagons	Repairing bridge Drainage Washing Wagons.		
	4th		Div' Dump. Drainage Corps Picture Ground Painting wagons.	ditto.	Dismantling Stage Observation Post (completed)—CHATEAU SEGARD.	Workshops Practice wiring Fatigues Painting wagons	1 Sgt & 8 men for 4 days course in pipe-pushing. Motor cycle received. Intermittent shelling of Camp Area from 10-0pm until 3.0am. 5th — no casualties	
	5th		Corps Picture Ground Workshops Painting wagons Div' Dump	Workshops Corps Picture Ground Painting wagons	Workshops Painting wagons.	Fatigues Workshops Repairing track		
H13d 6.2 and H21d 5.2	6th		Packing up, loading etc for move	As no 1.	As no 1	As no 1.	HQ, Transport Sect 1 moved from Camp at H26b3.7 to H13d 6.2 Sects 2,3+4 moved to H21b 5.2. 1 off. +10 OR rejoined from 5th Army Rest Camp. 15 OR proceeded to 5th Army Rest Camp for 14 days Coy. now under C.R.E. 8th Division	

2353 Wt. W2544/1454 700,000 5/15 D. D. & L. A.D.S.S./Forms/C. 2118.

202nd Field Coy RE

Instructions regarding War Diaries and Intelligence Summaries are contained in F. S. Regs., Part II. and the Staff Manual respectively. Title pages will be prepared in manuscript.

Army Form C. 2118.

WAR DIARY
or
~~INTELLIGENCE SUMMARY.~~
(Erase heading not required.)

VOLUME 21

Page Two

Place	Date 1917	Hour	Summary of Events and Information					Remarks and references to Appendices
			SECTION 1	SECTION 2	SECTION 3	SECTION 4	REMARKS	
YPRES Area H13d 6.2 and H21b 5.2	JULY 7		Corps Workshops Coy do.	Tracks 3, 6 + X	Tracks 3, 6 + X	Bunking Dugouts &c.		
	8		ditto	ditto	ditto	ditto		
	9		ditto	ditto	ditto	ditto		
	10		ditto	ditto	ditto	ditto		
	11		ditto	ditto	ditto	ditto		
H31b 3.5.	12		Cleaning up Camps etc	As No 1	As No 1.	As No 1.	HQ, Transport & Sect 1 moved from camp at H13d 6.2 to H31b 3.5. Sects 2, 3 & 4 moved from H21b5.2 to H31b3.5. Coy now under orders of CRE, 18th Divn.	
	13.		Making water carriers	As No 1.	As No 1	As No 1.	Also making 5 slide rules for Artillery, Sawing timber, loading wagons etc	
	14		ditto	ditto	ditto	ditto	ditto	
	15		ditto	ditto	ditto	ditto	ditto	
	16.		ditto	ditto	ditto	ditto	ditto	
	17.		ditto.	Workshops Fatigues	Workshops	Workshops	ditto	
	18		Water Point - Zillebeke Track No 2.	Workshops &c Loading wagons	Workshops Repairing Road	Repairing road. Cleaning out ditch.		
	19/20		Water Point - Zillebeke Making Track No 2 Washing Wagons	Removing Stores - Zillebeke Dump Unloading Wagons Workshops. Repairing Light Railway	Workshops Making Track No 2	Workshops Loading wagons. Repairing Light Railway	20/7/17. No 74143 Spr. TAYLOR G.W. slightly wounded.	

2353 Wt. W2544/1454 700,000 5/15 D. D. & L. A.D.S.S./Forms/C. 2118.

202nd Field Co RE

Instructions regarding War Diaries and Intelligence Summaries are contained in F. S. Regs., Part II. and the Staff Manual respectively. Title pages will be prepared in manuscript.

WAR DIARY
or
~~INTELLIGENCE SUMMARY.~~
(Erase heading not required.)

VOLUME 21 Page Three

Army Form C. 2118.

Place	Date 1917	Hour	Section 1	Section 2	Section 3	Section 4	Remarks	Remarks and references to Appendices
YPRES AREA H31 b 3.5	JULY. 21st		Making No 2 Track. Workshops.	Repairing Light Railway Loading Stores ZILLEBEKE Dump	Making Track No 2 Workshops.	Camp Fatigues Workshops		
	22nd		Making Track No 2 Workshops	Making Track No 2 ZILLEBEKE Dump Workshops	Workshops Fatigues	Making Track No 2 Constructing Bridge Filling Shell holes &c	Lt. T. B. BUCKLEY R.E. admitted to Hospital (Sick). 2Lt McCALLUM RE & details rejoined Coy. from TOURNEHEM.	
	23rd		Workshops.	Workshops	Workshops	Workshops.	Company moved from MICMAC Camp as follows :- Sects 1, 2, 3 & 4 to CHATEAU SEGARD (Area No 7) HQ, Transport & details to H26 b 3.7. Coy. came under orders of C.R.E. 30th Divn.	
H26 b 3.7 & CHATEAU SEGARD	24th.		Workshops ~~Camouflaging Promenade Trench Tor Top Dressing Stn~~ Track No 2	Workshops Fatigues	Workshops Camouflaging Promenade Trench Tor-Top Dsg Stn.	Workshops New HQ. - Stanley St. Drsg Stn. Maple St - Gears Reps.	No 556572 Spr FELTHAM C. & No 551082 Spr. Spencer F.J. (Gassed)	
	25/26		Workshops Track No 2 Dressing Stn. Dormy House " " Maple St.	Workshops Fatigues	Workshops Camouflaging Promenade Tr. Tor-Top Dressing Stn.	Workshops. New HQ. - Stanley St Dressing Station - Maple St	25/7/17. No 81360 - 2nd Cpl. T. Douglass wounded.	
	27		Workshops Dugout. Winnepeg St. Dressing Stn. Dormy House " " Maple St.	Workshops. Fatigues &c.	Workshops. Camouflaging Promenade Tr. Tor-Top Dressing Stn.	Workshops ~~New HQ. S~~ Dressing Station - Maple St.	9.0 p.m. Work cancelled. Company to 'stand by' until situation is cleared up - re enemy's retirement.	
	28th.		Water point - Promenade Tr Dugout Winnepeg St.	Workshops Fatigues	{ Camouflaging Promenade Tr. Tor Top Dsg Stn.	Dressing Stn. - Maple St.	Making camouflage.	
	29th		Water point - do	Workshops Fatigues	Tor Top Dsg Stn Camouflaging Promenade Tr.	Dressing Stn. - Maple St.	~~Coy standing by~~ HQ moved to Chateau Segard at 9.0 p.m.	

2353 Wt. W2544/1454 700,000 5/15 D. D. & L. A.D.S.S./Forms/C. 2118.

202nd Field Co R.E.

Instructions regarding War Diaries and Intelligence Summaries are contained in F. S. Regs., Part II. and the Staff Manual respectively. Title pages will be prepared in manuscript.

VOLUME 21

WAR DIARY
or
~~INTELLIGENCE SUMMARY.~~
(Erase heading not required.)

Army Form C. 2118.

Page Four

Place	Date 1917	Hour	Summary of Events and Information			Remarks and references to Appendices
H26b 3.7 & CHATEAU SEGARD	JULY		Section 1 and Section 3	Section 2 and Section 4	Remarks.	
	30th				Company 'standing by' & preparing for operations	
	31st		Sections 1 + 3 under Command of Lieut. C. H. COTTEW, R.E. left Assembly point at 5.30 AM and commenced making mule track from YEOMANRY POST to SANCTUARY WOOD. About 9.0 AM. enemy placed heavy barrage on 'No Man's Land' and SANCTUARY WOOD and Sections were compelled to take cover. Machine guns were also firing, searching 'No Man's Land' and SANCTUARY WOOD. 11-0 AM. shelling increased. At about 2.0 PM. Sections withdrew to MAPLE TRENCH, barrage still being exceedingly heavy. 5.15 P.M. order received from O.C. to return to CHATEAU SEGARD Casualties: Wounded O.R. 3	Sections 2 + 4 under Command of II Lieut. C.C. LINDSAY, R.E. left Assembly point about 5.50 A.M., and upon arrival at destination, commenced making mule track from SANCTUARY WOOD onwards. About 9.0 AM. heavy shelling and machine gun fire experienced, and Sections were forced to withdraw into such cover as was available. Shelling increased at about 11-0 AM. 2.0 PM. Section 2 were withdrawn to MAPLE TRENCH and Section 4 followed at about 3.0 P.M. 5.15 P.M. - received order from O.C. that all men were ~~to~~ to return to CHATEAU SEGARD. Casualties: Killed O.R. 3 Wounded O.R. 7 (Killed:- No 139840 2nd Cpl MARTIN R.C " 65039 Sapper RICHARDSON R " 81952 do BARRATT W	Company left CHATEAU SEGARD at 3.45 AM. July 31st 1917, and marched via Tracks H and 11 to Assembly point near DORMY HOUSE. Arrived Assembly point about 5.20 AM. O.C. reported to 21st Brigade H.Qrs, DORMY HOUSE at 5.30 AM, and left at 5.55 AM to reconnoitre mule track. Returned to DORMY HOUSE 8.10 AM. Another reconnaissance made from 12-0 noon to 1.30 P.M.	

202 FIELD COY
1/8/17 — 31/8/17 Vol 22

Vol 22

SECRET

WAR DIARY

of

202nd. FIELD COMPANY

ROYAL ENGINEERS

from 1st August 1917

to

31st August 1917

VOLUME No 22

202nd Field Co RE

Instructions regarding War Diaries and Intelligence Summaries are contained in F. S. Regs., Part II. and the Staff Manual respectively. Title pages will be prepared in manuscript.

WAR DIARY
or
~~INTELLIGENCE SUMMARY.~~
(Erase heading not required.)

VOLUME 22

Page One

Army Form C. 2118.

Place	Date 1917	Hour	Section 1	Section 2	Section 3	Section 4	Remarks	Remarks and references to Appendices
H26 b 3.7 & CHATEAU SEGARD	August 1st		Cleaning up &c	Cleaning up &c	Cleaning up &c	Cleaning up &c	Company drawn into Divisional Reserve	
	2nd		Left Chateau Segard at 9.30 AM, but were unable to work on mule track owing to heavy shelling.	Left CHATEAU SEGARD at 2.30 AM and worked for 6 hours on mule track between SANCTUARY WOOD and old enemy front line.	As No 1 Section	As Section 2.	Mule track fairly good from our old front line up to JACKDAW SUPPORT, but bad from YEOMANRY POST — old front line.	
	3rd						11-0 AM. — Company moved from CHATEAU SEGARD to DICKEBUSCH HUTS - H26 b 37. The men were buried at DICKEBUSCH NEW CEMETARY H11 d 9.1 No 139870 - 2ndCpl. MARTIN R.C. " 65039 - Sapper RICHARDSON R " 81952 - " BARRATT W	
	4th						Transport left DICKEBUSCH Huts at 9.0AM; remainder of Coy. left at 12.45 p.m. & embussed at DICKEBUSCH at about 3.30 p.m. — destination RAMSGAT FARM, near STEENVOORDE. 4/8/17. Lieut. C.H. COTTEW. transferred to II Corps School	
STEENVOORDE AREA	5th		Cleaning up, etc Erecting bivouacs	As No 1.	As No 1	As No 1.		
	6th		Squad Drill Rifle Exercises etc	As No 1	As No 1	As No 1	Bath made from tarpaulin sheet.	

A7092). Wt. W12839/M1293 750,000. 1/17. D. D & L., Ltd. Forms/C2118/14

202nd Field Coy R.E.

Instructions regarding War Diaries and Intelligence Summaries are contained in F. S. Regs., Part II. and the Staff Manual respectively. Title pages will be prepared in manuscript.

WAR DIARY
or
~~INTELLIGENCE SUMMARY.~~
(Erase heading not required.)

Army Form C. 2118.

VOLUME 22

Page Two

Place	Date 1917	Hour	Section 1	Section 2	Section 3	Section 4	Remarks	Remarks and references to Appendices
	AUGUST.							
MERRIS AREA	7th		Erecting bivouacs - horse lines Fatigues &c	As No 1	As No 1	As No 1	Company left PAMSGAT FARM at 8.0 a.m. & marched to MERRIS AREA.	
	8th		Cleaning wagons &c Squad Drill	Cleaning wagons &c Squad Drill Loading Pontoons (practice)	Cleaning wagons &c Squad Drill Loading pontoons (practice)	Cleaning wagons &c Squad Drill Loading Pontoons (practice)	Order received from 21st Bde to be prepared to move on 10th inst.	
	9th.		Squad Drill Rifle exercises Loading pontoons (practice)	Squad Drill Rifle Exercises	Squad Drill Rifle Exercises	Squad Drill Rifle Exercises	Div' Routine Orders notified award of MILITARY Medal to following N.C.O's & Men of 202nd Field Coy R.E. 36610 Sergt ROBERTS J.W. 83300 do WILLIAMS J. 81515 Sapper PEE W.H. 108490 " WHITTINGHAM F.	
	10th		Loading Wagons &c Rifle Exercises Dismantling bivouacs	As Sect 1	As Sect 1	As Sect 1.		
MONT VIDAIGNE	11th		Erecting bivouacs & horse lines	As Sect 1	As Sect 1	As Sect 1.	Company moved to M 21 b 3.2 (MONT VIDAIGNE)	
	12th		Fatigues	do	do	do		
	13th		Sq. Drill & Rifle Ex. Musketry Bayonet fighting	Phy. Drill & Rifle Ex. Knotting & Lashing Musky & Bayonet fighting	Phy. Drill & Bayonet fighting Gas Drill & Rifle Mechanism Extended Order Drill Knotting & Lashing	Squad Drill & Musketry Bayonet fighting Electric connections & Circuits Demolitions (theory)		
	14th		Field Day	Observation March & Map reading	Field Day	Observation March & Map reading	2/Lt Watkins and 2/Lt Aldred joined Coy as reinforcements	

A7092). Wt. W12839/M129 750,000. 1/17. D. D & L., Ltd. Forms/C2118/14.

Army Form C. 2118.

WAR DIARY
or
~~INTELLIGENCE SUMMARY.~~
(Erase heading not required.)

Instructions regarding War Diaries and Intelligence Summaries are contained in F. S. Regs., Part II. and the Staff Manual respectively. Title pages will be prepared in manuscript.

Volume 22.

page 3.

Place	Date	Hour	Summary of Events and Information: Sect 1	Sect 2	Sect 3	Sect 4	Remarks	Remarks and references to Appendices
M21 b 3.2	15th		Sq. Drill & Rifle Ex. Signalling Knotting & Lashing Bayonet fighting	Physical Drill Knotting & Lashing Weldon trestle	Physical Drl & Rifle Ex. Gas Drill - Knotting & Lashing Explosives	Sq. Drill & Musketry Bayonet fighting Musketry.		
N17c 1.1.	16th		Dismantling bivouacs & horselines & packing up. Re erecting above at new camp	As Sect 1.	As Sect 1	As Sect. 1	Coy. moved from M21 b 3.2 to N17c 1.1 (near KEMMELL) 100 Infy. attached for work & rations	
	17/18		RIDGE defences	As Sect 1	As Sect 1	As Sect 1.		
	19		Church parade	"	"	"		
	20		Ridge defences	"	"	"		
	21st		Overhauling toolcarts painting trestles	"	"	"		
N28 a 8.4.	22nd		Erecting bivouacs	"	"	"	Coy. moved to N28 a 8.4. Offs & NCOs reconnoitred line. Relieved 12th Austr. Field C RE. O.C. proceeded on leave, Capt. N.T. ELLIS RE in command. 2nd/Lt. C.C. LINDSAY, RE rejoined from Hospl 23rd inst. 1 NCO wounded 24th	
	23/24		Deepening & Revetting trenches in front line & Supports	"	"	"		
	25/26		do	"	"	"		
	27/29		do	"	"	"		
	30/31		do	"	"	"		

M. Ellis Capt RE
A/O.C 202nd Field Co RE.

A7092). Wt. W12839/M1297 750,000. 1/17. D. D & L., Ltd. Forms/C2118/14.

202 FIELD COY

1/SEP/17 — 30/SEP/17

Vol. 23

SECRET

VII 23

War Diary of 202nd Field Coy R.E.

from : Sept 1st 1917

to : Sept 30th 1917

VOLUME 23

202nd Field Co R.E.

Instructions regarding War Diaries and Intelligence Summaries are contained in F. S. Regs., Part II. and the Staff Manual respectively. Title pages will be prepared in manuscript.

Volume 23.

WAR DIARY
or
~~INTELLIGENCE SUMMARY.~~
(Erase heading not required.)

Page One

Army Form C. 2118.

Place	Date	Hour	Summary of Events and Information					Remarks and references to Appendices
			Section 1	Section 2	Section 3	Section 4	Remarks	
N28a.8.4 (Ypres Area)	1st		Deepening and revetting trenches in front line and supports. Night work	as No 1	as No 1	as No 1	3 ARP sheds for ammunition built at N21.d.6.6 Commenced 1st. completed 7th	
	2nd		do	do	do	do		
	3rd		do	do	do	do	Enemy aeroplanes fairly active bomb dropping night of 4/5th	
	4th		do	do	do	do		
	5th		do	do	do	do	2/Lieut C.C. LINDSAY proceeded on leave to UK on 6th. Lieut H RAINE RE joined Coy for duty on 6th	
	6th		do	do	do	do	Major J.E. Crippindall RE returned from leave to UK on 7.9.17 and proceeded to CRE HQ 30th Division same day as acting CRE.	
	7th		do	do	do	do		
	8th		do	do	do	do		
	9th		do	—	do	—	Nos 2 & 4 Sections, 80 att infantry and 600 Infantry working party built 200 yds of Breastwork at O.29c 29 on night of 9th/10th. Casualties 2 OR. slight remained on duty.	
	10th		do	as No 1	do	as No 1		
	11th		No work night of 11th. Brigade relief. Coy took over work on "Y" line from 201st Field Co RE and handed over work on front line and supports.					
	12th		Work on "Y" line Night work	Work on "Y" line Sandbagging, revetting etc	as No 2	as No 2		
	13/14th		Sandbagging & revetting 'Y' Line	As No 1	As No 1	As No 1	Erecting Nissen Huts & A.R.P Sheds	
	15/16th		Revetting etc 'X' & 'Y' Line	do	do	do	ditto	
	17/18th		do	do	do	do	ditto.- Lieut H RAINE, RE proceeded on leave to U.K. 2/Lt C.C. LINDSAY, RE rejoined from leave	

A7092). Wt. W12839/M1297 750,000. 1/17. D. D & L., Ltd. Forms/C2118/14.

202nd Field Co RE

Instructions regarding War Diaries and Intelligence Summaries are contained in F. S. Regs., Part II. and the Staff Manual respectively. Title pages will be prepared in manuscript.

WAR DIARY
or
~~INTELLIGENCE SUMMARY.~~
(Erase heading not required.)

Volume 23 — Page Two

Army Form C. 2118.

Place	Date 1917	Hour	Summary of Events and Information: Sect 1.	Sect 2	Sect 3	Sect 4	REMARKS	Remarks and references to Appendices
N 28 a. 8.4	Sept.							
	19		Revetting 'X' + 'Y' Line	as N°1	as N°1	as N°1	Erecting Nissen Huts & A.R.P. Sheds	
	20						No line work - Brigade relief.	
			During attack of 2nd & 5th Armies, 30th Division carried out a demonstration. The RE took part - the duty of the 202nd Field Co RE was to blow up a Concrete Dugout called "the GIANT" at O 12 c 22.65 Party consisting of iiLt. A. ALDRED, N° 83104 9Cpl. A.J. WARD, and 4 O.R. took part The charge was to have been 250 lbs Ammonal, Each man carried 50 lbs. The demolition was not carried out, as the Infantry were unable to clear the Dugout. Party had to remain out in shell holes all day, and returned under cover of dusk. CASUALTIES :- N° 185331 Sapper S.H. LEACH wounded severely (died 21/9/17) and N° 149564 Spr F. ROBINSON wounded.					
	21		Strong Points	As N°1	As N°1	As N°1	No 83102 a/Cpl PRESTWICH to N°2 Camp, ETAPLES for 2 months tour of duty. Building fireplace in G.O.C.s Hut; Clipping-Shed; Drying room; Nissen Huts; A.R.P. Sheds. O.C. rejoined from C.R.E.	
	22		OAK AVENUE OLIVE TRENCH STRONG POINTS	OLIVE TRENCH	HUTTING etc	As N°1	Sect. 1 + 4 moved into billets at GRAND BOIS. Work as above carried on.	
	23		do	Clearing OAK AVE.	do	do.	Work as above carried on.	
	24		—	Hutting, erecting harness shed etc	do	—	Work in line cancelled by order of C.R.E. owing to practice barrage. — work as above carried on.	
	25		do	Gumboot store RAVINE WOOD Reclaiming D.O.'s in DENYS WOOD	do	do.	Work as above	
	26/27		do	do	do	do	do.	
	28/29		do	do	do	do.	do	
	30		do	do	do	do	do. iiLt. W.C. McCALLUM, R.E. to Hospital (sick) Capt. N.T. ELLIS - 30 days leave to UK	

[signature] Major RE
O/C 202nd Field Co R.E.

A7092). Wt. W12839/M1297 750,000. 1/17. D. D & L., Ltd. Forms/C2118/14.

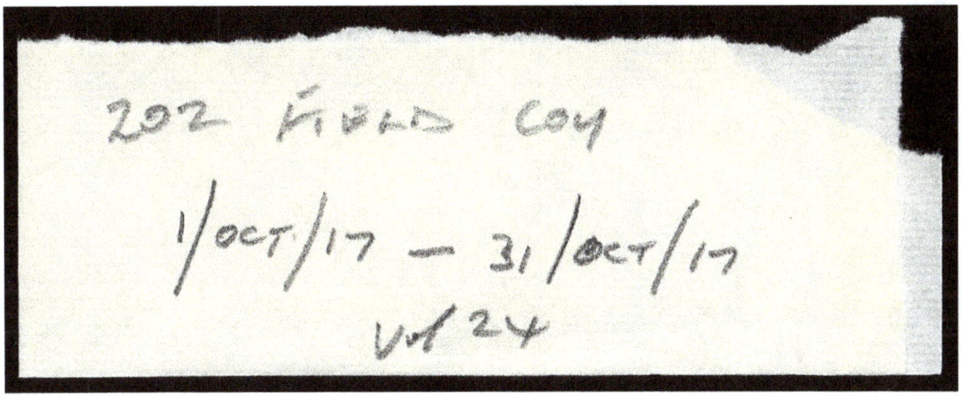

202 FIELD COY

1/OCT/17 – 31/OCT/17

Vol 24

WO 24

Ala.

SECRET.

WAR DIARY

OF

262ND FIELD COMPANY
ROYAL ENGINEERS

FROM 1ST OCTOBER 1917
TO
31ST OCTOBER 1917

VOLUME No 24.

202nd Field Co R E

Instructions regarding War Diaries and Intelligence Summaries are contained in F. S. Regs., Part II. and the Staff Manual respectively. Title pages will be prepared in manuscript.

WAR DIARY
or
~~INTELLIGENCE SUMMARY.~~
(Erase heading not required.)

VOLUME 24

Army Form C. 2118.

Page One

Place	Date	Hour	Summary of Events and Information					Remarks and references to Appendices
	1917		Sect 1.	Sect 2	Sect 3	Sect 4	Remarks	
N28a 8.4	Oct. 1/2		OAK AVENUE OLIVE TRENCH STRONG POINTS	Gum boot store RAVINE WOOD Reclaiming D.O's DENYS WOOD	HUTTING etc	As No 1	Half Section reliefs carried out each day 1st & 2nd inst. Sects 2 & 3 taking over work in line, & Sects 1 & 4 rear area work.	
	3		D.O's DENYS WOOD Camp work RAVINE DEFENCES	OLIVE TRENCH RAVINE DEFENCES OAK AVENUE	as Sect 2	Hutting, Clipping Shed, Drying Room.	Digging new Support line	
	4/5		D.O's DENYS WOOD Camp work RAVINE Defences	OLIVE TRENCH RAVINE Defences Digging trench between SPs 5 & 6 OAK AVENUE New Support Trench	As Sect 2	Hutting, Clipping shed, Drying Room	do	
	6/7		D.O's DENYS WOOD Shelters RAVINE WOOD RAVINE Defences Camp work	RAVINE Defences Digging trench between SPs 5 & 6 Oak Avenue Shelters Oak Support Wid. & deepening trench OLIVE TRENCH	As Sect 2	Hutting, Clipping shed, Drying room		
	8/9		D.O's DENYS WOOD Shelters RAVINE WOOD RAVINE Defences Camp Work	RAVINE Defences OAK AVENUE Shelters Oak Support Strong Points OLIVE TRENCH	As Sect 2	Hutting, Clipping shed, Drying room.		
	10		D.O's DENYS WOOD Shelters RAVINE WOOD RAVINE DEFENCES Camp Work	RAVINE Defences OAK AVENUE Shelters Oak Support Strong Points OLIVE TRENCH	As Sect 2	Hutting, Clipping shed, Drying room		

A7092). Wt. W12859/M1293 750,000. 1/17. D. D & L., Ltd. Forms/C2118/14.

202nd. Field Co. R.E

Instructions regarding War Diaries and Intelligence Summaries are contained in F. S. Regs., Part II. and the Staff Manual respectively. Title pages will be prepared in manuscript.

WAR DIARY
or
INTELLIGENCE SUMMARY.
(Erase heading not required.)

Volume 24

Army Form C. 2118.

Page Two.

Place	Date 1917	Hour	Sect. 1	Sect 2	Sect 3	Sect 4	REMARKS	Remarks and references to Appendices
N28 a 8.4	OCT. 11th		Camp Work	-	-	Hutting, Clipping shed, Drying room.	Sections 2+3 moved from GRAND BOIS to Coy HQ at N28a 8.4. owing to Section relief.	
	12th		Strong Points + Bn Soup Kitchen	Camp work &c	Hutting, Clipping Shed, Drying Room.	Shelter near Leaning Tower + Support Trench near Wall Farm	Attached Infantry on PIONEER LANE.	
	13th		Bn Soup Kitchen	Camp work &c	ditto.	-	All work and working parties cancelled night of 13/14th owing to bad weather.	
	14th		Strong. Points Bn Soup Kitchen Fixing Gas Curtains Bn HQ. SONEN FARM.	Ditto	ditto	Shelter near Leaning Tower + Support Trench near Wall Farm	Att. Infy on PIONEER LANE. and Reclaiming Dugouts.	
	15th		ditto	ditto	ditto	do.	Att Infy on PIONEER LANE and Reclaiming Dugouts	
	16th		ditto	ditto	ditto	ditto.	No Infy. Wkg parties ditto. Batt. relief	
	17th		ditto.	ditto	ditto.	ditto	Att. Infy on PIONEER LANE	
	18th and 19th		ditto	LEG COPSE Converting dugout to Gum Boot Store. O.7C 0.75 Const. 4 Shelters for new Coy HQ. Roofing Spray Baths LINDENHOEK	ditto Drying Rm finished	ditto	– ditto.	
	20th		-	LEG COPSE Conv. Dugout. Roof LINDENHOEK BATHS	ditto	.	No Infty Wkg parties. Brigade relief	

A7092). Wt. W12839/M1297 750,000. 1/17. D. D & L., Ltd. Forms/C2118/14.

202nd Field Co RE

Instructions regarding War Diaries and Intelligence Summaries are contained in F. S. Regs., Part II. and the Staff Manual respectively. Title pages will be prepared in manuscript.

Page 3

WAR DIARY
or
INTELLIGENCE SUMMARY.
(Erase heading not required.)

Volume 24

Army Form C. 2118.

Place	Date 1917	Hour	Summary of Events and Information					Remarks and references to Appendices
			Sect 1.	Sect 2.	Sect 3	Sect 4	Remarks	
I.28.a.8.4	OCT. 21st		Day off.	Day Off	Hutting &c. till 12 noon. Remainder of day off.	Day off	Half Section reliefs carried out each day. 21st and 22nd inst. Section 3 taking over work in line from Section 4. Section 4 taking over Hutting	
	22nd		Bn Soup Kitchen Bn HQ SONEN FM. Camp work	Gum boot Store LEG COPSE. Roofing LINDENHOEK BATHS. Completed.	Shelters near LEANING TOWER + SUPPORT TRENCH near WALL FM + M.G. Emp. in No 2 Strong point	Hutting &c. Clipping Shed	Att. Infantry on PIONEER LANE	
	23rd		do Picture Ground	Gum boot store LEG Copse	do	Hutting &c Clipping Shed	do. 2/Lt J.H SOMERSET to Hospital (Sick)	
	24th		Camp Work. Picture Ground	Making new Battn. HQ exc for entrance	do	do	Att Inf on PIONEER LANE	
	25th		do Sandbag revetting &c at REGENTS Dugouts + Picture Ground	do	do	do	do	
	26th		Camp work and Picture Ground	do	Shelters near LEANING TOWER Rest of Section night off	do.	do.	
	27/31st		do.	do	Shelters near Leaning Tower + M.G. emp. in 202 Strong Point	do.	do	

[signature] Major RE
O.C. 202nd FIELD CO. (COUNTY PALATINE) R.E.

A7092). Wt. W12839/M1297 750,000. 1/17. D. D & L., Ltd. Forms/C2118/14.

202 FIELD COY

1/NOV/17 — 30/NOV/17

VOL 25

Vol 25

SECRET

WAR DIARY
OF
202nd FIELD COY.
ROYAL ENGINEERS

from 1st. Nov. 1917
To.
30th Nov 1917

VOLUME No. 25

202nd Field Co RE

Instructions regarding War Diaries and Intelligence Summaries are contained in F. S. Regs., Part II. and the Staff Manual respectively. Title pages will be prepared in manuscript.

Page 1

WAR DIARY
or
INTELLIGENCE SUMMARY.
(Erase heading not required.)

Volume 25

Army Form C. 2118.

Place	Date 1917	Hour	Summary of Events and Information					Remarks and references to Appendices
			Section 1	Section 2	Section 3	Section 4	Remarks	
N 28.a.8.4	Nov 1		Camp work &c and Picture Ground	making new Batt HQ. Exc. for entrance	Hutting, Clipping Shed &c.	Shelters near LEANING TOWER	Nos. 3 + 4 Sections changed over work. No. 3 Section moved from N 28.a.8.4 to DRANOUTRE and No 4 Section moved from DRANOUTRE to N 28 a. 8.4. Att. Infy on PIONEER LANE	
	2		ditto and repair work at REGENTS DUGOUTS	Workshops and Camp Work	ditto	ditto	Att Infy on PIONEER LANE Capt. N.T. ELLIS RE rejoined Coy from 30 days leave to UK.	
	3		ditto	ditto	ditto	ditto	Att Infy on PIONEER LANE.	
	4		Part of Section day off. Remainder night work on Nos 2 + 3 Strong Points. Picture ground.	Day off	ditto	Part of Section day off. Remainder at Shelters near LEANING TOWER and M.G. Emp No 2 S.P.	Att Infy on PIONEER LANE	
	5		Erecting Blanket Store at TEA FARM No 2 + 3 S.P.s. PICTURE GROUND	Erecting new YMCA Shelter at WYTSCHAETE. Reclaiming and bunking D.O. at O20 a 0.8. RAMILLES CAMP imp. Camp work etc.	ditto and lagging Water pipes. Laundry, DRANOUTRE.	Shelters near LEANING TOWER and M.G. Emp. at No. 2 S.P.	ditto	
	6		ditto.	ditto	ditto	ditto Shelters near LEANING TOWER completed.	ditto 2/Lt. J.C. FISHER RE joined Coy for duty	
	7		ditto	ditto	ditto	M.G. Emp No 2 SP	Att Infy on PIONEER LANE.	
	8		-	-	ditto	-	Orders received for Coy to move on 9th. All men called in from outside work. Att Infy rejoined their Battns in afternoon. No 3 Section rejoined Coy from DRANOUTRE in evening.	

A7092). Wt. W12839/M1297 750,000. 1/17. D. D & L., Ltd. Forms/C2118/14.

202nd Field Co RE

Instructions regarding War Diaries and Intelligence Summaries are contained in F. S. Regs., Part II. and the Staff Manual respectively. Title pages will be prepared in manuscript.

Page 2

WAR DIARY
or
INTELLIGENCE SUMMARY.
(Erase heading not required.)

Volume 25

Army Form C. 2118.

Place	Date 1917 Nov	Hour	Section 1	Section 2	Section 3	Section 4	Remarks	Remarks and references to Appendices
	9		-	-	-	-	Coy moved from N28.a.8.4. (leaving at 9.30 am) to BAILLEUL at 1pm. Coy Office, 67 Rue de la Gare.	
	10		-	-	-	-	Morning spent washing wagons, cleaning equipment &c. Afternoon off.	
	11		-	-	-	-	Coy moved from BAILLEUL to H18 b.0.5 on West side of YPRES. Transport left BAILLEUL at 9.30 am and arrived at destination at 3pm. Dismounted part of Coy. embussed in The Grand Place, BAILLEUL at 11-30 am and arrived at H18 b.0.5 at 2pm. Rest of day spent erecting shelters &c. Lieut. C.C. LINDSAY RE to 2nd Army Central School, WISQUES. for course of instruction	
	12		-	-	-	-	At 6.0 am 1 Officer and 3 NCOs went over work to be taken over from 6th Canadian Field Co. of Engineers and at 9.0 am OC, 3 Section Officers and 2 NCOs went over the work. In the evening O.C, 1 Sec Offr, and Nos. 2 and 4 moved into YPRES to take over billets vacated by two Sections of 6th Canadian Field Coy	
	13		-	-	-	-	3 OR from each Section went over work No 3 Section moved into billets in YPRES Transport moved to VLAMERTINGHE	
	14		-	Repairs to billets improvements &c.	-	-	No 4 Section took first shift on road repairing on SEINE - ZONNEBEKE ROAD. No 3 Section took second shift instead of a section of 201st Field Co RE by arrangement between O.C's Companies. Working party from 9th K.R.R.	
	15		-	Road repairing on SEINE - ZONNEBEKE Road.	Repairs to billets improvements &c	Repairs to billets improvements &c	Owing to enemy shell fire, no work was possible on road. No. 1 Section moved from H18.b.0.5 to YPRES. Relief of 6th Canadian Field Company Complete. Working party from 9th K.R.R.	

A7092). Wt. W12839/M1297 750,000. 1/17. D. D & L., Ltd. Forms/C2118/14.

202nd Field Co RE

Instructions regarding War Diaries and Intelligence Summaries are contained in F. S. Regs., Part II. and the Staff Manual respectively. Title pages will be prepared in manuscript.

Page 3

WAR DIARY
or
INTELLIGENCE SUMMARY.
(Erase heading not required.)

Volume 25

Army Form C. 2118.

Place	Date 1917 Nov.	Hour	Section 1	Section 2	Section 3	Section 4	Remarks	Remarks and references to Appendices
	16		Road Repairing on SEINE-ZONNEBEKE ROAD. Road very much damaged by enemy's heavy shell fire of previous day.	Repairs and improvements to billets &c	Repairs and improvements to Billets &c	Repairs and improvements to Billets &c.		
	17		Repairs & improvements to billets etc.	Repairs and improvements to Billets &c	Repairs and improvements to Billets &c	Road Repairing on SEINE-ZONNEBEKE RD		
	18.		Repairs and improvements to Billets etc.		Road Repairing SEINE-ZONNEBEKE RD. Only 1½ hrs work done owing to enemy shell fire.	Repairs to Billets &c.		
	19		Repairs to road ZONNEBEKE TO SEINE		Billet repairs, Fatigues, etc.			
	20		Repairs to Billets &c		Repairs to and making sides for Bogie wagons at KANSAS X roads			
	21		BRIDGE HOUSE TO KANSAS CROSS, Road Repairs. 20 OR. on night patrol duty in two shifts on the same road, repairing breaks.					
	22.		ditto		ditto		ditto	Lt HRAINE RE to Hospital (Sick)
	23		ditto		ditto		ditto.	Orders received to move on 24th. night patrol parties called in.

A7092). Wt. W12839/M1297 750,000. 1/17. D. D & L., Ltd. Forms/C2118/14.

Instructions regarding War Diaries and Intelligence Summaries are contained in F. S. Regs., Part II. and the Staff Manual respectively. Title pages will be prepared in manuscript.

202nd Field Co RE

WAR DIARY
or
INTELLIGENCE SUMMARY.
(Erase heading not required.)

Page 4

Volume 25

Army Form C. 2118.

Place	Date	Hour	Summary of Events and Information					Remarks and references to Appendices
	1917 Nov		Section 1	Section 2	Section 3	Section 4	Remarks	
	24th	-	-	-	-	-	Billets in YPRES and work handed over to 234th Field Coy R.E. Company (dismtd portion) paraded at 10.30am and marched to I 31 a central (VOORMEZEELE) arriving at destination at 12 noon. 1 N.C.O. and 8 O.R. reported to HQ. 89th Bde RFA for work on Gun positions and OPs. Transport moved from VLAMERTINGHE to N 5 d.5.5	
	25th	-	Horse Standings at H 32 d.2.2.	Rest of ~~do No1~~ Company cleaning and draining camp etc.	Improving Bty positions &c			
	26th	.	do	As No 1.	Camp work &c Improving Bty positions	As No 1 and repairing baths CHIPPEWA CAMP.		
	27th	.	do	do	do. & Sandbag revetting huts at I 26 c 4.6 & flooring &c	do.		
	28th	.	do	do	do	do.		
	29th		do	do.	do	do		
	30th	-	do	do	do	do		

[signature]

Major R.E.

O.C. 202ND FIELD CO, (COUN[illegible]) R.E.

2353 Wt. W2544/1454 700,000 5/15 D. D. & L. A.D.S.S./Forms/C. 2118.

202 FIELD COY
1/DEC/17 — 31/DEC/17
Vol 26

Vol 26

WAR DIARY

of

202ND FIELD COY. ROYAL ENGINEERS

from 1st December 1917
to
31st December 1917.

VOLUME No 26

202nd Field Co RE

WAR DIARY
or
~~INTELLIGENCE~~ SUMMARY.

Army Form C. 2118.

Instructions regarding War Diaries and Intelligence Summaries are contained in F. S. Regs., Part II. and the Staff Manual respectively. Title pages will be prepared in manuscript.

Page 1 (*Erase heading not required.*) Volume 26

Place	Date 1917	Hour	Summary of Events and Information: Section 1	Section 2	Section 3	Section 4		Remarks and references to Appendices
	Dec.							
	1		Horse standings at H32 c 9.1	Horse standings at H32. c.9.1 and H30 c 1.6.	Camp work &c. Work on Battery positions and repairs at VIJERHOEK Baths	Horse standings at H32 c 9.6		
	2		do	do	do	do.	No 1 Section moved from H32 c 9.1 to Company camp.	
	3		Moved from Camp at I31 a central to STIRLING CASTLE and relieved a Section of 201st Field Co RE, who took over billets vacated by No 1 Section	do	Moved from Camp at I31 a central to STIRLING CASTLE and relieved a Section of 201st Field Co RE who took over billets vacated by No 3 Section.	do		
	4		Work on PERTH AVENUE continuing trench J21 B.0.1. to J21 b.35.15.	–	Reclaiming 2 German Dugouts Nos 206 – 207 at J19 a.7.8. Building latrine and improving German dugout at J13 d.7.0. Casualties. Spr T. BERRY wounded (Died in 2nd CCS on 5th.)	–	O.C. No 4 Section Officer & Nos. 2 & 4 Sections moved from Camp at I31 a Central to STIRLING CASTLE. HQ Section moved to Transport lines. Office left at I31 a central.	
	5		ditto.	R. Batty HQ J20 d 2.9. Enlarging & draining 1 Kitchen and making new Kitchen	J19 a 7.8. Clearing out and repairing entrances to 3 German D.Os. J19 a 8.5. Clearing and repairing tunnel dugout (RE Billet). Clearing out old German trench & dugout at J13 c 7.1.	Reclaiming dugouts. Putting billets in good order. Building new Kitchen at HQ.		

202nd Field Co RE

Instructions regarding War Diaries and Intelligence Summaries are contained in F. S. Regs., Part II. and the Staff Manual respectively. Title pages will be prepared in manuscript.

Page 2

WAR DIARY
or
~~INTELLIGENCE~~ SUMMARY.
(Erase heading not required.)

Volume 26

Army Form C. 2118.

Place	Date	Hour	Summary of Events and Information					Remarks and references to Appendices
	1917 Dec		Section 1	Section 2.	Section 3	Section 4	Remarks	
	6th		Continuation of PERTH AVENUE	Bn Kitchen at J 20 d 2.9.	I 30 a RFA billets, erecting Elephant shelters and work on old German dugouts as on 5th	Improving RFA billets and work as on 5th	Casualties:- No Spr W.C. Allen } wounded No 2/Cpl Watkins }	
	7th		do and making Electric Light Signal boxes	do and improvements to Coy. billets	Work on RFA billets & Camp improvements. Cleaning and deepening JASPER AVENUE	Reclaiming dugouts and Camp improvements	A few enemy shells fell around Company billets about 10 pm.	
	8th		Continuation of PERTH AVENUE and making electric Light Signal boxes	Bn Kitchen at J 20 d 2.9. and work on PERTH AVENUE	Reclaiming old German dugouts Work on RFA dugouts	Reclaiming + cleaning dugouts	Casualties att. Infantry wounded one Lieut P. Cook 2/Yorks Regt temporarily att. to Coy.	
	9th		do	do	do	do		
	10th		Claiming and Cleaning dugouts also cleaning MENIN RD TUNNEL	do	do	Work on PERTH AVENUE		
	11th		do	Right Bn Cookhouse and Support Bn Cookhouse	do	do		

D. D. & L., London, E.C.
(A7883) Wt. W509/M1672 350,000 4/17 Sch. 52a Forms/C/2118/14

202nd Field Co RE

Instructions regarding War Diaries and Intelligence Summaries are contained in F. S. Regs., Part II. and the Staff Manual respectively. Title pages will be prepared in manuscript.

Page 3.

WAR DIARY
or
~~INTELLIGENCE SUMMARY.~~
(Erase heading not required.)

Volume 26.

Army Form C. 2118.

Place	Date 1917	Hour	Section 1	Section 2	Section 3	Section 4	Remarks	Remarks and references to Appendices
	Dec 12th		Reclaiming dugouts and work on MENIN Road Tunnels	R. Bath Cookhouse and Drying Room at J19a 9.8	Reclaiming Dugouts RFA work	J.13 a.5.3 Cleaning and Pumping out dugout	Transport moved from N5 d 5.5 to ANZAC Camp.	
	13th		do	do and Support Bn Cookhouse	do	Cleaning MENIN road tunnel		
	14th		do	do and Drying Room	do	PERTH AVENUE		
	15th		do and Gum Boot Store at CANADA TUNNELS	do and reclaiming dugout	do	do		
	16th		do	Drying Room & reclaiming dugouts	do	do		
	17th		do and work on switch track	do and making barbed wire concertinas	do	Work on Pillboxes Repairing E Track		
	18th		do	do	Making barbed wire concertinas	Work on C.T. Support to front line Repairs to E Track		
	19th		WIRING from J22a 6.9 to J22a 35.65 Reclaiming Dugouts Work on MENIN Road Tunnel, & Gum Boot Store	Drying Room, Reclaiming Dugouts repairs to E Track	Work on PERTH AVENUE RFA work	Reclaiming Pill boxes. Repairs to E Track. Work on PERTH AVENUE		

202nd Field Co. RE

Instructions regarding War Diaries and Intelligence Summaries are contained in F. S. Regs., Part II. and the Staff Manual respectively. Title pages will be prepared in manuscript.

Page 4

WAR DIARY
or
~~INTELLIGENCE~~ SUMMARY.
(Erase heading not required.)

Volume 26

Army Form C. 2118.

Place	Date	Hour	Section 1	Section 2	Section 3	Section 4	Remarks	Remarks and references to Appendices
	20th		Reclaiming Dugouts. Work on MENIN RD Tunnel. Gum Boot Store at CANADA TUNNELS	Drying Room. E Track and Concertina wire making. Reclaiming Pill boxes	Work on PERTH AVENUE. RFA work	Reclaiming Pillboxes. Work on E Track. Making barbed wire concertinas. R. Bn. HQ. Drainage	Night of 20/21st. prolonged enemy gas shell bombardment	
	21st		do	do	do	do	Half of each Section returned to Back area and relieved half Sections of 200th FIELD Co. RE, and took over work. 2/Lt TOMKINSON. 11th S. LANCS Rgt temp. att. to Coy	
	22nd		A32.d.0.1. Horse Standings	H32 d.0.1 Horse Standings	BEDFORD Ho. YMCA Hut. HORNBY SIDING. Bomb store. RFA work, etc	A30 d.1.3. Horse Standings. H30 c 2.6. erecting QMS Stores	Remainder of Company returned to Back area and 200th FIELD Co RE took over forward work.	
	23rd		do	do	do	do		
	24th		do	do	do and Gum boot Drying Room at H36 b5.7	do	2/Lt A. ALDRED R.E. to Hosp (Sick). Lieut P. COLK 2/Yorks Rgt att. to Coy. to Hosp (Sick). Lieut C. C. LINDSAY RE rejoined from CRE's HQ 30th Division	
	25th		Holiday	Holiday	Holiday	Holiday		
	26th		H32 d.0.1 Horse Standings	H32 d.0.1 Horse Standings. Erecting Bechet Huts at SWAN CHATEAU	As on 24th	as on 24th	Capt N. T. ELLIS RE transferred to 201st Field Co RE as O.C. Coy. Lieut C. C. LINDSAY RE appointed 2nd in Command vice Capt ELLIS.	

2353 Wt. W2544/1454 700,000 5/15 D. D. & L. A.D.S.S./Forms/C. 2118.

202nd Field Coy RE

Army Form C. 2118.

WAR DIARY
or
INTELLIGENCE SUMMARY.
(Erase heading not required.)

Instructions regarding War Diaries and Intelligence Summaries are contained in F. S. Regs., Part II. and the Staff Manual respectively. Title pages will be prepared in manuscript.

Page 5 Volume 26

Place	Date 1917 Dec	Hour	Section 1	Section 2	Section 3	Section 4	Remarks	Remarks and references to Appendices
	27th		H32 d.0.1 Horse Standings	H32 d.0.1 Horse Standings Erecting Decket [illegible] at SWAN CHATEAU	BEDFORD HOUSE YMCA [illegible] Stn. [illegible] SIDING [illegible] Boot and [illegible] Room	H30 d.1.3 Horse Standings &c		
	28th		do	do	do	do	Half of No 1 Section moved from WARBOURG Camp to Coy HQ. Lieut. H. RAINE rejoined Coy from Hosp	
	29th		do	do	do	do	Half of each Section moved up to CANADA TUNNELS and relieved 4 half Sections of 201st FIELD CO RE	
	30th		Excavating for & erecting shelters in strong points.	As No 1.	Work on Battery positions at I 28.b.6.3. 150 yds Barbed wire put out from J26.b.35.85 onwards. Strong points. J 20 d. 3.2. and J26 a. 8.9.	As No 3	Remainder of Coy with Lieut C.C. LINDSAY RE moved to CANADA TUNNELS.	
	31st		do.	do	RFA batty positions Fixing frames for Gas Blankets at Torr Top Tunnels Wiring	Wiring. Digging strong Point J 20 d 3.2 and J26.a 8.9.	Major F.E. Chippindall RE proceeded on leave to U.K.	

C.C. Lindsay Lieut RE.
A/O.C. 202nd Field Coy RE

D. D. & L., London, E.C. (A7883) Wt. W89/M1672 350,000 4/17 Sch. 52a Forms/C/2118/14

202 FIELD COY

1/JAN/17 – 31/JAN/17

Vol 27

Vol 27

SECRET

WAR DIARY

OF

202nd FIELD Co.

ROYAL ENGINEERS

from 1st Jan. 1918
to 31st Jan. 1918.

VOLUME No 27

202nd Field Co RE

Instructions regarding War Diaries and Intelligence Summaries are contained in F. S. Regs., Part II, and the Staff Manual respectively. Title pages will be prepared in manuscript.

Page 1

WAR DIARY
or
~~INTELLIGENCE SUMMARY.~~
(*Erase heading not required.*)

Volume 27

Army Form C. 2118.

Place	Date 1918	Hour	Section 1	Section 2	Section 3	Section 4	Remarks	Remarks and references to Appendices
	Jan 1st		Work on Strong Points	as No 1	— WIRING	—	2/Lt H.A.WATKINS RE wounded night of 1st/2nd. Evac. to C.C.S.	
	2nd		do and wiring	as No 1.	— WIRING	—		
	3rd		do	do	— WIRING	—	Handing over to 84th Field Co RE. Cyclist proceeded to Horse Lines.	
	4th		-	-	-	-	Transport and cyclists marched to GODEWARSVELDE. Remainder of Company moved from CANADA TUNNELS to Horse Lines.	
	5th		-	-	-	-	Dismounted part of Coy marched to DICKEBUSCH and entrained at 7.30 pm arriving at EBLINGHEM at 12.30 am on the 6th. Transport moved from GODEWARSVELDE to REAUMONT arriving at 7 pm. Dismounted portion arrived at destination at 3 am on the 6th.	
	6th		-	-	-	-	Settling down in new billets. Coy HQ at A18 d 15.30 Sheet 36A	
	7th		Drill &c in morning afternoon off	as No 1	as No 1	as No 1.		

A6945 Wt. W11422/M1160 350,000 12/16 D. D. & L. Forms/C./2118/14.

202nd Field Co RE

Instructions regarding War Diaries and Intelligence Summaries are contained in F. S. Regs., Part II. and the Staff Manual respectively. Title pages will be prepared in manuscript.

Page 2

WAR DIARY
or
~~INTELLIGENCE SUMMARY.~~
(Erase heading not required.)

Volume 27

Army Form C. 2118.

Place	~~Date~~ Jan 1918	Hour	Section 1	Section 2	Section 3	Section 4	Remarks	Remarks and references to Appendices
	8th.		Kit Inspection &c. Remainder of day off.	As No 1	As No 1	As No 1	Very bad weather.	
	9th.		Preparing for move	As No 1	As No 1	As No 1.		
	10th		–	–	–	–	Company paraded at 10.30 pm and marched to STEENBECQUE Station.	
	11th						Coy entrained at STEENBECQUE at 6.30AM arriving at LONGEAU at 2.30pm. and marched to CASTEL arriving at 7.50 pm.	
	12th		Cleaning Harness &c	As No 1	As No 1	As No 1	2/Lt E.C. ALLERTON R.E joined Coy for duty	
	13th		–	–	–	–	Coy paraded at 8.15AM. and marched to ARVILLERS. arriving at 2.40pm. 2/Lieut J.C. FISHER, R.E proceeded on leave to UK.	
	14th		–	–	–	–	Coy paraded at 8.15AM and marched to MARGNY arriving at 2.20pm.	

D. D. & L., London, E.C. (A7833) Wt. W80/M1672 350,000 4/17 Sch. 52a Forms/C/2118/14

202nd Field Co RE

Instructions regarding War Diaries and Intelligence Summaries are contained in F. S. Regs., Part II, and the Staff Manual respectively. Title pages will be prepared in manuscript.

WAR DIARY
or
~~INTELLIGENCE SUMMARY~~.
(Erase heading not required.)

Army Form C. 2118.

Page 3 Volume 27.

Place	Date 1918	Hour	Summary of Events and Information					Remarks and references to Appendices
	Jan		Section 1	Section 2	Section 3	Section 4	Remarks	
	15th.		Squad Drill Map Reading Gas Helmet drill	Rifle Exercises Knots and Lashings Map Reading	Squad Drill Map Reading Knots and Lashings	Rifle Exercises Map Reading Knots & Lashings.		
			———	Recreational	Training ———			
	16th.		Rifle Exercises Knots & Lashings Musketry	Squad Drill Demolitions Gas Helmet Drill	Rifle Exercises Field Geometry Musketry	Squad drill Strong Points & obstacles Bayonet Fighting		
			———	Recreational	Training ———			
	17th.		do	do	do	do		
	18th.		-	-	-	-	Coy paraded at 9.30 am and marched from MARGNY to HERLY, arriving at destination at 12.15 pm	
	19th.		-	-	-	-	Coy paraded at 2.30 pm and marched to NESLE arriving at destination at 3.50 pm. Coy HQ No 1 RUE DES POISSONNIERS. Major J.E. Chippindall RE rejoined from leave to UK.	
	20th.		-	-	-	-	Whole of Company working on new 5th Army HQ under orders of CRE, 5th Army Troops.	
	21st		-	-	-	-	ditto 2/Lt C.R. TOMKINSON rej. Battn. (11th S. Lancs R)	
	22nd		-	-	-	-	ditto	

D. D. & L., London, E.C. (A7883) Wt. W603/M1672 350,000 4/17 Sch. 52a Forms/C/2118/14

202nd Field Co RE.

Instructions regarding War Diaries and Intelligence Summaries are contained in F. S. Regs., Part II. and the Staff Manual respectively. Title pages will be prepared in manuscript.

Page 4

WAR DIARY
or
~~INTELLIGENCE SUMMARY.~~
(Erase heading not required.)

Volume 27

Army Form C. 2118.

Place	Date 1918	Hour	Section 1	Section 2	Section 3	Section 4	Remarks	Remarks and references to Appendices
	Jan 23rd		-	-	-	-	Whole of Coy working on 5th Army HQ	
	24th						- ditto -	
	25th						ditto	
	26th		no 1 Section under 2/Lt A. ALDRED RE moved to LIANCOURT FOSSE for work at HATTENCOURT under CRE 5th Army Troops.	-	-	-	nos 2. 3 & 4 Sections working on 5th Army HQ	
	27th		work at HATTENCOURT Prisoners Cage				ditto in morning. afternoon off duty	
	28th		do				nos 2. 3 & 4 Sections working on 5th Army HQ. 2/Lieut J.A.H BURFORD of 201st Field Co RE temporarily attached to Coy for duty	
	29th		do.				nos 2. 3 & 4 Sections working on 5th Army HQ	
	30th		do				ditto	
	31st		do				ditto. 2/Lieut J.C FISHER RE rejoined from leave to U.K.	

[signature] Major R.E.
O.C. 202ND FIELD CO, (COUNTY PALATINE) R.E.

202 FIELD COY
1/2/18 – 28/2/18
Vol 28

Vol 28

SECRET

WAR - DIARY
of
202ND FIELD COY ROYAL - ENGINEERS

From - 1st February 1918
To — 28th February 1918

VOLUME No 28

202nd Field Co RE

Instructions regarding War Diaries and Intelligence Summaries are contained in F. S. Regs., Part II, and the Staff Manual respectively. Title pages will be prepared in manuscript.

Page 1

WAR DIARY
or
INTELLIGENCE SUMMARY.
(Erase heading not required.)

Volume 28

Army Form C. 2118.

Place	Date 1918	Hour	Summary of Events and Information					Remarks and references to Appendices
	Feby		Section 1	Section 2	Section 3	Section 4	Remarks	
	1st		Work at HATTENCOURT. Moved from LIANCOURT FOSSE and rejoined Coy at NESLE in the evening.	-	-	-	2, 3 & 4 Sections working on 5th Army HQ	
NESLE	2nd		-	-	-	-	Whole of Company working on 5th Army HQ 2/Lieut A ALDRED RE proceeded on leave to U.K.	
	3rd		-	-	-	-	Whole of Company working on 5th Army H.Q.	
	4th		-	-	-	-	- ditto -	
	5th		-	-	-	-	- ditto -	
	6th		-	-	-	-	- ditto -	
	7th						- ditto -	

A6945 Wt. W11422/M1160 350,000 12/16 D. D. & L. Forms/C./2118/14.

202nd Field Co. R.E.

Instructions regarding War Diaries and Intelligence Summaries are contained in F. S. Regs., Part II. and the Staff Manual respectively. Title pages will be prepared in manuscript.

Page 2

WAR DIARY
or
~~INTELLIGENCE SUMMARY.~~
(Erase heading not required.)

Volume 28.

Army Form C. 2118.

Place	Date 1918.	Hour	Section 1.	Section 2.	Section 5.	Section 4.	Remarks.	Remarks and references to Appendices
NESLE	Feby							
	8th	.	~	~	~	~	Whole of Company working on 5th Army H.Q. Lieut H. Raine rejoined from Hospital. 2/Lieut J.C. Fisher and 2/Lieut J.A.H. Burford left to join 201st FIELD Coy	
	9th	.	~	~	~	~	Whole of Company working on 5th Army H.Q. 2/Lieut J.C. Fisher and 2/Lieut J.A.H. Burford rejoined Coy.	
	10th	.	~	~	~	~	Whole of Company working on 5th Army H.Q.	
	11th	.	~	~	~	~	- ditto -	
	12th	.	~	~	~	~	- ditto -	
	13th		~	~	~	~	Finishing off work on 5th Army H.Q. Half of Company employed in the afternoon packing and cleaning up ready to move.	
	14th		Paraded at 8.a.m. & moved by lorry to FLUQUIÈRES and marched to billet at LeHAMEL	Paraded at 8am, Entrained at NESLE 8-45 a.m. detrained at FORESTE and marched to billet in ROUPY arriving at 12 noon. Remainder of day settling down and repairing billets	Paraded at 8 a.m entrained at NESLE 8-45 a.m. detrained at FORESTE, and marched to billet in SAVY		Transport and cyclists moved by road to FLUQUIERES arriving at 3-30 pm.	

A6945 Wt. W11422/M1160 350,000 12/16 D. D. & L. Forms/C./2118/14.

202nd Field Coy R.E.

Instructions regarding War Diaries and Intelligence Summaries are contained in F. S. Regs., Part II, and the Staff Manual respectively. Title pages will be prepared in manuscript.

Page 3.

WAR DIARY
or
~~INTELLIGENCE~~ SUMMARY.
(*Erase heading not required.*)

Volume 28.

Army Form C. 2118.

Place	Date 1918	Hour	Summary of Events and Information					Remarks and references to Appendices
	Feby.		Section 1	Section 2	Section 3	Section 4	Remarks	
ROUPY	15th			N.C.O's proceeded on reconnaissance of work in the line. Sections repairing billets			Enemy aircraft very active at night. A few bombs were dropped in the region of Coy. H.Q.	
"	16th		Subsector "E" making redoubt & S.P.	Wiring at P.8 & repairing billets	Wiring as No 2	Laying out S.P's in subsector "D."		
"	17th		do	do	do	do	2nd Lieut. H.A.WATKINS rejoined Coy. for duty	
"	18th		do	do	do	do	Capt. C.C. Lindsay proceeded on leave to U.K. 2nd Lieut A. Aldred rejoined Coy. from leave. 2/Lt E.C. ALLERTON R.E. to 18th Corps Gas School for Course of Instruction	
"	19		do.	do	do	do.		
"	20		Constructing fire bays & comm. trench	D & E Sectors. Const. firebays and shelters	Wiring and repairing billets.	Taping & setting out in D Sector.		
"	21		do	do	do	do		
	22nd		do	D & E Sectors const. Firebays &c.	do	do.		

A6945 Wt. W11422/M1160 350,000 12/16 D. D. & L. Forms/C./2118/14.

202nd Field Co RE

Instructions regarding War Diaries and Intelligence Summaries are contained in F. S. Regs., Part II. and the Staff Manual respectively. Title pages will be prepared in manuscript.

WAR DIARY
or
~~INTELLIGENCE SUMMARY.~~

(Erase heading not required.)

Army Form C. 2118.

Page 4 Volume 28

Place	Date 1918 FEB	Hour	Section 1	Section 2.	Section 3	Section 4	Remarks	Remarks and references to Appendices
ROUPY	23rd		E Subsector making fire & C.T's	D Subsector firebays & C.Ts	ETREILLERS Village Defences	work on D Sector (North)	2/Lt E CALLERTON RE from Course at 18th Corps Gas School	
	24th.		do	do	do	do		
	25th		do	do	do	do		
	26th.		do	do	do	do	Company manned Battle Positions (test) at 10.15 pm	
	27th		do & wiring	do	do	do		
	28th		Taping out new work. Erecting notice boards	Taping out new work, &c. Erecting notice boards	Preparing for new work and rifle practice	Preparing for new work. Erecting notice boards	No working parties	

[signature] Major R.E.
O.C. 202ND FIELD CO, (COUNTY PALATINE) R.E.

A6945 Wt. W11422/M1160 350,000 12/16 D. D. & L. Forms/C./2118/14.

Sketch A. Method of detonating Ammonal tube

Plan.

Ammonal Tube in Casing

Elevation.

Wood Plug bored in 2 places for detonators

Dry Guncotton Primer

The Ammonal is enclosed in a tin tube about 3" diam! – it does not appear to matter if tube is not watertight.
The tube itself is in a light wood frame as per sketch.

[illegible] Major RE
O/C 202nd Field Co. RE

17/12/16.

App. 1.

30th Div.

202nd FIELD COMPANY, R.E.

M A R C H

1 9 1 8

30

SECRET

WAR DIARY of

202nd FIELD Co R.E

from 1st March 1918
to 31st March 1918

Volume No 29

Vol 29

202nd Field Co. R.E.

Instructions regarding War Diaries and Intelligence Summaries are contained in F. S. Regs., Part II. and the Staff Manual respectively. Title pages will be prepared in manuscript.

Page 1

WAR DIARY
or
INTELLIGENCE SUMMARY.
(Erase heading not required.)

Army Form C. 2118.

Volume 26

Place	Date	Hour	Summary of Events and Information					Remarks and references to Appendices
	MAR 1918		Section 1	Section 2	Section 3	Section 4	Remarks	
ROUPY	1st		E. North Sector. Fire and Communication Trenches	D. South Sector. Trenches & C.Ts. Taping Trenches. Fixing boards	Excavating for shelters. No working party. (ETREILLERS)	D North Sector. Making concertinas & pegging out. No working party		
	2nd		E North Sector. Work on platoon shelters. 10 O.R. sent as guides to 18th K.L.R. for working parties.	ditto	ETREILLERS defences excavating tunnels	D North Sector. Digging & levelling parapets. No working party		
	3rd		E North Sector. Fire trenches &c.	ditto and shelters for platoon HQ	ditto	D North Sector. Work on Redoubt & Keep.		
	4th		ditto & wiring	ditto	ditto	ditto	Lieut H RAINE R.E. proceeded on leave to UK. (5.3.18 to 20.3.18).	
	5th		Wiring and digging C.Ts	Digging Trenches. Taping out shelters	ditto	ditto		
	6th		ditto.	ditto.	Camp work (No infantry digging party)	ditto.		
	7th		Erecting shelters, fixing gas screens &c.	Digging Trenches, wiring &c. (No infantry working party)	Wiring and erecting notice boards. No infantry working party.	ditto	Capt. C.C. LINDSAY, R.E. rejoined Coy from leave to UK.	

A6945 Wt. W11422/M1160 350,000 12/16 D. D. & L. Forms/C./2118/14.

202nd Field Co. R.E.

Instructions regarding War Diaries and Intelligence Summaries are contained in F. S. Regs., Part II. and the Staff Manual respectively. Title pages will be prepared in manuscript.

Page 2

WAR DIARY
or
INTELLIGENCE SUMMARY.
(Erase heading not required.)

Volume 29

Army Form C. 2118.

Place	Date MAR	Hour	Section 1	Section 2	Section 3	Section 4	Remarks	Remarks and references to Appendices
ROUPY	8th		Digging C.Ts and Wiring &c. E. NORTH Sector	Digging Trenches Fixing Gas Curtains etc D SOUTH Sector	Wiring. Excavating for trenches and for shelters &c ETREILLERS DEFENCES	Work on Redoubt &c D NORTH Sector		
	9th		Day off (No Infy parties)	Day off (No Infy parties)	Setting out tapes for wiring Fixing M.G. boards & setting out shelters (No Infy parties)	ditto		
	10th		E NORTH Sector Wiring, Digging CTs &c	Digging Trenches Taping out Work on shelters D SOUTH sector	Fixing shelters, Preparing for wiring. (No Infy parties)	Day off (No Infy parties)		
	11th		E NORTH Sector Digging C.T's. Fixing Gas curtains. etc.	D SOUTH Sector. Digging trenches Work on shelters &c.	ETREILLERS DEFENCES Putting up wire entanglement. Excav. trenches & shelters. Work on Bde Baths.	D. NORTH Sector Work on Redoubt, Bomb Store &c.	O.C. Company, Major J.E. CHIPPINDALL R.E. admitted to Hospital (Sick)	
	12th		E NORTH SECTOR Wiring, Digging C.T. Fixing Gas Curtains Erecting shelters Making L.G. Emp. etc	D SOUTH Sector Digging trenches Shelters, etc. Fixing Gas Curtains.	ETREILLERS defences Erecting wire entanglements. Excav trenches etc.	D. NORTH Sector Work on Redoubt Bomb Store &c.		

A6945 Wt. W11422/M1160 350,000 12/16 D. D. & L. Forms/C./2118/14.

202nd Field Coy R.E.

Instructions regarding War Diaries and Intelligence Summaries are contained in F. S. Regs., Part II. and the Staff Manual respectively. Title pages will be prepared in manuscript.

Page 8

WAR DIARY
or
INTELLIGENCE SUMMARY.
(Erase heading not required.)

Volume 29

Army Form C. 2118.

Place	Date Mar	Hour	Summary of Events and Information					Remarks and references to Appendices
			Section 1	Section 2	Section 3	Section 4	Remarks	
	13th		E. NORTH Sector. Digging C. Ts. L.G. Emp. etc.	D. SOUTH Sector Digging trenches Taping out etc	ETREILLERS defences Wiring. Excav. trenches etc Work at Baths	D. NORTH Sector Work on Redoubt. M.G. emp.		
	14th		Wiring. Digging C. Ts etc.	ditto.	ditto	ditto		
	15th		ditto	ditto	ditto	ditto		
	16th		ditto and work on Breastwork.	ditto	ditto	ditto		
	17th		Day off. NO WORKING	Day off PARTIES	Day off (INFANTRY)	Day off FOR BATTLE ZONE	Major J.E. CHIPPINDALL R.E. rejoined Company from Hospital.	
	18th		E NORTH Sector Digging C.Ts etc	D SOUTH Sector Digging C.Ts. Excavating for and erecting shelters, etc	ETREILLERS defences Wiring. Excav. Trenches. Work at Baths, etc.	D NORTH Sector Work on redoubt Wiring. etc.		
	19th		Do ditto and work on Breastwork	ditto	ditto	ditto.		

A6945 Wt. W11422/M1160 350,000 12/16 D. D. & L. Forms/C./2118/14.

202nd Field Co R.E.

Instructions regarding War Diaries and Intelligence Summaries are contained in F. S. Regs., Part II. and the Staff Manual respectively. Title pages will be prepared in manuscript.

WAR DIARY
or
~~INTELLIGENCE SUMMARY.~~
(Erase heading not required.)

Army Form C. 2118.

Page 4. Volume 29.

Place	Date	Hour	Summary of Events and Information	Remarks and references to Appendices
	Mar. 1918			
	20th		Whole of Company working on BATTLE ZONE	2/Lieut. H.A.WATKINS R.E. transferred to No 1 SEIGE COY R.A. R.E. (Army C.E. XVIII Corps)
	21st		Intense bombardment by enemy Artillery opened out at 4.30 a.m. Company manned Battle Positions in ROUPY KEEP, afterwards being relieved by Infantry at 5.45 a.m. Coy. then moved to, and assembled at, FLUQUIERES. A number of shells fell in ROUPY as the Coy was vacating the village. FLUQUIERES was shelled intermittently by H.V. Guns all day. At 2.40 p.m. Company received orders to move to the Quarry near AVIATION WOOD (F25d) and arrived at 3.40 p.m. After standing by till 9.30 p.m. Coy moved to AUBIGNY and were billeted there awaiting further orders.	Casualties. 2/Lt. A. ALDRED R.E. wounded (Shell back) No. 179991 Spr. HOULDEN. J (wounded) (Shell neck) Lieut. H. RAINE R.E. rejoined Coy from leave to U.K.
	22nd		In the morning Coy. dug a trench outside AUBIGNY but were called back before it was finished and moved from AUBIGNY to HAM. O.C. reported to C.R.E. on arrival at HAM. Afterwards Coy dug trenches on west side of HAM as Rear Bridgehead Defences. Company moved into HAM (under orders from C.R.E.) and were billeted alongside the Canal for the night, prior to wiring the HAM defences along the Canal.	
	23rd		At about 4 a.m. the enemy attacked HAM and Company left billets and took up a position just outside the town astride the ERCHEU Road. Afterwards being relieved by Infantry, Company retired to ESMERY HALLON and O.C. reported to 90th Brigade (Infty) HQ. following which Company took up a position on the rear side of ESMERY HALLON. Orders received afterwards to move to a position in front	Casualties. KILLED. Lieut. H. RAINE R.E. WOUNDED No. 470108 Sgt GRIEVE R. No. 134805 Corpl LOVEGROVE J. No. 145610. Spr DAVIDSON J. No. 83368. Spr JOHNSON H.

A6945 Wt. W11422/M1160 350,000 12/16 D. D. & L. Forms/C./2118/14.

202nd Field Co RE

Instructions regarding War Diaries and Intelligence Summaries are contained in F. S. Regs., Part II. and the Staff Manual respectively. Title pages will be prepared in manuscript.

WAR DIARY
or
~~INTELLIGENCE SUMMARY.~~
(Erase heading not required.)

Army Form C. 2118.

Page 5 — Volume 29

Place	Date	Hour	Summary of Events and Information	Remarks and references to Appendices
	Mar 1918			
	23rd (cont)		of ESMERY HALLON. Company arrived in position at 1.20 pm and dug in. Late on in afternoon positions were heavily shelled by enemy artillery. At night Company was relieved by 21st Infantry Bde Details and after Tool Carts had arrived proceeded to put the village of ESMERY HALLON in a state of defence. i.e. Loopholing walls and digging trenches (along with 200th & 201st Field Coy. RE)	
	24th		Half way through the work of making the defences of ESMERY: HALLON, Company had to "Stand To", and later on, after "Standing Down", went into billets in ESMERY-HALLON and spent the remainder of the night resting. Orders had been received that when the defences of ESMERY HALLON were complete the Company was to assemble at the Quarry behind ESMERY-HALLON. The Company was making its way there when the enemy attacked. Coy. then took up a position on a line running across the fields behind ESMERY-HALLON. Shortly afterwards orders were received to fall back (together with 200th and 201st Field Coys RE) across the Canal to assist the 279th Infantrie Regt. (French) to dig a line of trenches on the slope in front of ERCHEU village. Work was completed at 4 p.m and Coy moved back to SOLENTE, spending the night in huts in that village.	Casualties No 83438. Dvr LITTLER T. wounded
	25th		The Coy dug trenches in front of SOLENTE during the morning and in the afternoon moved back to Horse Lines at ROIGLISE and encamped there. At 11.30 pm Company	

A6945 Wt. W11422/M1160 350,000 12/16 D. D. & L. Forms/C./2118/14.

202nd Field Coy RE

Instructions regarding War Diaries and Intelligence Summaries are contained in F. S. Regs., Part II. and the Staff Manual respectively. Title pages will be prepared in manuscript.

Page 6

WAR DIARY
or
~~INTELLIGENCE SUMMARY.~~
(Erase heading not required.)

Volume 29

Army Form C. 2118.

Place	Date	Hour	Summary of Events and Information	Remarks and references to Appendices
	Mar 1918			
	25th (cont)		paraded and marched off to PLESSIER.	
	26th		A halt of 2 hours was made at BOUCHOIR for breakfast, and Coy arrived at PLESSIER at 11a.m. In the afternoon Coy moved to HANGEST to await orders. Late in the afternoon Coy moved back to PLESSIER, and, assisted by 30th Divisional R.E. Dump Party, dug trenches in front of the village.	
	27th		Coy dug a line of trenches in front of the village of LE HAMEL, and at night manned a position (together with 23rd Entrenching Battalion, 172nd Tunnelling Coy R.E. and 2 Corps Special Brigade R.E) running from the wood South of PLESSIER to the AVRE river. About midnight Coy withdrew to PLESSIER after orders had been received from C.R.E. to move back to ROUVREL.	
	28th		3 Pontoon wagons arrived at 5.30 a.m. and carried the Sappers back to ROUVREL. Transport moved from SAUVILLERS to ROUVREL and rejoined Coy. Remainder of day spent in resting	
	29th		Coy assisted French Engineers to prepare the crossings of the river at MORIEL for defence, and on completion of work required by the French moved back again to the village of ROUVREL. Mounted Section moved to SAINS.	Casualty No. 155199 Spr WILSON J. wounded

A6945 Wt. W11422/M1160 350,000 12/16 D. D. & L. Forms/C./2118/14.

202nd Field Co. RE

Instructions regarding War Diaries and Intelligence Summaries are contained in F. S. Regs., Part II. and the Staff Manual respectively. Title pages will be prepared in manuscript.

Page 7.

Army Form C. 2118.

WAR DIARY

or

~~INTELLIGENCE SUMMARY.~~

(Erase heading not required.)

Volume 29

Place	Date	Hour	Summary of Events and Information	Remarks and references to Appendices
	Mar. 1918 30th		Coy moved off at 10 A.M. to SALEUX where the Dismounted Portion of the Coy. entrained at 5 p.m. for ST VALERY - SUR - SOMME. Mounted Section proceeded by road	
	31st		Coy arrived at ST VALERY - SUR - SOMME at 12.30 a.m. and marched to the village of WATIEHURT, arriving at 5 a.m.	

[signature] Major RE.

O.C. 202nd FIELD Co. R.E.

A6945 Wt. W11422/M1160 350,000 12/16 D. D. & L. Forms/C./2118/14.

SECRET

No 32

Vol 30

WAR DIARY

of

202ND FIELD COY

R. E

FROM 1ST APRIL 1918

to

30th APRIL 1918

VOLUME No. 30.

202nd Field Co RE

Instructions regarding War Diaries and Intelligence Summaries are contained in F. S. Regs., Part II. and the Staff Manual respectively. Title pages will be prepared in manuscript.

Page 1.

WAR DIARY
or
~~INTELLIGENCE~~ SUMMARY.
(Erase heading not required.)

Volume 30.

Army Form C. 2118.

Place	Date	Hour	Summary of Events and Information	Remarks and references to Appendices
	April 1918			
	1st.		Dismounted portion of Coy on drill &c during morning. Mounted portion arrived in afternoon	
	2nd.		Coy on drill &c.	
	3rd.		Preparing for move & wagon and harness cleaning	
	4th.		Packing wagons &c.	
	5th.		Coy paraded at 12.40 pm and marched to WOINCOURT, entraining at 7 pm for PROVEN.	
	6th.		Coy arrived and detrained at PROVEN at 10 pm., and marched to WHEATFIELD CAMP 28/A14 b 8.6 arriving at 1 pm. Transport arrived at 2pm.	
	7th.		Coy moved to YSER CANAL BANK at 28/C13 c 2.2 arriving at 1.30pm. Transport moved to ARRACOURT CAMP 28/B22 a.	
	9th.		Officers and Section Sergeants went round new work in BATTLE ZONE. Company employed cleaning camp &c. 2/Lt C.P. GARRARD RE joined Coy for duty.	

A6945 Wt. W11422/M1160 350,000 12/16 D. D. & L. Forms/C./2118/14.

202nd Field Co RE

Instructions regarding War Diaries and Intelligence Summaries are contained in F. S. Regs., Part II. and the Staff Manual respectively. Title pages will be prepared in manuscript.

Page 2

WAR DIARY
or
~~INTELLIGENCE SUMMARY.~~
(Erase heading not required.)

Army Form C. 2118.

Volume 30.

Place	Date April 1918	Hour	Summary of Events and Information: Section 1	Section 2	Section 3	Section 4	Remarks	Remarks and references to Appendices
	9th		COMEDY FARM Digging revetting drainage & preparing for shelters	BATTERY COPSE Shelters (excavation)	COMEDY FARM Digging revetting drainage and preparing for shelters	BATTERY COPSE Shelters (excavation) work on Light Railway		
	10th		ditto	ditto	ditto	ditto.	2/Lieut. T.D.S. BAYLEY R.E Joined Coy. for duty	
	11th		CARDIFF N + CARDIFF S Digging for drains & clearing sites for draining	ditto	ditto	ditto.		
	12th		ditto.	ditto	ditto.	ditto.	2/Lieut. E.C. ALLERTON R.E. admitted to Hospital (Sick)	
	13th		ditto.	ditto	ditto	ditto. Work on demolition of bridges over YSER CANAL.		
	14th		ditto and assisting No 4 Section on work of demolition of Bridges	ditto and as No. 1.	ditto and as No. 1.	Work on demolition of bridges over YSER CANAL		
	15th		CARDIFF N & S Digging drains	BATTERY COPSE Work on shelters	COMEDY FARM Digging revetting drainage	ditto ~~[illegible]~~		

A6945 Wt. W11422/M1160 350,000 12/16 D. D. & L. Forms/C./2118/14.

202nd Field Co RE

Instructions regarding War Diaries and Intelligence Summaries are contained in F. S. Regs., Part II. and the Staff Manual respectively. Title pages will be prepared in manuscript.

Page 3.

WAR DIARY
or
~~INTELLIGENCE SUMMARY.~~
(Erase heading not required.)

Volume 30

Army Form C. 2118.

Place	Date April 1918	Hour	Section 1	Section 2	Section 3	Section 4	Remarks	Remarks and references to Appendices
	16th		Dismantling Nissen Huts at HUDDLESTONE CAMP	Dismantling Nissen Huts at HUDDLESTONE CAMP.	as No 1	Work on preparing for demolition of bridges over YSER CANAL		
	17th.		Dismantling and loading NISSEN HUTS.	Dismantling and loading NISSEN HUTS	Dismantling NISSEN HUTS	ditto	Coy with exception of No 4 Section were relieved by Belgian Engineers, and moved to LOTHIAN CAMP 28/B23 b 2.2	
	18th.		-	-	-	-	No. 4 Section handed over bridge demolitions to Belgian Engineers at 7 am. and rejoined Coy at LOTHIAN CAMP. Company moved off at 10 am and marched to G.16.c.6.0 (near BUSSEBOOM)	
	19th		28/H25 c.0.8 digging trench.	28/G30 b9.4. digging and clearing trenches	28/G 24 central. Clearing out old trenches	G24 b 3.2 to G24 a 9.8 Renovating trenches	Casualties. Killed. 179143 Spr TAYLOR G.W. Wounded. 145610 " DAVIDSON J.	
	20th		-	-	-	-	Coy paraded at 11 a.m. and marched to H33a.5.2 and came under orders of G.O.C. 21st Infy Bde. 2/Lieut D. McCALLUM RE joined Coy for duty.	
	21st		Digging and draining Section Posts from SHELLEY FARM to TRIANGULAR WOOD			SPOIL BANK, Dugouts BRASSERIE and ST ELOI. Preparations for demolitions		

A6945 Wt. W11422/M1160 350,000 12/16 D. D. & L. Forms/C./2118/14.

202nd Field Co. R.E.

Instructions regarding War Diaries and Intelligence Summaries are contained in F. S. Regs., Part II. and the Staff Manual respectively. Title pages will be prepared in manuscript.

WAR DIARY
or
~~INTELLIGENCE SUMMARY.~~
(Erase heading not required.)

Army Form C. 2118.

Page 4 Volume 30

Place	Date April 1918	Hour	Summary of Events and Information					Remarks and references to Appendices
			Section 1	Section 2	Section 3	Section 4	Remarks	
	22nd		21st BDE H.Q. Sandbagging and strengthening cellar	ST ELOI CRATER to SHELLEY FARM Constructing posts	CANAL BANK (I33 d. 5.4) Demolishing remains of 2 foot bridges.	SPOIL BANK DUGOUTS. ST ELOI and VOORMEZEELE Preparations for demolitions. Section moved to Shelters on banks of DICKEBUSCH LAKE (H35 a 3.9)	CASUALTIES WOUNDED 470108 Sgt GRIEVE R. 83104 Cpl WARD A 99784 Spr BOLTON R WOUNDED & GASSED 154001 Spr SENIOR G GASSED 83003 Spr LYNCH T. 474630 Spr FLINTHAM J. 153950 Spr MANSELL W. 59451 Pnr McKARELL H. 81681 Spr JONES W	
	23rd		ditto	Section resting	ditto and moved to House at H35 a3.9)	Work as 22nd		
	24th					ditto	HQ and Nos. 1 & 3 Sections moved to H35 a 3.9 arriving at 12 noon	
	25th		Enemy opened out a heavy bombardment at 3 a.m., using a large quantity of Gas Shells, subsequently attacking. Coy. wore box respirators from 3 a.m. to 8 a.m. and stood by all day. At night Nos. 1 and 3 Sections erected wire entanglements in front of HILL 60.				CASUALTIES KILLED No.96745 Spr McBURNIE W GASSED 2/Lt T.D.S. BAYLEY R.E No.99763 Spr PERCIVAL J. No. 66685 Pnr SIMSON W.	
	26th		Nos. 1 & 3 Sections arrived back at billets at 2.15 am and Coy moved at 6 am. to Camp at H16c 7.0 arriving at 7.30 a.m. In the evening No 2 Section and part of No 4 Section wired Strong Point at H22 a. 5.1. Remainder of Coy. moved to ~~[illegible]~~ N. 15 a. 1.6 being joined by the Sections on wiring on completion of work.				CASUALTIES KILLED No. 81705 2/Cpl WALKER S. WOUNDED No. 48471 Spr CUTTER W.G No. 81515 Spr PEE W.H. No 83064 L/Cpl HOUGHTON G.	

D. D. & L., London, E.C.
(A8004) Wt W1771/M2031 750,000 5/17 Sch. 52 Forms/C2118/14

WAR DIARY

or

~~INTELLIGENCE SUMMARY.~~

(Erase heading not required.)

Instructions regarding War Diaries and Intelligence Summaries are contained in F. S. Regs., Part II. and the Staff Manual respectively. Title pages will be prepared in manuscript.

Army Form C. 2118.

Page 5 Volume 30

Place	Date	Hour	Summary of Events and Information	Remarks and references to Appendices
	April 1918 27th		At 3 am ~~2/Lt [illegible] FISHER RE with~~ 2 O.R. blew up lock 7 over YPRES-COMINES CANAL after withdrawal of 21st BDE. At night Company dug posts to hold a Company between DICKEBUSCH LAKE and HALLEBAST CORNER. Casualties WOUNDED No 83102 Cpl PRESTWICH R. No 19878 2/Cpl BERRY WAE No 42177 Pnr PITCHER J.	
	28th		Nos 1, 2, 3 and 4 Sections wiring at BRASSERIE, near VOORMEZEELE.	
	29th		Nos. 2 & 4 Sections repairing trench at H36c.7.4. Nos 1 & 3 Sections night off.	
	30th		Nos 1, 2 & 3 Sections repairing trench at H36b and d. No 4 Section night off.	

[signature] Major RE
O.C. 202nd Field Co RE
1. 5. 1918

A6945 Wt. W11422/M1160 350,000 12/16 D. D. & L. Forms/C./2118/14.

202 FIELD COY
1/MAY/18 – 31/MAY/18
VOL 31

SECRET

War Diary

of

202nd Field Coy R.E.

May 1st 1918

to

May 21st 1918.

Vol 31

Volume 31

Pages 1 to 5

202nd. Field Co RE

Instructions regarding War Diaries and Intelligence Summaries are contained in F. S. Regs., Part II. and the Staff Manual respectively. Title pages will be prepared in manuscript.

WAR DIARY
or
~~INTELLIGENCE SUMMARY.~~

(Erase heading not required.)

Page 1 Volume 31

Army Form C. 2118.

Place	Date MAY 1918	Hour	Summary of Events and Information	Remarks and references to Appendices
			Section 1 / Section 2 / Section 3 / Section 4	
	1st		Coy. repairing trenches.	
	2nd		Dismounted portion of Coy paraded at 11 am and moved to ST LAWRENCE CAMP (28/G.11 c 5.2) arriving at 12.45 p.m.	
	3rd		Awaiting orders. Orders received at 11 p.m. for Company to assemble at Horse Lines by 8 a.m. on 4th.	
	4th		Dismounted portion of Coy paraded at 4 am and marched to Horse Lines at 27/L14 a 8.8. In the afternoon, whole of Coy moved to 27/E 20. b. 2.5.	
	5th		Company on drill etc. O.C. went over work on the STEENVOORDE LINE with G.O.C. 21st Infantry Bde.	
	6th		Dismtd portion of Coy paraded at 12 noon and marched to PAMSGAT (Sheet 27/Q1 c 05.10).	

D. D. & L., London, E.C. (A8004) Wt W1771/M2031 750,000 5/17 Sch. 52 Forms/C2118/14

202nd Field Co RE

Instructions regarding War Diaries and Intelligence Summaries are contained in F. S. Regs., Part II. and the Staff Manual respectively. Title pages will be prepared in manuscript.

Page 2.

WAR DIARY
or
~~INTELLIGENCE~~ SUMMARY.

(Erase heading not required.)

Volume 31

Army Form C. 2118.

Place	Date MAY 1918	Hour	Section 1	Section 2	Section 3	Section 4	Remarks	Remarks and references to Appendices
STEENVOORDE AREA.	7th		Setting out trenches, and camp fatigues	As No. 1.	As No. 1.	As No. 1	Mounted portion of Company moved to PAMSGAT arriving at 2.15 pm.	
-"-	8th				Drill etc Afternoon - Baths		Nos. 1. 2 and 4 Sections moved to billets at 27/P 12 c. Rest of morning camp fatigues, drill etc. afternoon - baths	
-"-	9th		Wiring near ABEELE	Drill etc	Drill etc	Wiring near ABEELE	Nos 1 2 & 4 Sections moved back to PAMSGAT in afternoon and evening	
-"- LEDERZEELE AREA	10th						Orders received to move. Company marched off at 9.0 am to LEDERZEELE Area (ABBEVILLE G12 a & b) and arrived at destination about 5-0 p.m. Capt C.C. LINDSAY. RE entrained St. Omar to reconnoitre new Area & to site rifle ranges etc. Lt J.B. FROST. RE joined Coy for duty from C.E. V Corps	
	11th						Orders received for Coy. to entrain at St. Omar at 9.0 p.m. Company with transport marched to St. Omar and entrained about 9.0 pm.	
EU.	12th						Detrained at Eu about 2-0 pm. Coy & transport marched to Hutments in BELGIAN ~~Cavalry~~ Artillery Camp, Eu.	

D. D. & L., London, E.C. (A8004) Wt W1771/M2031 750,000 5/17 Sch. 52 Forms/C2118/14

202nd FIELD Coy. R.E.

Instructions regarding War Diaries and Intelligence Summaries are contained in F. S. Regs., Part II. and the Staff Manual respectively. Title pages will be prepared in manuscript.

WAR DIARY
or
~~INTELLIGENCE SUMMARY.~~
(Erase heading not required.)

Page 3

Volume 31

Army Form C. 2118.

Place	1918 Date MAY	Hour	Section 1	Section 2	Section 3	Section 4	Remarks.	Remarks and references to Appendices
EU AREA	13th						Sections 1, 2, 3 & 4 – with 2 days rations moved for work on rifle ranges & Sanitary arrangements in Brigade Area. Sections located as follows:- Sect 1 :- near BETHENCOURT; Sect 2 :-; Sects 3 & 4 :- MILLE-BOSC. O.C. assumed duties of Acting C.R.E. & visited HQrs No 34 Santy. Sect re erection of latrines, water-supply etc. Capt. LINDSAY, R.E. made reconnaissance of new Area for report to Div¹ HQ.	
	14th		Erection of latrines etc. for American camps	Making rifle & M.G. ranges	Erection of latrines etc. and water supply.			
	15th		do	do	ditto.		HQrs & transport moved to Sheet ABBEVILLE 6 F 1.3. CRE. took over papers etc. from O.C.	
	16th						HQrs & transport moved to billets near Water Mill SW. BOUVAINCOURT. Sheet ABBEVILLE 6 F 82.33.	
	17th		do	do	ditto			
	18th		do	do	ditto.			

D. D. & L., London, E.C.
(A8004) Wt W1771/M2031 750,000 5/17 Sch. 52 Forms/C2118/14

202nd Field Coy R.E.

Instructions regarding War Diaries and Intelligence Summaries are contained in F. S. Regs., Part II. and the Staff Manual respectively. Title pages will be prepared in manuscript.

Page 4

WAR DIARY
or
~~INTELLIGENCE SUMMARY.~~
(Erase heading not required.)

VOLUME 31

Army Form C. 2118.

Place	1918 Date MAY	Hour	Summary of Events and Information					Remarks and references to Appendices
			Section 1	Section 2	Section 3	Section 4	Remarks	
Eu Area	19th		Erection of latrines etc for American Camps + surrounding villages	Making rifle & M.G. ranges	Erection of latrines and water supply		Capt. C.C. LINDSAY. R.E. thrown from his horse and admitted to Hospital with Contused Back. Sections only worked half-day	
	20th		ditto	ditto	ditto		O.C. proceeded to Eu, and took over work from C.R.E. who moved to LE THIL to keep in touch with 35th AMERICAN Div' Engrs. MAJOR CHIPPINDALL, RE therefore assumed duties of Acting C.R.E.	
	21st		ditto	ditto	ditto			
	22nd		Latrines and Ablution benches	ditto	Latrines, water supply + rifle + M.G. ranges.			
	23rd		ditto	ditto	ditto		Parties of 35th AMERICAN Div' Engrs instructed in making rafts and Control of Pontoons etc.	
	24th		ditto	ditto	ditto		Ditto	
	25th		ditto	ditto	ditto		Ditto	
	26th						Inspection parade. No work remainder of day.	
	~~27th~~		ditto	ditto	ditto		Thus far, difficulty in obtaining stores necessary for erection of Rifle & M.G ranges	

D. D. & L., London, E.C. (A8004) Wt W1771/M2031 750,000 5/17 Sch. 52 Forms/C2118/14

202nd Field Coy R.E.

Instructions regarding War Diaries and Intelligence Summaries are contained in F. S. Regs., Part II. and the Staff Manual respectively. Title pages will be prepared in manuscript.

Page 5

WAR DIARY
or
~~INTELLIGENCE SUMMARY.~~
(Erase heading not required.)

VOLUME 31

Army Form C. 2118.

Place	1918 Date MAY	Hour	Summary of Events and Information					Remarks and references to Appendices
			Section 1	Section 2	Section 3	Section 4	Remarks	
Eu Area	28th		Latrines, Ablution trenches etc.	Making Rifle & M.G. ranges	Latrines, Water Supply, Rifle and M. G. ranges.		II Lt. E.C. ALLERTON, R.E. and 3 N.C.O's (Reinforcements) joined Company.	
	29th		do	do	ditto			
	30th		do	do	ditto		One motor cycle & sidecar on loan from 30th M.T. Coy. (Frame No. 6068 - DOUGLAS)	
	31st		do	do	ditto			

[illegible]
Major R.E.
O/C 202nd Field Coy R.E.

D. D. & L., London, E.C.
(A8004) Wt W1771/M2031 750,000 5/17 Sch. 52 Forms/C2118/14

202 FIELD COY

1/JUN/18 — 30/JUNE/18

Vol 32

Secret

Vol 32

War Diary

of

202nd Field Coy R.E.

from

June 1st 1918

to

June 30th 1918.

Volume 32

202nd Field Coy RE

Instructions regarding War Diaries and Intelligence Summaries are contained in F. S. Regs., Part II. and the Staff Manual respectively. Title pages will be prepared in manuscript.

Page 1

WAR DIARY
or
~~INTELLIGENCE SUMMARY.~~
(Erase heading not required.)

VOLUME 32

Army Form C. 2118.

Place	Date 1918 MAY	Hour	Section 1	Section 2	Section 3	Section 4	Remarks	Remarks and references to Appendices
EU AREA	1		Latrines, Ablution benches etc	Making rifle & M.G. ranges.	~~Latan~~ Rifle & M.G. ranges	Latrines, Ablution benches etc	Capt. LINDSAY, R.E. rejoined Unit from Hospl.	
	2		do	do	do	do.	O/C made tour round rifle ranges.	
	3		do	do	do	do. Baths at Eu.	Lt. LANNON, R.E. (Asst. Adjt. 30th Divl RE) attached to 33rd AMERICAN DIVN to ascertain stores likely to be required in the near future.	
	4		do	do	do	do.		
	5		do	do	do	do.	" Lt. LANNON, R.E. rejoined from att. to 33rd Am. Divn. Motor cycle + sidecar returned to 30th M.T. Coy.	
	6		do	do.	do	do. Baths at LeLieu Dieu		
	7		do	do	do	do.		
	8		do	do	do	do.		
	9		-	-	-	-	Rifle + B.R. inspection, etc.	
	10		Latrines, Ablution benches etc. Baths GAMACHES	Making rifle & M.G. ranges	Rifle + MG ranges. Water Supply Sept Meules	Baths. Eu do LeLieu Dieu	Total of 500 latrine seats installed in Southern Area to date.	
	11		do	do	do	do		

D. D. & L., London, E.C.
(A8004) Wt W1771/M2031 750,000 5/17 Sch. 52 Forms/C2118/14

202nd Field Coy R.E.

Instructions regarding War Diaries and Intelligence Summaries are contained in F. S. Regs., Part II. and the Staff Manual respectively. Title pages will be prepared in manuscript.

WAR DIARY
or
~~INTELLIGENCE~~ ~~SUMMARY~~.
(Erase heading not required.)

Army Form C. 2118.

Page 2

VOLUME 32

Place	1918 Date May	Hour	Section 1.	Section 2.	Section 3.	Section 4.	Remarks	Remarks and references to Appendices
EU AREA.	12		Latrines, Ablution benches, Baths GAMACHES	Rifle & M.G. ranges	Rifle ranges. Water Supply SEPT MEULES	Eu Baths LE LIEU DIEU do		
	13		do	do	do	do.		
	14/15		do	do	do Water troughs for horses	do.		
	16		–	–	–	–	Rifle & B.R. inspection etc. C.R.E. rejd. Divn. MAJOR CHIPPINDALL relinquishes duties of A/C.R.E. & rejd. Coy. Hdqrs.	
	17		Latrines, Ablution benches, Baths GAMACHES	Rifle & M.G. ranges	Rifle Ranges, Water Supply, SEPT MEULES Horse troughing	Eu Baths LE LIEU DIEU Baths		
	18		do	do	do	do	Orders received to prepare to move on 20th. Detachments ordered to rejoin Coy Hdqrs.	
	19						Preparing to move. Detachments rejd. Coy Hdqrs.	
NOLETTES.	20						Coy. paraded 5-0 a.m. & marched to NOLETTES arriving about 2-30 p.m. LT. FROST R.E. & 8 O.R. left at BOUVAINCOURT to hand over to relieving Unit of 21st Divn.	
FONTAINE-SUR-MAYE	21						Orders received at 1-30 A.M. to move to FONTAINE-SUR-MAYE. Dismtd. details moved by lorry and transport by road.	

D. D. & L., London, E.C.
(A8004) Wt W1771/M2031 750,000 5/17 Sch. 52 Forms/C2118/14

202nd Field Coy RE

Instructions regarding War Diaries and Intelligence Summaries are contained in F. S. Regs., Part II. and the Staff Manual respectively. Title pages will be prepared in manuscript.

Page 3

WAR DIARY
or
~~INTELLIGENCE SUMMARY.~~
(Erase heading not required.)

Army Form C. 2118.

VOLUME 32

Place	Date 1918	Hour	Summary of Events and Information: Section 1	Section 2	Section 3	Section 4	Remarks	Remarks and references to Appendices
	June							
FONTAINE-SUR-MAYE	22nd		Drill	Drill	Drill	Drill		
	23rd		–	–	–	–	Rifle & B.R. inspection etc.	
	24th		Squad Drill &c Musketry Knotting & Lashing Gas Drill	Gas & Rifle Drill &c Knotting & Lashing Ext. Order ~~Drill~~ Physical Drill	Rifle Exercises Knotting & Lashing Gas Drill Physical Drill	As Sect 2	Lt. FROST RE & 8 O.R. rejoined Company	
	25th		Drill Weldon Trestle Gyn, Shears & Derricks	Drill Demolitions Extended Order	Drill Use of Spars & Tackle Field Geometry	As per Sect 2	Orders received to be prepared to move on 27th.	
	26		Gas & Rifle Drill Squad Drill.	Extended Order Knotting & Lashing	Extended Order Semaphore Sig.	Extended Order Knotting & Lashing	Orders received about 11·30 a.m. to move to FOREST-MONTIERS. Company marched off at 2-0 p.m. Major J.E. CHIPPINDALL granted leave in France. Capt. C.C. LINDSAY a/g O/C Company.	
FOREST-MONTIERS	27						Orders received to entrain RUE at 11-45 p.m. Coy marched off 7-0 p.m.	
GANSPETTE	28						Coy. detrained AUDRICQ and marched to GANSPETTE	
	29		Drill	Drill	Drill	Drill		
	30.						Rifle & B. R. inspection. Upon instructions of A.D.M.S. all men were taken from billets, & put into bivouacs — owing to the prevalence of Influenza.	

C.C. Lindsay Capt. RE
a/g O/C 202nd Field Coy RE

D. D. & L., London, E.C.
(A8004) Wt W1771/M2031 750,000 5/17 Sch. 52 Forms/C2118/14

202 FIELD COY

1/July/18 - 31/July/18

Vol. 33

W.O. 95/33

SECRET.

WAR DIARY

of

202ND FIELD COY ROYAL ENGINEERS

from. 1-~~8~~7-18 to 31-~~8~~7-18.

VOLUME No 33

202nd Field Coy RE

Instructions regarding War Diaries and Intelligence Summaries are contained in F. S. Regs., Part II. and the Staff Manual respectively. Title pages will be prepared in manuscript.

Page One

WAR DIARY
or
~~INTELLIGENCE SUMMARY.~~
(Erase heading not required.)

Army Form C. 2118.

VOLUME 33

Place	Date July 1918	Hour	Summary of Events and Information					Remarks and references to Appendices
			Section 1	Section 2	Section 3	Section 4	Remarks	
GANSPETTE	1		Rifle Range	Rifle Range	Rifle Range	Rifle Range	Coy. granted use of Second Army "A" range	
	2		Drill Musketry Demolitions Knotting & Lashings	Drill Musketry Weldon Trestle	Drill Musketry Demolitions. Knotting & Lashings	Drill Musketry Gyns & Shears		
	3		Ext. Order Drill Gas do Semaphore Sign. Weldon Trestle	Drill Gas Drill Semaphore Sign Knotting & Lashing Demolitions	Ext. Order Drill Gas do Semaphore Sign Gyns & Shears	Drill Gas Drill Semaphore Sign Knotting & Lashing Demolitions		
	4		Drill Musketry Demolitions Gyns & Shears	Drill Gas Drill Knotting & Lashing Derricks	Drill Musketry Demolitions Weldon Trestle	Drill Gas Drill Knotting & Lashing Derricks	Maj. J.E. CHIPPINDALL, R.E. rejd. from leave in France	
	5		Rifle Range	Rifle Range	Rifle Range	Rifle Range	Coy granted use of Second Army "A" range. 5 O.R. granted leave in France.	
	6		Drill Scheme	Drill Scheme	Drill Scheme	Drill Scheme	1 NCO to R.E. Training School ROUEN for Field Coy Course of 3 weeks duration	

D. D. & L., London, E.C.
(A8004) Wt W1771/M2031 750,000 5/17 Sch. 52 Forms/C2118/14

202nd Field Coy RE

Instructions regarding War Diaries and Intelligence Summaries are contained in F. S. Regs., Part II. and the Staff Manual respectively. Title pages will be prepared in manuscript.

Page Two

WAR DIARY
or
~~INTELLIGENCE SUMMARY.~~
(Erase heading not required.)

VOLUME 33.

Army Form C. 2118.

Place	Date 1918	Hour	Section 1	Section 2	Section 3	Section 4	Remarks	Remarks and references to Appendices
GANSPETTE	JULY 7						Company Sports in field. Packing up for move.	
	8						Company moved to KINDERBELCK.	
STEENVOORDE AREA	9th						Company moved at 9-45 AM and marched to NOORDPEENE. At 7-15 pm Coy. marched to bivouacs near STEENVOORDE map.ref. Q14 d 7.8. Arrived 12-0 midnight.	
	10th		Drill	Drill	Drill	Drill		
	11th		Drill	Drill	Drill	Drill	Preparing to move	
GODEWAERSVELDE Area.	12th						Coy. moved at 10-0 a.m. HQrs + transport marched to Q4d 99.05 + the 4 Sections to STEEN AKKER R2b. All officers made reconnaissance of line + scene of work. Lt. GARRARD leave in France to 20/7/18	
	13th		Digging trenches; making templates; Setting out; Wiring Reserve line.				Infantry working party of 90.	
	14th/15th		As for 13th also clearing fore ground between trenches + wire entanglement.				No Infy. Working party. MAJOR J.E. CHIPPINDALL RE to Hospl. (sick) Capt. C.C. LINDSAY RE assumed command of Coy.	
	16th		Digging trenches; clearing crops + revetting; High Wire entanglements; trench drainage.				120 Pioneers working party.	

D. D. & L., London, E.C.
(A8004) Wt W1771/M2031 750,000 5/17 Sch. 52 Forms/C2118/14

202nd Field Coy RE

Instructions regarding War Diaries and Intelligence Summaries are contained in F. S. Regs., Part II. and the Staff Manual respectively. Title pages will be prepared in manuscript.

Page Three

WAR DIARY
or
~~INTELLIGENCE SUMMARY.~~
(Erase heading not required.)

VOLUME 33

Army Form C. 2118.

Place	Date 1918	Hour	Summary of Events and Information	Remarks and references to Appendices
	JULY		Section 1 / Section 2 / Section 3 / Section 4 — Remarks	
GODEWAERSVELDE Area	17th		Digging trenches; clearing hedges & Crops. Wiring, drainage, & building blocks — O/C rejd Coy. from Hospital	
	18th		ditto — Coy. carried out practice of manning "Army Line" from 1·0 a.m. to 5.30 a.m.	
	19th		ditto.	
	20th		ditto also Bde. Hdrs. dugouts.	
	21st		Wiring front line, Cutting hedges & fixing notice boards Bde Hdrs. Dugouts & drainage.	
	22nd		ditto. — 2/Lieut. J.C. FISHER, R.E. granted leave in FRANCE 23/7/18 to 1/8/18. 2/Lt GARRARD rejd. from leave.	
	23rd		Wiring front line, Spider web wiring, fixing notice boards, excavating for Bde Hdrs, Salving material.	
	24th/25		Excavations for Bde Hdrs + revetting. Laying out new Reserve Bde Hdrs at R11 b 90.85. Fixing notice boards.	
	26th/27		Erecting Shelters. Excavating + revetting drain. Salving material	
	28th		ditto.	

D. D. & L., London, E.C.
(A8604) Wt W1771/M2031 750,000 5/17 Sch. 52 Forms/C2118/14

202nd Field Co RE

Instructions regarding War Diaries and Intelligence Summaries are contained in F. S. Regs., Part II. and the Staff Manual respectively. Title pages will be prepared in manuscript.

Page Four

WAR DIARY
or
INTELLIGENCE SUMMARY.
(Erase heading not required.)

Army Form C. 2118.

VOLUME 53

Place	Date 1918	Hour	Summary of Events and Information					Remarks and references to Appendices
			Section 1	Section 2	Section 3	Section 4	Remarks	
GODEWAERSVELDE AREA	JULY 29th		Erecting Shelters.	revetting & excavating	for drains	Salving materials	Lt. E.C. ALLERTON R.E. leave to U.K. 30/7/18 to 13/8/18	
	30th			ditto	Camouflaging.			
	31st			ditto.				

[signature] Major R.E.
OC 202nd Field Coy R.E.

D. D. & L., London, E.C.
(A8004) Wt W1771/M2031 750,000 5/17 Sch. 52 Forms/C2118/14

202 Field Coy

1/8/18 – 31/8/18

Vol 34

WR 34

SECRET

WAR DIARY

OF

202ND FIELD COY. R.E.

From:- 1st August 1918
To:- 31st August 1918

202nd Field Coy RE

Instructions regarding War Diaries and Intelligence Summaries are contained in F. S. Regs., Part II. and the Staff Manual respectively. Title pages will be prepared in manuscript.

WAR DIARY
or
INTELLIGENCE SUMMARY.

(Erase heading not required.)

Page 1. Volume 34.

Army Form C. 2118.

Place	Date 1918	Hour	Summary of Events and Information: Section 1	Section 2.	Section 3.	Section 4.	Remarks.	Remarks and references to Appendices
GODEWAERSVELDE ~~AREA~~ AND BOESCHEPE Area.	August. 1st		R. 16.b. 90.85. for Ad. Div. H.Q. - Interior of dugouts, drains and filling in	Making New Dugouts Fixing Exterior and making New Entrances, bead cover.	Erecting shelters for Bde H.Q. R. 2d. 5.9 and fitting same with gas curtains.	as No 1 and 2 Sections - also Salving of material	Ref. map sheet 1/10000 BERTHEN. 12 MINERS (attached) working on MINED DUGOUTS (from 6th S.W.B. Pioneers)	
	2nd		Ditto -		- Ditto -	- Ditto -	11 MINERS (attached) working on MINED DUGOUTS. 2/Lieut. J. C. Fisher RE. Joined Coy from leave in France.	
	3rd		Ditto -		Ditto.	Ditto.	17 Miners (attached) working on MINED DUGOUTS Work at R. 16b. 90.85 HANDED OVER TO C.R.E 35th Div.	
	4th		- Day	off work -	Day off.	Day off.	2 Off - 42 OR attended 59th Bde Special Service (Church) 1 Off 60 OR attended Army Church Service	
	5th		Paraded 6.30 AM at STEEN AKKER and marched to Coy REAR H.Q. Q4d 99.05 on Rem: of day settling down in camp Erecting Ckhouses, latrines and a 25 yd Rifle Range.		Continued work Bde H.Q. -	Paraded 6.30 AM at STEEN AKKER and marched to Q4d 99.05 Settling in Camp and General fatigues	Lieut J.B. Frost Granted leave to PARIS 5/8/18 - 12/8/18.	
	6th		Squad Drill Musketry Ex. Order drill	Squad drill Rifle Exercises Knots & Lashing Ex. Order Drill.	Working on Bde. H.Q.	Squad drill Ext. Order Drill, Musketry	2/Lieut. J.C. FISHER left for RE T.C. ROUEN.	
	7/8th		ditto	ditto	ditto	ditto		

D. D. & L., London, E.C.
(A8004) Wt W1771/M2031 750,000 5/17 Sch. 52 Forms/C2118/14

202nd Field Coy. R.E.

Instructions regarding War Diaries and Intelligence Summaries are contained in F. S. Regs., Part II. and the Staff Manual respectively. Title Pages will be prepared in manuscript.

Page Two

WAR DIARY
or
~~INTELLIGENCE SUMMARY~~
(Erase heading not required.)

Volume 34.

Army Form C. 2118.

Place	Date	Hour	Summary of Events and Information					Remarks and references to Appendices
			SECTION 1	SECTION 2	SECTION 3	SECTION 4.	REMARKS:-	
WESTOUTRE AND LOCRE AREA	1918 AUGUST 9th						All Sections moved up to shelters near WESTOUTRE to commence work in [illegible] Division takes over line from ~~SHPER~~ SCHERPENBERG to MOUNT NOIR	from 35th Div.
	10/11th		Reconnoitring work handed over by 203rd Fld Co. R.E.				Work in LOCRE and HOSPICE Sectors taken over from 203rd Field Co. R.E. 35th Division	
	12th		Making Infantry Coy H Qrs in left and right sub Sectors Camouflaging trench on MOUNT ROUGE				No 4 Section attached to 90th Bde in LOCRE SECTOR. No 1 Section attd to 21st Bde in HOSPICE SECTOR	
	13th		Do.	Working on their own Billets	Working on their own Billets	Working for 90th Brigade		
	14th		Infantry Coy H.Qrs for 21st Brigade	Ditto	Ditto	on Infy Coy H.Qrs Ditto	II LIEUT. BURFORD leave to U.K. 14-8-1918 to 28-8-1918.	
	15th		Do.	Ditto.	M.G. Dugouts and Shelters	Ditto.	II LIEUT. E.C. ALLERTON Afd from leave in U.K.	
	16th		Do	Ditto.	Ditto.	Ditto.		
	17th		Do.	Ditto	Ditto	Ditto.		
	18th		Do.	Ditto	Ditto	Ditto	MAJ. J.E. CHIPPINDALL R.E. to hospital (Sick) CAPTAIN C.C. LINDSAY R.E. assumed command of Coy.	
	19th		Do.	Ditto.	Ditto	Ditto.		
	20th		Do.	Ditto	Ditto	Ditto.		
	21st		Took part in local operations under II LIEUT E.C. ALLERTON	Took part in local operations Six men attd to Infantry	Ditto	Ditto		

2449 Wt. W14957/M90 750,000 1/16 J.B.C. & A. Forms/C.2118/12.

202nd Field Coy. R.E.

Instructions regarding War Diaries and Intelligence Summaries are contained in F. S. Regs., Part II. and the Staff Manual respectively. Title pages will be prepared in manuscript.

WAR DIARY
or
~~INTELLIGENCE SUMMARY.~~
(Erase heading not required.)

Page Three — Volume 34

Army Form C. 2118.

Place	Date 1918	Hour	Summary of Events and Information: SECTION 1	SECTION 2	SECTION 3	SECTION 4	REMARKS	Remarks and references to Appendices
WESTOUTRE and LOCRE Area.	August 21st (CONTD)		Attached to 21st Bde for Wiring purposes. Assembled 10.30 pm 20th inst. in Shell Holes behind Front line near LOCRE HOSPICE. Between 10.30 pm and Zero hour (2:05 am) they carried wiring material up to M 29 b 20.85 (Sheet 27) About 3 am commenced to wire from M. 29 B 2.2 to approx. M 29 B 5.7 (300 yds) Party withdrew at 4.20 am on completion of job. Casualties NIL.	with Bangalore Torpedoes. The Section was attached to 90th Brigade for making tracks, and was divided into four parties of two men each, one party reporting to each Company of Assaulting Infantry. Each Party carried one Bangalore Torpedo but none of these were used as no uncut wire was encountered. Two of these men were wounded by M.G. Fire. Remainder of Section 2 was divided into two parties - one party under 2LIEUT C.P. GARRARD, RE the other under Sergt CRYSTAL D.C.M. - both parties	See Page Two	See Page Two	—	

D. D & L., London, E.C.
(A8:04) Wt W:771/M2031 750,000 5/17 Sch. 52 Forms/C2118/14

202ND Field Coy R.E.

Instructions regarding War Diaries and Intelligence Summaries are contained in F. S. Regs., Part II. and the Staff Manual respectively. Title pages will be prepared in manuscript.

WAR DIARY
or
INTELLIGENCE SUMMARY.
(Erase heading not required.)

Page Four — Volume 34

Army Form C. 2118.

Place	Date	Hour	Summary of Events and Information					Remarks and references to Appendices
			No 1 SECTION	No 2 SECTION	No 3 SECTION	No 4 SECTION	REMARKS	
WESTOUTRE and LOCRE AREA	1918 August 21st (Continued)		See Pages 2 and 3	were employed on Tracks. Party under 2nd LIEUT GARRARD, R.E. encountered 7 men of the enemy lying in a Shell Hole - all these were taken Prisoners and handed over to the Infantry. This was largely due to the coolness of CORP. S.R. SLOUGH.	See Page 2.	See Page 2		
	22nd		Section under 2nd Lieut E C ALLERTON, R.E. endeavoured to erect wire defences in area of operations on 21st near LOCRE HOSPICE but were prevented by enemy Barrage.	Standing by.	Standing by	Standing by	2/LIEUT E C ALLERTON R.E. wounded	
	23rd		Started work on A.D.S. near CANADA CORNER and M.G. DUGOUT BLUE LINE	~~Standing~~ Started work on BLUE LINE	Started work on Adv Bde H Qrs at REDAN WOOD	Handing over all work in 90th Bde Area to 201 Field Coy R.E.	~~2/LIEUT E C ALLERTON R.E. wounded~~	
	24th		Ditto	Ditto	Ditto	Working for 21st Bde in HOSPICE SECTOR on [illegible] Coy H.Q.	BLUE LINE is 2nd Line of [illegible] CANADA CORNER to MONT ROUGE. 100 Infantry [illegible] and 2 [illegible]	

A5834 Wt. W4973/M687 750,000 8/16 D. D. & L. Ltd. Forms/C.2118/13.

202nd Field Coy R.E.

Instructions regarding War Diaries and Intelligence Summaries are contained in F. S. Regs., Part II. and the Staff Manual respectively. Title pages will be prepared in manuscript.

WAR DIARY

or

~~INTELLIGENCE SUMMARY.~~

(Erase heading not required.)

Page Five — Volume 34

Army Form C. 2118.

Hour, Date, Place	Summary of Events and Information				Remarks and references to Appendices
	No 1 SECTION	No 2 SECTION	No 3 SECTION	No 4 SECTION	
Aug. 25th 1918 {Westoutre and Locre Area.	Worked on A.D.S. near CANADA CORNER and M.G. DUGOUT BLUE LINE	Worked on BLUE LINE	Worked on Advanced Brigade H Qrs. at REDAN WOOD	Worked for 21st Bde. in HOSPICE SECTOR on tunnelled Coy. H Qrs.	
" 26th "	Ditto	Ditto	Ditto	Ditto	
" 27th "	Ditto	Ditto	Ditto	Ditto	
" 28th "	Ditto	Ditto	Ditto	Ditto	
" 29th "	Ditto	Ditto	Ditto	Ditto	
" 30th "	Ditto	Ditto	Ditto	Ditto	2/LIEUT D. McCALLUM. R.E left for 2nd Army School of Instruction.
" 31st "	Repairing LOCRE-DRANOUTRE NEUVE EGLISE ROAD	Making Adv. Bde H Qrs. at BEAVER HALL on MOUNT KEMMEL.	Same as No 1	Same as No 1 and 3	2/LT. J.A.H. BURFORD rejd from leave in UK on 30/8/18. Enemy retired from MOUNT KEMMEL to NEUVE EGLISE–LINDENHOCK RIDGE on 31st

[illegible signature]
Captain R.E.
A/O.C. 202nd Field Coy R.E.

(73989) W4141—463. 400,000. 9/14. H.&J.Ltd. Forms/C. 2118/10.

202 FIELD COY

1/SEP/18 — 30/SEP/18

VOL 35

202nd Field Coy. R.E.

Instructions regarding War Diaries and Intelligence Summaries are contained in F. S. Regs., Part II. and the Staff Manual respectively. Title pages will be prepared in manuscript.

Page 1.

WAR DIARY
or
INTELLIGENCE SUMMARY.
(Erase heading not required.)

Volume 35.

202 Fd Coy RE

Army Form C. 2118.

Vol 35

Place	Date 1918	Hour	Summary of Events and Information					Remarks and references to Appendices
			Section 1.	Section 2	Section 3	Section 4	Remarks	
WESTOUTRE AREA.	Sept 1st		Standing by in Reserve	Working extra accom. for Bde H.Q. at BEAVER HALL KEMMEL.	Demolishing concrete obstacles on DRANOUTRE – DAYLIGHT CORNER Rd	Completed draining DRANOUTRE – DAYLIGHT Corner Rd [illegible]		
	2nd		Working on DRANOUTRE DAYLIGHT CORNER Rd & making it passable for Heavy Artillery.	Working on Bde H.Q. BEAVER HALL	As No 1	Standing by		
	3rd		Standing by. All bathed in afternoon	Working on Bde H.Q. BEAVER HALL	As No 1	As No [illegible]	Transport Lines [illegible]	
	4th		Putting up baths & accomodation for the 1/6 CHESHIRES at LOCRE CHATEAU	All [illegible] baths and held in reserve remainder of day	Working on accom. for R.I.R. & 23rd LONDON Regt	Putting [illegible] and [illegible] Transport lines [illegible]	2/Lieut. [illegible] GARRARD awarded the M.C. No 13[illegible] Corporal SLOUGH S.R. awarded the D.C.M.	
	5th		Baths & accom at LOCRE CHATEAU	As No 1	Accom for R.I.R. & 2/23rd LONDON Regt	Transport Lines		
	6th		Baths & accom at LOCRE CHATEAU	As No 1	Accom for R.I.R. & 2/23rd LONDON Regt	Transport Lines		
	7th		Transport Lines	Baths & accom at LOCRE CHATEAU	Accom for R.I.R. & 2/23rd LONDON Regt	As 1st		
KEMMEL AREA	8th		All four sections moved forward to N.26.c.5.0.				Capt LINDSAY [illegible] with C.R.E.	[illegible]
	9th		All sections employed making billets, salving materials, & settling					

(A9175) Wt W2358/P360 600,000 12/17 D. D. & L. Sch. 52a. Forms/C2118/15.

202nd Field Coy R.E.

Instructions regarding War Diaries and Intelligence Summaries are contained in F. S. Regs., Part II, and the Staff Manual respectively. Title pages will be prepared in manuscript.

Page 2

Army Form C. 2118.

WAR DIARY or INTELLIGENCE SUMMARY.

(Erase heading not required.)

VOLUME 35

Place	Date	Hour	Summary of Events and Information: Section 1	Section 2	Section 3	Section 4	Remarks	Remarks and references to Appendices
KEMMEL AREA	1916. SEPT 10th		All sections employed on making billets				Heavy enemy shelling [illegible] billet area. [illegible]	
	11th		All sections moved to new billets [illegible] at N 31 [illegible]				Major H. I. LEE [illegible] took over command.	
	12th		All sections employed making new billets and [illegible] around billets				Lieut J. B. [illegible] took over No 3 Section	
	13th		All sections employed as on 12th				[illegible]	
	14th		Making billets & improvements [illegible]	[illegible] billets [illegible]	Work on New Bde H.Q. at TYRO FARM M36 a [illegible] Working party of 50 Inf	Making billets & [illegible]		
	15th.		Removing [illegible] from [illegible] at M.31 a 1.5. & work on billets	Working on billets & camp improvements	Work on Bde H.Q. M36a 9.2 [illegible] the work Working party of 50 Inf	2 Billets [illegible] Erecting [illegible]		
	16th		Working on [illegible] dugouts [illegible] & billets	Working on billets	Bde H.Q. at M36 a 9.2 [illegible] of 50 Inf	[illegible] site of building [illegible] ADS at M.29 a 6.6.		
	17th		Erecting framework preparatory to fixing camouflage on DRANOUTRE DAYLIGHT Corner Rd	Working on billets	Bde HQ M.36a 9.2 W.P. of 25 Inf	ADS M.29 a 6.6 building and started clearing sites for shelters		
	18th		Road screening T.1.b.2.9 collecting & preparing for erection of camouflage Supervising training for RFA (DONEGAL Fm) N.32.d.5.4	Working on billets N.31 a 9.3	Bde H.Q. 36 a 9.2 [illegible] of 25	[illegible] YMCA [illegible] M.34 [illegible] N.32 a 6.6 [illegible] Accom. 30 men (93rd Fld Amb) Wkg Pty of 24 RAMC		

(A9175) Wt W2358/P360 600,000 12/17 D. D. & L. Sch. 52a. Forms/C2118/15.

202nd Field Coy RE.

Instructions regarding War Diaries and Intelligence Summaries are contained in F. S. Regs., Part II. and the Staff Manual respectively. Title pages will be prepared in manuscript.

Page 3.

WAR DIARY
or
INTELLIGENCE SUMMARY.
(Erase heading not required.)

Volume 35

Army Form C. 2118.

Place	Date 1918	Hour	Summary of Events and Information: Section 1	Section 2	Section 3	Section 4	Remarks	Remarks and references to Appendices
KEMMEL AREA	Sept. 19th		T.1.b.2.95. erecting camouflage 60x ... also salving material ...	Work on billets	Bde H.Q. at M.36a.9.2 W.P. of 45	ADS. M.35 ... repairs of ADS and making shelter for 30 men ... at M.34 c.3.3 W.P. of 22 RAMC	... Taking over work from 23rd ... R.E.	
			M.32a.5.4 DONEGAL Fm. Supt. RE mining					
	20th		Taking over & started work on New ADS at N.31.d.2.1 (Mining commenced ...)	Work in Billets	New Bde H.Q. at M.36a ... W.P. 45	Shelters for 30 men of Fld Amb at ADS / M.29.a.66 and repg Church Army hut M.34.c.3.8. W.P. of 23 RAMC	... R.E. Leave to UK 24/9/18 ...	
	21st		Mined dugout for ADS N.31.d.2.1 / 11 miners & W.P. of 39 Inf	Salving material & work on Bay Billets	New Bde. H.Q. at M.36a.9.2. W.P. of 39 Inf	Accom for Fld Amb & Church Army hut also repairing ADS building W.P. of 15 RAMC		
	22		Mined dugout for ADS at N.31.d.2.1 / 11 Miners & 40 RAMC W.P.	Screening NEUVE EGLISE DRANOUTRE Rd. 180x / BOSCHE screening recovered & made up	New Bde H.Q. M.36a.9.2 W.P. 42 Inf	Shelters for 98th Fld Ambce / W.P. of 23 RAMC		
	23rd		Mined dugout for ADS. N.31.d.2.1 / 11 Miners 40 RAMC / All RAMC withdrawn from work for 72 hrs	Erected 60x screening at corner T.18.a.10.25. / Carried timber & Camp shelter from NEUVE EGLISE to EMU Fm. Erected shelter at EMU Fm. (Day) W.P. of 12	Bde H.Q. at M.36a.9.2 No W.P.	Shelter for 98th Fld Ambce		
	24th		Mined dugout for ADS (N.31.d.2.1) / 1 RAMC with ...	EMU Fm. erecting shelters	Bde H.Q. M.36a.9.2 (completed) W.P. 25	Shelter for 98th Fld Ambce		

(A9175) Wt W2358/P369 600,000 12/17 D. D. & L. Sch. 52a. Forms/C2118/15

202nd Field Coy RE

Instructions regarding War Diaries and Intelligence Summaries are contained in F. S. Regs., Part II. and the Staff Manual respectively. Title pages will be prepared in manuscript.

Page 4

WAR DIARY
or
INTELLIGENCE SUMMARY.
(*Erase heading not required.*)

Volume 35.

Army Form C. 2118.

Place	Date	Hour	Summary of Events and Information	Remarks and references to Appendices
	1918 Sept		Section 1. / Section 2 / Section 3. / Section 4. / Remarks	
KEMMEL AREA	25th		Company relieved by 200th Field Company RE. [Remarks: Transport lines moved to same location.]	
			Moved to new billets at M 9 d 0 7 for work in Back Area	
			No 1 Section took over work from 201st Fld Coy at MONT NOIR	
			Remainder of Company took over work on billets etc at WESTOUTRE from 201st Fld Co RE	
WESTOUTRE AREA	26th		Section 1: MONT NOIR CHATEAU const. CRE'S Mess & improving billets at WESTOUTRE / 10. W.P. — Section 2: Improvements to billets at WESTOUTRE & HORSE LINES — Section 3: Billets in WESTOUTRE — Section 4: Making baths at WESTOUTRE. W.P. 20. Fixing [illegible] at M 9 d 0 7. W.P. 19.	
"	27th		Section 1: MONT NOIR CHATEAU const. CRE'S Mess & improving billets at WESTOUTRE — Section 2: Improving billets at Horse Lines WESTOUTRE — Section 3: Billets in WESTOUTRE — Section 4: Making baths at WESTOUTRE	
KEMMEL AREA	28.		Whole of dismounted portion of Company moved to [illegible] billets at N 31 a 0 8. Dressing [illegible] WESTOUTRE W.P. 22	
			Whole of dismounted portion employed in [illegible]	
	29		Whole company employed on road [illegible] from TRUSSTRAAT CABARET via BELL Fm to MIDDLE Fm. Road made [illegible] for [illegible] Transport as far as O 32 a 2 4	
			Reconnaissance [illegible] No 3 [illegible] No 1 [illegible] Roads. No 2 [illegible] CABARET [illegible] MESSINES [illegible]	
			Y Road [illegible] La PLUS DOUVE Fm, GABION Fm	
			Snipers House, MESSINES Rd at [illegible]	
	30th.		No 1 & 2 [illegible] No 3 [illegible]	
			Evening shelling at [illegible]	
			ARMOUR Fm (N 33 d 4 [illegible]) No 2 [illegible] Clearing roads from N 35 a 3 8 to O 31 [illegible] YPRES [illegible]	

(A9175) Wt W2358/P360 600,000 12/17 D. D. & L. Sch. 52a. Forms/C2118/15.

[illegible] Capt RE
O.C. 202 Field Co R.E.

Vol 36

WAR DIARY.

202nd FIELD COMPANY. ROYAL ENGINEERS.

FROM 1st OCTOBER to 31st OCTOBER.
1918.

VOLUME 36.

202nd Field Coy R.E.

Instructions regarding War Diaries and Intelligence Summaries are contained in F. S. Regs., Part II. and the Staff Manual respectively. Title pages will be prepared in manuscript.

WAR DIARY
or
INTELLIGENCE SUMMARY.
(Erase heading not required.)

Page 1 Volume 36.

Army Form C. 2118.

Place 1918	Date	Hour	Summary of Events and Information					Remarks and references to Appendices
			Section 1	Section 2	Section 3	Section 4	Remarks	
October	1st		Whole of dismounted [illegible]	[illegible]	[illegible]	[illegible] at O.23 [illegible]		
			Nos 1 & 3 sections moving in the forenoon	[illegible]	[illegible]	Nos 2 & 4 at [illegible]		
	2nd		Making billets at O.17.d 3.6.	Clearing and repairing roads [illegible]	[illegible]	from O.24 [illegible]	[illegible] proceeded on leave [illegible]	
				to O.18.a [illegible]				
	3rd		do.	Clearing road & digging drains [illegible]	[illegible]	O.24 [illegible]		
				to O.18.d.9.5				
	4th		Completing billets at O.17.c 3.6.	[illegible]	[illegible]	[illegible]		
	5th		Whole of Company [illegible]	[illegible]	[illegible]	O.13 [illegible] 35	[illegible]	
			[illegible] 1 & 2 [illegible] 6th [illegible] Pioneers	[illegible]	[illegible]	[illegible]	[illegible]	
			[illegible] 50 yds and repaired [illegible]	[illegible]	[illegible]			
	6th		Working on PLANK Rd O.13.d [illegible] 35 (No Pioneers working)		[illegible] Road. [illegible]	[illegible] Nos 1 & 2 [illegible] from 7.00 hrs to 1.30 [illegible] HOUTHEM Road	[illegible] 2nd Army School	
	7th		Plank Road (O.13.d [illegible] 35) 50 yds planking laid. 400 yds ditching completed. 40 Pioneers carrying & assisting		[illegible] on HOUTHEM Road. Keeping road in good state [illegible]		[illegible] FISHER [illegible] from leave in U.K.	

(A9175) Wt W2358/P360 600,000 12/17 D. D. & L. Sch. 52a. Forms/C2118/15.

202nd Field Coy. R.E.

Instructions regarding War Diaries and Intelligence Summaries are contained in F. S. Regs., Part II. and the Staff Manual respectively. Title pages will be prepared in manuscript.

Page 2

WAR DIARY
or
INTELLIGENCE SUMMARY.
(Erase heading not required.)

Volume 36

Army Form C. 2118.

Place	Date	Hour	Section 1	Section 2	Section 3	Section 4	Remarks	Remarks and references to Appendices
1918. October	8th		PLANK ROAD. Total of [illegible] yds planked & [illegible] completed. Carrying existing camouflage [illegible]. [illegible] 140 Pioneers		Erecting camouflage screen [illegible]	SOUTHERN Road [illegible] keeping in good repair		
	9th		[illegible] yds planked. Working party [illegible] Pioneers		Erecting camouflage [illegible] SOUTHERN Road	Repairing		
	10th		All sections working on New Plank Road. Two shifts. Nos 1 & 2 Secs 06.00 till 12.00. Nos 3 & 4 12.00 to 18.00. 264 yards planked, 90 formations made. Half Company of Pioneers working on each shift.				O.C. reconnoitred roads & tracks in the forward area	
	11th		All sections working on New Plank Road in two shifts as on the 10th. Sections shelled off the job at 16.00 and 19.00 hours. Half company of Pioneers to each shift. Total planked 370 yards. Formations 100 yds.				[illegible] & [illegible] & C.R.E. [illegible] for [illegible]	

(A9175) Wt W2358/P360 600,000 12/17. D. D. & L. Sch. 52a. Forms/C2118/15.

202nd Field Coy. R.E.

Instructions regarding War Diaries and Intelligence Summaries are contained in F. S. Regs., Part II, and the Staff Manual respectively. Title pages will be prepared in manuscript.

Page 3

WAR DIARY
or
INTELLIGENCE SUMMARY.
(Erase heading not required.)

Volume 36

Army Form C. 2118.

Place	Date	Hour	Summary of Events and Information	Remarks and references to Appendices
October	1918		Section 1 / Section 2 / Section 3 / Section 4 / Remarks	
	12th		All sections working on Plank Road [illegible]	
			Total planked 48½ yds [illegible] 100 yds	
			Half Company of [illegible] [illegible] [illegible] at intervals after [illegible] hours	
	13th		Sects 1 & 2 on New Plank Rd. No 3 & 4 [illegible] by [illegible] [illegible] Fisher, 2nd Lt McCallum and [illegible]	
			from 0300 hrs till 1200 hrs [illegible] [illegible] 3 O.R. [illegible] [illegible]	
			[illegible]	
	14th		All sections [illegible] in Battle [illegible] [illegible] with [illegible] [illegible] 3rd [illegible]	
			Nos 1, 3 & 4 [illegible] [illegible] [illegible] [illegible] [illegible]	
			No 1. BICKSTRAAT REDOUBT under 2/Lt [illegible] RE	
			" 3. WHITE [illegible] POST " 2/Lt McCallum RE	
			" 4. [illegible] 2/Lt Fisher RE	
			No 2 Section [illegible] [illegible] [illegible]	
			At 04.45 hrs [illegible] [illegible] 2nd [illegible] [illegible] (R [illegible])	
			At 06.15 No 2 Sect received orders from O.C. [illegible] [illegible] and reported	
			at Reserve Bde HQ (Schoonveld Farm) (P 22 c [illegible])	

(A9175) Wt W2358/P360 600,000 12/17 D. D. & L. Sch. 52a. Forms/C2118/15.

202nd Field Coy, RE

Instructions regarding War Diaries and Intelligence Summaries are contained in F. S. Regs., Part II. and the Staff Manual respectively. Title pages will be prepared in manuscript.

WAR DIARY
or
INTELLIGENCE SUMMARY.
(Erase heading not required.)

Page 4 Volume 33

Army Form C. 2118.

Place	Date	Hour	Summary of Events and Information	Remarks and references to Appendices
October	1918		Section 1 / Section 2 / Section 3 / Section 4 / Remarks	
	14th	(cont)	No. 2 Section stood to at [illegible] H.Q. and were withdrawn at 06.00 hrs	
			on the 15th. No. 1 Sect. returned to H.Q. at 13.30 hrs.	
			" 3 " " at 12.20 hrs.	
			" 4 " " at 14.10 hrs.	
	15th.		No. 2 Section Standing by in Billets. Nos. 3 & 4 started work on Plank Rd at	
			06.00 hrs. No. 3 sect. sent to reconnoitre & repair bridges over — Casualties	
			the Canal between WERVICQ & COMINES. No. 3 Sect. relieved — Major K. J. LEE (slight scalp wound	
			by No. 1 sect. who placed two foot bridges over the river LYS 1 on — remained at duty)	
			each side of WERVICQ. 5 O.R. wounded — Spr. BROOKES S.E., KERSHAW F., TAYLOR A. (since died of wounds), LEADBITTER M., TURNER H.	
			No. 4 Section worked on Plank Road until 12.00 hrs.	
			No. 1 Section returned to billets at 07.30 on the 16th & also — all evacuated	
			part of No. 3 Section.	
	16th		Whole of Company standing by awaiting orders. — Lt. C. F. GARRARD proceeded on leave to U.K.	

(A9175) Wt W2358/P360 600,000 12/17 D. D. & L. Sch. 52a. Forms/C2118/15.

202nd Field Coy RE

Instructions regarding War Diaries and Intelligence Summaries are contained in F. S. Regs., Part II, and the Staff Manual respectively. Title pages will be prepared in manuscript.

Page 5

WAR DIARY
or
INTELLIGENCE SUMMARY.
(Erase heading not required.)

Volume 36

Army Form C. 2118.

Place	Date	Hour	Summary of Events and Information	Remarks and references to Appendices
October	1918		Section 1 — Section 2 — Section 3 — Section 4 — Remarks	
	17th		Whole of Company moved to new location at P.12 c.4.1.	
			Section 2 & 4 left on Trestle wagons to construct a bridge	
			across the river LYS near HALLUIN. Work could not be proceeded with until	
			17.00 hrs owing to the enemy holding the opposite bank of the river. At 17.00 hrs	
			the enemy cleared, and a Weldon trestle bridge (for Infantry [illegible]) was	
			constructed. Finished at 24.00 hrs.	
			Nos 1 & 3 sections moved to P.12 c.4.1 and awaited	
			orders. Nos 2 & 4 sections stayed in [illegible] at Q.21 central	
			(Near BOUSBECQUE)	
	18th		Nos 1 & 3 sections joined Nos 2 & 4 at Q.27 central [illegible] at 06.00 hrs	
			arriving at Q.27 central at 08.10 hrs. Nos 2 & 4 sect [illegible]	
			at 12 [illegible] and worked on bridge.	
			[illegible] moved to Q.30 a.3.3. along with Nos 1 & 3 sect.	
			Nos 2 & 4 joined at Q.30 a.3.3. Transport lines	
			moved to R.30 a.8.8	

(A9175) Wt W2358/P360 600,000 12/17 D. D. & L. Sch. 52a. Forms/C2118/15.

202nd Field Coy R.E.

Instructions regarding War Diaries and Intelligence Summaries are contained in F. S. Regs., Part II, and the Staff Manual respectively. Title pages will be prepared in manuscript.

Page 6.

WAR DIARY
or
INTELLIGENCE SUMMARY.
(*Erase heading not required.*)

Volume 36.

Army Form C. 2118.

Place	Date	Hour	Summary of Events and Information					Remarks and references to Appendices
October	1918		Section 1.	Section 2	Section 3.	Section 4	Remarks	
	19th		Inspection of whole Company including [illegible]					
			Bridging [illegible]	Bridging [illegible]	As No 1 sect	As No 2 sect		
			08 00 till 12 30	12 30 till 13 00				
	20th		06 30 till 12 30	As No 1.	12 30 till 13 30	As No 3.	Whole Coy working on bridge [illegible]	
	21st		18 30 " 00 30 (21st) 06 30 " 12 30		00 30 " 06 30		LYS [illegible] Heavy Pontoon Bridge)	
			Work was continuous until bridge was completed				[illegible]	
							2/Lt FROST [illegible] for leave.	
	22nd		Whole Coy with Transport moved to N 28 c 3 7					
	23rd		Whole Coy standing by awaiting orders					
	24th		Three sections (Nos 1, 3 & 4) moved to RUDDERVOORDE (T 11 d 5 1)					
			One section (No 2) moved to COYGHEM (U 19 c) [illegible] awaiting orders)					
	25th		Whole Company standing to awaiting orders					
	26th		Nos 1, 3 & 4 employed at COYGHEM [illegible] the cutting & preparing timber					
			and other material for approaches of Pontoon Bridge					
			No 2 Standing to awaiting orders.					

202nd Field Coy R.E.

Instructions regarding War Diaries and Intelligence Summaries are contained in F. S. Regs., Part II. and the Staff Manual respectively. Title pages will be prepared in manuscript.

Page 7

WAR DIARY
or
INTELLIGENCE SUMMARY.
(Erase heading not required.)

Volume 38

Army Form C. 2118.

Place	Date	Hour	Summary of Events and Information					Remarks and references to Appendices
	October 1918		Section 1.	Section 2	Section 3	Section 4	Remarks	
	27th		Employed at COYGHEM cutting timbers & preparing material for Pontoon bridge	Building bridge across Canal at Lock No 5. 1 Off & 12 O.R. (Pioneers) assisting	Employed collecting [illegible] at COURTRAI [illegible] same to COYGHEM	As No 1 section		
	28th		As on 27th	Awaiting orders except for 1 NCO & 2 sappers at ST GENOIS inspecting rafts etc. 1 Off & 11 Spr on bridge at Lock No 5	As on 27th	As on 27th	Nos 1, 3 & 4 Sect moved to [illegible] otherwise as worked as on 27th	T.17.d.1.1.
	29th		As on 27th	7 men making rafts. 1 N.C.O & 2 men taking rafts up to 6th CHESHIRES. 1 N.C.O. & 3 spr working on bridge at Lock No 5	As on 27th	As on 27th		

(A9175) Wt W2358/P360 600,000 12/17 D. D. & L. Sch. 52a. Forms/C2118/15.

202nd Field Coy R.E.

Instructions regarding War Diaries and Intelligence Summaries are contained in F. S. Regs., Part II. and the Staff Manual respectively. Title pages will be prepared in manuscript.

Page 8

WAR DIARY
or
INTELLIGENCE SUMMARY.
(Erase heading not required.)

Volume 36

Army Form C. 2118.

Place	Date	Hour	Summary of Events and Information					Remarks and references to Appendices
October	1918.		Section 1.	Section 2	Section 3	Section 4	Remarks	
	29/30th		"Standing to"	Preparing taking up raft. Working on bridge at Chateau. Also putting handrail on bridge at Lock No 5.	"Standing to"	"Standing to"		
	30/31st		Moving to new billets	Working on bridge as on 29/30th. Constructing rafts for Infantry	As No 1	As No 1	All sections moved during the day to U.3.a.7.3.	[illegible]

[illegible] Capt
O.C. 202ND FIELD CO. R.E.
(COUNTY PALATINE) R.E.

Vol 37

SECRET

WAR DIARY of

202nd Field Co. R.E.

from 1st November

to 30th November 1918

VOLUME 37

202nd Field Co. R.E.

Instructions regarding War Diaries and Intelligence Summaries are contained in F. S. Regs., Part II. and the Staff Manual respectively. Title pages will be prepared in manuscript.

WAR DIARY
or
INTELLIGENCE SUMMARY.
(Erase heading not required.)

Page 1 Volume 34

Army Form C. 2118.

Place	Date	Hour	Summary of Events and Information					Remarks and references to Appendices
			Section 1	Section 2	Section 3	Section 4	Remarks	
October	1st		Standing to	Putting Light bridge over stream	Section Cyclists reconnoitring roads	Same as No 3.		
	2nd		Standing to	Standing to	Making Barrel rafts at Billets	Standing to		
	3rd		Standing to	Making Petrol tin rafts at Billets	Ditto.	Standing to		
	4th		½ Section making rafts at River Lys. Rem. of Sect. loading & sorting material at COYGHEM	Making Petrol tin rafts at Billets	Standing to	Making rafts at Canal	2/Lieut C. G. Garrard RE rejoined Coy from leave	
	5th		Making rafts at River	Standing to	Standing to	Standing to		
	6th		Whole Coy moved to New location at O.18 a.2.2 Transport joins dismounted portion of Coy					
	7th		Making Cookhouses and Drying Sheds	Working at KNOKKE DUMP	Making cookhouses and Drying shed	Standing by in Billets	13722 Corp Reece E. Awarded the D.C.M. for gallantry in the field on 17-10-18. Lieut J. B. Frost RE rejoined Coy from Hospital	

(A9175) Wt W2358/P360 600,000 12/17 D. D. & L. Sch. 52a. Forms/C2118/15.

202nd Field Co R.E.

Instructions regarding War Diaries and Intelligence Summaries are contained in F. S. Regs., Part II. and the Staff Manual respectively. Title pages will be prepared in manuscript.

Page 2

WAR DIARY
or
INTELLIGENCE SUMMARY.
(Erase heading not required.)

Volume 37

Army Form C. 2118.

Place	Date	Hour	Summary of Events and Information					Remarks and references to Appendices
			Section 1	Section 2	Section 3	Section 4.	Remarks	
October.	8th		Making Cookhouses and Drying shed	Preparing Girders for Footbridge	Working at KNOKKE DUMP	Making Piers for bridge on River		
	9th		Moved to new billets at P.33c.05.05 and started work on bridge at V.10c immediately	Moved in the afternoon to new billets at P.33c.05.05	Same as No 1.	Same as No 2	All 4 Sections worked on bridge at V.10c and completed bridge before leaving	
	10th		All 4 Sections working in shifts day and night on Super heavy Pontoon Bridge at V.10c.4.4				Transport moved to area P.33c and joined by Company with Transport	
	11th		Working shifts on Super Heavy Pontoon Bridge	Working shifts on Super heavy Pontoon Bridge	Working shifts on Super Heavy Pontoon Bridge	Working shifts on Super heavy Pontoon Bridge	moved to ESCANAFFLES the Sections moving on completion of shifts	
	12th		- ditto.	- ditto.	- ditto.	. ditto.	Bridge completed at 11 a.m.	
	13th		All Sections on reliefs looking after Bridge					

(A9175) Wt W2358/P360 600,000 12/17 D. D. & L. Sch. 52a. Forms/C2118/15.

202nd Field Co RE

WAR DIARY
or
INTELLIGENCE SUMMARY.
(*Erase heading not required.*)

Army Form C. 2118.

Instructions regarding War Diaries and Intelligence Summaries are contained in F. S. Regs., Part II, and the Staff Manual respectively. Title pages will be prepared in manuscript.

Page 3

Volume 37

Place	Date	Hour	Summary of Events and Information					Remarks and references to Appendices
October			Section 1	Section 2	Section 3	Section 4	REMARKS	
	14th		Whole Company cleaning up Equipment.					
	15th		Squad Drill in Forenoon	Squad Drill in Forenoon	Squad Drill in Forenoon	Squad Drill in Forenoon		
	16th		ditto	ditto	ditto	ditto		
	17th		ditto	ditto	ditto	ditto	2/Lieut D McCallum leave to UK.	
	18th		Whole Coy moved to ROLLEGHEM.					
	19th		Squad & Rifle Drill	Squad & Rifle Drill	Squad & Rifle Drill	Squad & Rifle Drill		
	20th		do.	do.	do.	do.		
	21st		do	do.	do.	do.		
	22nd		do.	do	do	do		
	23rd		do.	do	do.	do.		
	24th		do.	do.	do.	do.		
	25th		do.	do.	do.	do.		
	26th		do.	do.	do.	do		
	27th		do.	do.	do.	do		

(A9175) Wt W2358/P360 600,000 12/17 D. D. & L. Sch. 52a. Forms/C2118/15.

202nd Field Co RE, Page 4 — Volume 37

Instructions regarding War Diaries and Intelligence Summaries are contained in F. S. Regs., Part II. and the Staff Manual respectively. Title pages will be prepared in manuscript.

WAR DIARY
or
INTELLIGENCE SUMMARY.
(Erase heading not required.)

Army Form C. 2118.

Place	Date	Hour	Summary of Events and Information	Remarks and references to Appendices
October				
	28th		½ Coy proceeded to ESCANAFFLES and dismantled light Pontoon bridge	
			Rem. of Coy cleaning and packing up ready to move	
	29th		Whole Coy and Transport moved to LA VIGNETTE	Lieut Garrard to Hospital
	30th		Ditto Ditto CROIX-AU-BOIS	

[signature]
Major RE
OC 202nd Field Co RE

(A9175) Wt W2358/P360 600,000 12/17 D. D. & L. Sch. 52a. Forms/C2118/15.

SECRET

VR 38

War Diary
~OF~
202nd Field Coy RE.
FROM:- Decr 1st 1918
TO:- Dec 31st 1918.

Volume 39

Instructions regarding War Diaries and Intelligence Summaries are contained in F. S. Regs., Part II. and the Staff Manual respectively. Title pages will be prepared in manuscript.

Page 1

WAR DIARY
or
~~INTELLIGENCE SUMMARY.~~

(Erase heading not required.)

Volume 39

Army Form C. 2118.

Place	Date	Hour	Summary of Events and Information	Remarks and references to Appendices
	1918			
CROIX DU BOIS	Decr 1st		Company continued move as far as BAC-ST. MAUR.	
BAC ST. MAUR	" 2nd		Whole Company left BAC ST. MAUR and moved to ST. FLORIS.	
ST FLORIS	" 3rd		Whole Company moved off from ST FLORIS and arrived at AIRE where the N.C.O. and Men and Animals were billetted in the French Artillery Barracks.	
AIRE	" 4th		The whole Company was employed on Fatigue around Barracks and settling down in Billets.	
"	" 5th		Whole Company employed principally on putting the Billets (Aire Barracks) in a Sanitary condition, such as Erecting Latrines, Cookhouses, Fire appliances &c and making wire Beds for Barrack Rooms.	
"	" 6th		As on 5-12-1918	
"	" 7th		As on 6-12-18	
"	" 8th		Company attended Church Parade (C of E) and were inspected in Drill order by OC Company.	2/Lt McCALLUM and 3 Ors [illegible] Ball [illegible]
"	" 9th		Company employed on general work on Billets &c One party of Painters worked at R.E. Dump. AIRE.	
"	" 10th		All Sections worked in Barracks. A party of Painters employed at RE Dump AIRE.	
"	" 11th		As on 10-12-18 and a Party was also employed at RE Workshops. AIRE	
"	" 12th		As on 11-12-18	CAPT. C.C. LINDSAY, RE proceeded on Leave to U.K
"	" 13th		The whole Company marched to LA LACQUE for Baths.	
"	" 14th		Company employed on Fatigues (scrubbing Equipment &c) from 8.30am - 11am Company paraded in Skeleton Order for inspection at 11am	
"	" 15th		Company attended Church Parade.	
"	" 16th		Inspection Parade and Presentation of Medal Ribands by G.O.C. 30th (British) Division Company employed generally on Barrack work after 2pm	
"	" 17th		Company employed on General work in Barracks, at RE Dump, AIRE and at RE Workshops AIRE	
"	" 18th		As on 17th Decr	LT. J. C. FISHER, RE [illegible] D. McCALLUM, RE [illegible] Ball
"	" 19th		Barracks were inspected by Corps Commander XIX Corps. Company employed as on 18th	
"	" 20th		Company employed as on 18-12-18.	

(A9175) Wt W2358/P360 600,000 12/17 D. D. & L. Sch. 52a. Forms/C2118/15.

Instructions regarding War Diaries and Intelligence Summaries are contained in F. S. Regs., Part II. and the Staff Manual respectively. Title pages will be prepared in manuscript.

Page 2

WAR DIARY ~~or~~ INTELLIGENCE SUMMARY. Volume 39

(*Erase heading not required.*)

Army Form C. 2118.

Place	Date	Hour	Summary of Events and Information	Remarks and references to Appendices
	1918			
AIRE	Dec 21		Company employed as on December 20th 1918	
"	" 22		Portion of Company attended voluntary Church Parade (C of E) Remainder of Company employed on Fatigues to 1200 hrs	
"	" 23		Company employed as on 21-12-18	2/Lt J.A.H. Burford RE to U.K. leave
"	" 24		As on 23rd Dec.	Capt C.C. Lindsay rejoined from U.K. leave
"	" 25		Christmas Day. Company attended Divine Service	
"	" 26		Boxing Day. Check parade 1000 hours	
"	" 27		Company employed as on 24-12-18	
"	" 28		As on 27-12-18	
"	" 29		General work in Barracks & making preparations for moving to Dunkirk on 30-12-18	
"	" 30		Company - with Transport - entrained at AIRE and moved to Camp at DUNKIRK	Capt. C.C. Lindsay went on French leave 4 days.
DUNKIRK	" 31		Whole Company employed on preparing Camp. Erecting Nissen Huts. Cookhouses Etc	

H. J. [signature illegible]
Major RE
OC 202nd Field Company RE
2-1-1919

(A9175) Wt W2358/P360 600,000 12/17 D. D. & L. Sch. 52a. Forms/C2118/15.

SECRET

30/

V8 39

War Diary
of
202nd Field Co. R.E.
from
1st Jany. 1919
to
31st Jany. 1919.

Instructions regarding War Diaries and Intelligence Summaries are contained in F. S. Regs., Part II, and the Staff Manual respectively. Title pages will be prepared in manuscript.

Page 1

WAR DIARY ~~or~~ ~~INTELLIGENCE SUMMARY.~~

(Erase heading not required.)

Volume 40.

Army Form C. 2118.

Place	Date	Hour	Summary of Events and Information	Remarks and references to Appendices
	1919.			
DUNKIRK	Jan 1.		Company moved by march route from camp at Dunkirk to camp at MALO-LES-BAINS (near Dunkirk) and was employed in General Camp work.	
MALO-LES-BAINS	" 2		Company employed (a) on erecting Nissen Huts in Camp (b) on Off-loading Wagons &c and (c) general camp work.	
	" 3		Company employed as on 2/1/1919.	
	" 4		As on 3/1/19. (Three men also employed on levelling and pegging out site for Stables for Horse Demobilization Camp, MALO-LES-BAINS.	
	" 5		Erecting Nissen Huts, commencing excavations of foundations for Stables. Off-loading Wagons Etc.	
	" 6.		As on 5/1/19.	
	" 7.		As on 6/1/19 and laying out and digging post holes.	× MAJOR R. [illegible] LEE, R.E. left for U.K. for duty. CAPT C.C. LINDSAY. R.E. assumed command of Company
	" 8		As on 7/1/19. Two Huts erected in "A" Camp (Personnel Camp).	
	" 9.		Wiring area around around P of W. camp, and all work in that camp completed. Part of Coy employed off-loading material.	
	" 10.		Erecting Stabling. Erecting Troughing at Canal. Wire fence around P of W camp completed.	2nd LT. J.A.H. BURFORD. R.E. left on temp.y attachment to [illegible] CORNWALL WKS. CO. R.E. at DUNKIRK

(A9175) Wt W2358/P360 600,000 12/17 D. D. & L. Sch. 52a. Forms/C2118/15.

Instructions regarding War Diaries and Intelligence Summaries are contained in F. S. Regs., Part II, and the Staff Manual respectively. Title pages will be prepared in manuscript.

Page 2

WAR DIARY

~~or~~

~~INTELLIGENCE SUMMARY.~~

(Erase heading not required.)

Volume 40

Army Form C. 2118.

Place	Date	Hour	Summary of Events and Information	Remarks and references to Appendices
	1919			
MALO-LES-BAINS	Jan 11.		As on 10/1/1919.	
	" 12		Sunday. No work done.	
	" 13.		Erecting Stabling. Building Cook house & Latrine in P. of W. Camp. Erecting Troughing at Canal and distributing pipes along pipe-line.	
	" 14.		As on 13/1/19.	
	" 15.		-Do-	
	" 16		Ditto and erecting Men's Kitchen in Personnel Camp.	
	" 17		Ditto and making excavations for Reservoirs.	
	" 18.		Erecting Stabling, Men's Kitchen and Latrines. Levelling off ground in "C" Camp (Camp for 1500 Horses) and making Ramps.	
	" 19.		Sunday. No work executed.	
	" 20.		Erecting Stabling in "C" Camp. Erecting Men's Kitchen Latrines in "A" Camp (Personnel Camp) and Erecting Engine, digging Pipe Track and excavations for Reservoir for water supply.	
	" 21		As on 20/1/19.	Capt. C. [illegible] Lindsay R.E. [illegible] Lieut. [illegible] R.E. Assumed Command of Coy
	" 22		" " 21/1/19 but no work done in "A" (Personnel) Camp.	

(A9175) W: W2358/P360 600,000 12/17 D. D. & L. Sch. 52a. Forms/C2118/15.

Instructions regarding War Diaries and Intelligence Summaries are contained in F. S. Regs., Part II. and the Staff Manual respectively. Title pages will be prepared in manuscript.

Page 3

WAR DIARY
or
~~INTELLIGENCE SUMMARY.~~ Volume 40
(Erase heading not required.)

Army Form C. 2118.

Place	Date	Hour	Summary of Events and Information	Remarks and references to Appendices
	1919.			
MALO-LES-BAINS	Jan 23		As on 22/1/1919.	
	" 24		Ditto and fitting Engine Pump for water supply	
	" 25		Erecting Stables in "C" (Horse) Camp. Work on P of W Camp. Laying 4" main and making excavations for Reservoir and building Engine Shed	
	" 26		Sunday. No work done	
	" 27		As on 25/1/19 and making Ramps in "C" (Horse) Camp.	
	" 28		Erecting Nissen Huts in "A" (Personnel) Camp. Erecting Stables in "C" (Horse) Camp. Laying 4" main and branches. Fitting up Engine Pump and erecting Engine Shed. Minor work to accessory buildings in "B" (~~Personnel~~ P of W) Camp	
	" 29		As on 28/1/1919	
	" 30		Erecting Nissen Huts in "A" Camp. Minor work in "B" Camp. Roofing Stables with corrugated iron in "C" Camp. Laying 4" main and Roofing Reservoir at the Canal for Water. Levelling entrance tracks in "X" Site (for Horse Tents) and ditto in "Y" Site. One Horse Tent erected in "Y" Site	
	" 31		As on 30/1/19	

J. B. [illegible] Lieut. R.E.
for O.C. 202nd Field Coy. R.E.

Instructions regarding War Diaries and Intelligence Summaries are contained in F. S. Regs., Part II. and the Staff Manual respectively. Title pages will be prepared in manuscript.

WAR DIARY
or
INTELLIGENCE SUMMARY.
(*Erase heading not required.*)

Army Form C. 2118.

VOLUME 41

Place	Date	Hour	Summary of Events and Information	Remarks and references to Appendices
			40	
CONFIDENTIAL				
			WAR DIARY	
			202ND FIELD COY	
			ROYAL ENGINEERS	
			FEBRUARY 1919	
			O.C. 202ND FIELD CO. (COUNTY PALATINE) R.E.	

(A9175) Wt W2358/P360 600,000 12/17 D. D. & L. Sch. 52a. Forms/C2118/15.

202 Field Coy R.E. Page 1 Volume 41

Instructions regarding War Diaries and Intelligence Summaries are contained in F. S. Regs., Part II. and the Staff Manual respectively. Title pages will be prepared in manuscript.

WAR DIARY
or
INTELLIGENCE SUMMARY.
(Erase heading not required.)

Army Form C. 2118.

Place	Date	Hour	Summary of Events and Information	Remarks and references to Appendices
MALO LES BAINS	FEB 1st		Working on pipe line reservoir and erection of stable do do do	
	2nd		Sunday no work done	
	3rd		Working on reservoir pipe line stabling and erecting Nissen Huts	
	4th		do do do do	
	5th		do do do do	
	6th		do do do do	
	7th		do do do do	
	8th		do do do do	
	9th		Sunday no work done CRE Dunkirk inspected work in Land.	CAPT H.T. JOHNSON ASSUMED COMMAND
	10th		The whole Coy employed on hutting and water supply	LIEUT FISHER TO UK for demobilisation.
	11th		do do do do	
	12th		do do do do General Stewart D.W. inspected work on Camp	
	13th		do do do do	
	14		do do do do	
	15th		do do do do	Lt FROST Leave to UK

(A9175) Wt W2358/P360 600,000 12/17 D. D. & L. Sch. 52a. Forms/C2118/15.

Instructions regarding War Diaries and Intelligence Summaries are contained in F. S. Regs., Part II. and the Staff Manual respectively. Title pages will be prepared in manuscript.

Page 2

WAR DIARY
or
INTELLIGENCE SUMMARY.
(Erase heading not required.)

Army Form C. 2118.

Place	Date	Hour	Summary of Events and Information	Remarks and references to Appendices
	16th		Sunday no work done	
	17		Coy employed on hutting, water supply, stabling etc	
	18th		Station pumping from reservoir by Canal to Storage [illegible]. Coy working on [illegible] etc	
	19th		Water supply on to Horse troughs. Hutting etc	
	20th		Replacing steam pipe by [illegible]. Other work same as 19th	
	21st		Putting in steam pipe for water [illegible]. Work as on 20th	
	22nd		Banking up sides of [illegible]. Hutting etc	
	23rd		Sunday no work done.	
	24th		Coy working on Stabling, erecting ablution sheds etc. Divl General visited the Coy	
	25th		Coy working on Camp, stabling, ablution sheds, huts etc. C.R.E. Division inspected Camp	
	26th		Work as on 25th	
	27th		do do	
	28th		do do	

[illegible signature]
Capt. R.E.
O.C. 202nd FIELD CO.
(COUNTY PALATINE) R.E.

(A9175) Wt W2358/P360 600,000 12/17 D. D. & L. Sch. 52a. Forms/C2118/15.

War Diary

of

202nd Field Coy R.E

for

Feb. 1919

R 22nd Field Company. R.E.

WAR DIARY
or
INTELLIGENCE SUMMARY.
(Erase heading not required.)

Army Form C. 2118.

Instructions regarding War Diaries and Intelligence Summaries are contained in F. S. Regs., Part II, and the Staff Manual respectively. Title pages will be prepared in manuscript.

Page. VOLUME 42

Vol 41

Place	Date	Hour	Summary of Events and Information	Remarks and references to Appendices
	MARCH	1919		
NALO	1st		Company working on Embarkation Camp (Horses) - Erecting Stabling and Huts for Personnel	
LES-BAINS.	2nd		Sunday - No work done.	
	3rd		Company employed as on 1st March.	
	4th		do	
	5th		do	
	6th		do	
	7th		do	
	8th		do	
	9th		Sunday - No work done	
	10th		Company working on Embarkation Camp (Horses) Erecting Stabling &c, and Scottish Churches Hut	
	11th		Company employed as on 10th March.	
	12th		do	
	13th		do	
	14th		do	
	15th		do	
	16th		Sunday - No work done.	

(A9175) Wt W2358/P363 600,000 12/17 D. D. & L. Sch. 52a. Forms/C2118/15.

Army Form C. 2118.

WAR DIARY
or
INTELLIGENCE SUMMARY.
(*Erase heading not required.*)

Instructions regarding War Diaries and Intelligence Summaries are contained in F. S. Regs., Part II, and the Staff Manual respectively. Title pages will be prepared in manuscript.

Page 2. VOLUME 42.

Place	Date	Hour	Summary of Events and Information	Remarks and references to Appendices
	17th		Company working on Embarkation Camp (Horses) · Maintenance of Stabling · Huts &c.	
	18th		— do — do —	
	19th		— do — do —	
	20th		— do — do —	
	21st		— do — do —	
	22nd		— do — do —	
	23rd		Sunday. No work done.	
	24th		Company working on Embarkation Camp (Horses) Maintenance of Stabling · Huts &c	
	25th		— do — do —	
	26th		— do — do —	
	27th		— do — do —	
	28th		— do — do —	
	29th		— do — do —	
	30th		Sunday, No work done	
	31st		Company employed as on 24th March.	

J. B. Frost Capt. RE
for O. C. 202 Fd. Co

(A9175) Wt W2358/P360 600,000 12/17 D. D. & L. Sch. 52a. Forms/C2118/15.

War Diary

of

202nd Field Coy R.E

for

March 1919

7/8 30

202nd Coy. R.E.

Army Form C. 2118.

Instructions regarding War Diaries and Intelligence Summaries are contained in F. S. Regs., Part II. and the Staff Manual respectively. Title pages will be prepared in manuscript.

WAR DIARY
or
~~INTELLIGENCE SUMMARY~~ for July 1919
(Erase heading not required.)

4R 45 Cancelled

Place	Date	Hour	Summary of Events and Information	Remarks and references to Appendices
Dunkirk	1st to 4th		Routine	
"	4th		Preliminary Orders for Disbandment of Coy. received from R.E. L of C. per C.R.E. Dunkirk	
"	5th		Preparations for disbanding Coy & for handing in Coy. Stores.	
"	6th to 10th		Routine	
"	11th		Waggons & Stores entrained to proceed to Ordnance Depot BEAUMARAIS, CALAIS	
"	16th		Stores arrived at Beaumarais; Documents of Coy forwarded to Records	
"	17th		Men demobilised	
Beaumarais	18th		Stores checked & receipt received from O.O. Beaumarais	
Dunkirk	20th		O.C. proceeds for demobilisation, disbandment of Coy completed.	

(A9175) Wt W2358/P360 600,000 12/17 D. D. & L. Sch. 52a. Forms/C2118/15.

[signature] Lieut

www.ingramcontent.com/pod-product-compliance
Lightning Source LLC
Chambersburg PA
CBHW080913230426
43667CB00015B/2665